A Golden Hands PATTERN BOOK

CROCHET

A Golden Hands PATTERN BOOK

CROCHET

RANDOM HOUSE   NEW YORK

© Marshall Cavendish Limited 1972
All rights reserved under International and Pan-American
Copyright Conventions. Published in the United States
by Random House, Inc., New York, and simultaneously in
Canada by Random House of Canada Limited, Toronto.
The greater part of the material published in this book
was first published by Marshall Cavendish Ltd. in "Golden
Hands." The British edition entitled *The Golden Hands
Book of Crochet* was published by William Collins Sons
& Co Ltd.

Library of Congress Cataloging in Publication Data
Crochet: a Golden hands pattern book.
Originally published under title: The Golden hands book
of crochet.
"The greater part of the material published in this book
was first published . . . in 'Golden hands.'"
1. Crocheting—Patterns.   I. Golden hands.
TT820.G73   1973   746.4'4   72-11422
ISBN 0-394-48575-0

Manufactured in the United States of America
First American Edition

CONTENTS

About this book . . . .

Here is a special collection of garments for
every member of your family, and a variety
of colorful and original items to enhance
your home.
There are layettes and playsuits for babies;
shawls, smocks and dresses for mothers and
teenage daughters; good-looking sweaters for
dads, and rugs, tablecloths and curtains for the
house.
The collection is technically definitive, too.
It should encourage the beginner and
challenge the expert.
If you are a newcomer to the craft of
crochet, then turn to our Crash Course on
page 121, which will guide and instruct you
to that stage of confidence and skill that
will enable you to tackle everything in the
book. We suggest that you start with a
simple item, such as the baby's playsuit in
granny squares on page 9 and then move
on to the more complicated designs.
Crochet can be a totally absorbing and
worthwhile hobby—even more so when it
involves those nearest to you. You can save
money, delight your family and friends
with gifts, and provide a satisfying and
creative outlet for your leisure time.

YARN MANUFACTURERS' ADDRESSES

In case of difficulty in obtaining any yarns featured in this book, please write directly to the following manufacturers' addresses to find out the location of your nearest retailer.

American Thread and **Dawn** yarns by—
American Thread
High Ridge Park
Stamford, Connecticut 06905.

Bear Brand, Botany, Bucilla and **Fleisher** yarns by—
Bernhard Ulmann Co.
Division of Indian Head
30-20 Thomson Avenue
Long Island City, New York 11101.

Bernat yarns by—
Emile Bernat & Sons Co.
Uxbridge, Massachusetts 01569.

Brunswick yarns by—
Brunswick Worsted Mills Inc.
Pickens, South Carolina 29671.

Coats & Clark's yarns by—
Coats & Clark's
430 Park Avenue
New York, New York 10022.

Columbia-Minerva yarns by—
Columbia-Minerva Corp.
295 Fifth Avenue
New York, New York 10016.

Reynolds yarns by—
Reynolds Yarns Inc.
215 Central Avenue
East Farmingdale, New York 11735.

Spinnerin yarns by—
Spinnerin Yarn Co. Inc.
230 Fifth Avenue
New York, New York 10001.

Unger yarns by—
William Unger & Co.
230 Fifth Avenue
New York, New York 10001.

CROCHET ABBREVIATIONS

alt	alternate(ly)
approx	approximate(ly)
beg	begin(ning)
ch	chain
cont	continu(e) (ing)
dec	decrease
dc	double crochet
dtr	double treble
foll	follow(ing)
gr(s)	group(s)
hdc	half double crochet
in	inch(es)
inc	increase
No.	number
patt	pattern
rem	remaining(ing)
rep	repeat
RS	right side
sc	single crochet
ss	slip stitch in crochet
sp	space
st(s)	stitch(es)
tog	together
tr	treble crochet
WS	wrong side
yd(s)	yard(s)
yrh	yarn around hook

SYMBOLS

An asterisk (*) shown in a pattern row denotes that the stitches shown after this sign must be repeated from that point.
Square brackets [] denote directions for larger sizes in the pattern.
Parentheses () denote that this section of the pattern is to be worked for all sizes.
Gauge—this is the most important factor in successful knitting and crochet. Unless you obtain the gauge given for each design, you will not obtain satisfactory results.

YARNS AND GAUGES

Yarns and qualities vary from year to year and country to country. The secret of using this book at any time, in any country, is to use a yarn which crochets up to the right gauge. To check, crochet a gauge sample before embarking on a garment. The hook size is only a guide. The point is to have the right number of stitches and rows to the inch. To do this you may need to use a hook a size larger or smaller than suggested because some people crochet more loosely or tightly than others.

Photographs by Camera Press   Kjell Nilsson, 48, 49,
51, 52, 62, 63. GMN, 33, 38, 61.
Uggla, 39, 50, 59, 77. Hans o Peter, 55, 56, 57, 58.
Seiden & Almgren, 60. Kamerabild,
23, 24, 32, 37. Ed-Foto, 22. Femina Design, 29.
Simis Press, 14, 15, 17, 18, 19, 20, 21,
25, 26, 27, 34, 35, 64, 68, 74.
John Carter, 36. Pingouin,
65. Twilley, 16. Chris Lewis, 31, 69, 70, 71, 72, 73.
Design by Pam Dawson, 43, 45, 46, 47.

Diagrams by: Barbara Firth
             and by courtesy of J.P. Coats
             UK Ltd.

77 designs for the Family

1

Up-to-the-minute play-suit (overblouse, shorts and bonnet) in easy Granny Squares. Make it in bright contrast colors, or in an interesting mixture—like sugar ▸pink, raspberry and navy, or in soft muted shades of pastel.

*Crochet
Size: to fit 20/22 inch chest.*

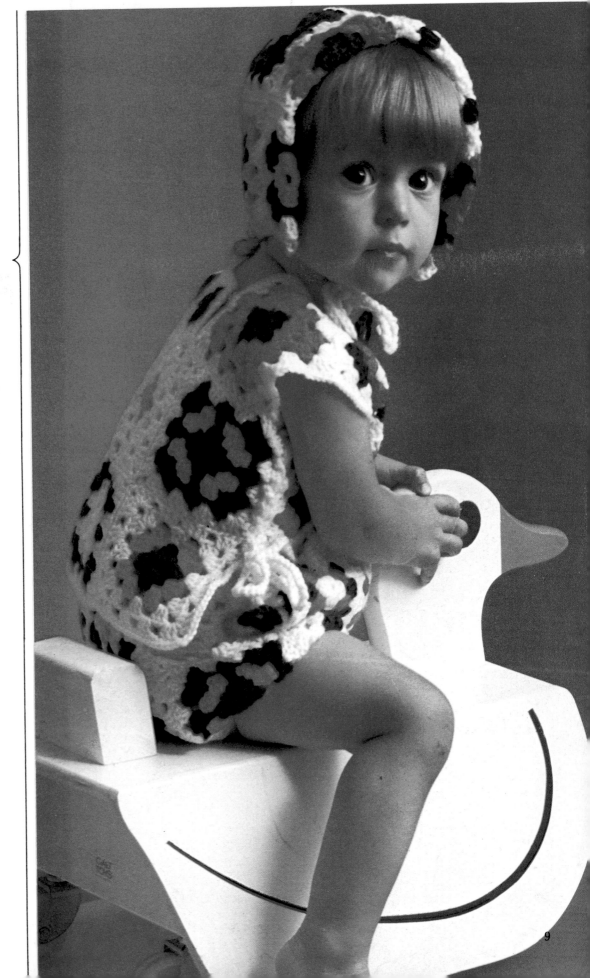

Cuddly poncho with matching, separate pixie helmet. The poncho is lavishly fringed and doubles as a practical carrying shawl.

Crochet
Size: to fit an 18/20 inch chest.

3

Slipper/shoes worked in a crunchy stitch, with ribbon slotted tie straps.

Crochet
Size: heel to toe, 4¾ inches.

4

Crib or carriage cover knitted in a lovely deep "waffle" stitch, using yarn double for extra warmth. The edging is worked in crochet, also using yarn double.

Knit and crochet
Size: 30 inches by 21½ inches.

5

Christening robe
with a delicate
frill around the neck
and sleeves, a neat
little bodice, and a
cascade of lacy skirt
falling from the
ribbon trim.

Crochet
Size: to fit 18/20 inch
chest.

6

All-in-one jumpsuit
and hooded jacket with
optional embroidered
ribbon trim.

Crochet
Sizes: to fit 20 [22]
inch chest.

7

Candy striped maxi top
in summer weight cotton.
Matching pants are
solid colored with contrast
edging.

Crochet
Size: to fit 18/20 inch
chest.

8

For little girls, a lacy, openwork sleeveless pants suit, with ribbon bows on the shoulders. Crisp cotton makes it cool for summer days.

Crochet
To fit 20 [22:24] inch chest.

9

Two-color, striped bathrobe that looks just as good on a boy or a girl. The "belt" is attached to the bodice and skirt to make an all-in-one garment.

Crochet
Sizes: to fit 22 [24] inch chest.

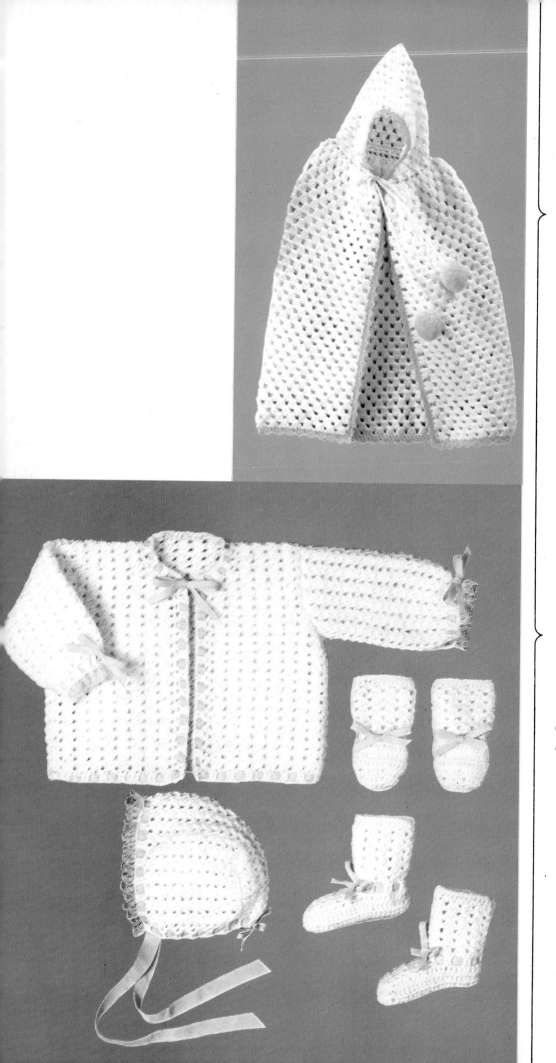

10

Hooded cape trimmed with shell edging.

Crochet
Size: from birth to 6 months.

11

Dainty set with trimmings of lace and ribbon on coat, bonnet, bootees and mittens.

Crochet
Sizes: jacket to fit 22 [24] inch chest.

12

Merry little dress with
a dropped waistline and
brief, contrasting mini-
skirt in a shell pattern.

Crochet
Sizes: to fit 21 [23]
inch chest.

13

Pick pale yellow for this dress with ribbon trim. The bodice is worked in double crochet, and the skirt is worked in large and small shells, with the same pattern repeated in the sleeves.

Crochet
Size : to fit 22 [24:26] inch chest.

14

A beautifully shaped single-breasted coat with flap pockets and shoulder tabs. The coat and matching hat are crocheted in half doubles.

Crochet
Sizes: to fit 22 [24:26] inch chest.

15

Pretty dressing gown worked in open diamonds. Buttoned to the neck at the front, it can be trimmed with a cord belt.

Crochet
Sizes: to fit 22 [24] inch chest.

16

A bright, striped poncho worked entirely in double crochet, finished with a lavish fringing. It is made in two sections, which make for easy shaping.

Crochet
Sizes: to fit 6/8 [8/10 : 10/12] years.

17

Half-belted coat and matching, head hugging hat. The coat has a flared skirt and a fitted bodice with collar.

Crochet
Sizes: to fit 24 [26] inch chest.

18,19

Comfortable crochet swim trunks for a boy. Worked in three-color stripes. The girl's bikini has neat fitting pants and the top is fastened with a ring at the front. Worked in panels of shell stitch and double crochets

Crochet
Sizes: boy's trunks to fit 24 [26:28:30] inch hips, girl's bikini to fit 24 [26:28:30] inch chest

20, 21

Crochet traditionally
spells femininity.
The matching pullover
and jacket can be
worked in a wide
range of sizes.

Crochet
Sizes 32-50 inch bust.

22

Work the motifs
separately. Then join them
into this appealing
matching jacket and
beret.

Crochet
Sizes 34-36 inch bust.

23, 24

For a beautiful
summer outfit, crochet
this sleeveless cotton
dress and matching
casual cover-up.
Special features—the
oval neckline and
three-quarter sleeved
jacket.

Crochet
Sizes 34-40 inch bust.

25

To crochet: a beach-wear stunner! The set comprises a well-fitting bikini and long, sleeveless jacket to match.

Crochet
Sizes 32-38 inch bust.

26

Another glamorous beach outfit. Smart bikini with co-ordinating cover-up.

Crochet
Sizes 32-36 inch bust.

27

Accessorize your beach outfit with this Garbo-like hat and matching bag in shiny straw.

Crochet
Size Average head.

28

Cut a dash in this striking toreador bolero. Work the flower motifs separately. Then join them together to make up the garment.

Crochet
Sizes 34-36 inch bust.

29

Add a touch of romance to a special outfit with this lavishly fringed, triangular shawl. The crocheted squares are bordered with simple chains.

Crochet.

30

This fashionably styled trouser suit will be an extremely useful addition to any wardrobe.

Crochet Sizes: 32–35 inch bust.

31

This long jacket is cleverly designed for the minimum of making up.

Crochet Sizes: 34[37:40] inch bust.

32

*Far left Easy raglan
sleeves, a soft collar
and two patch pockets
make this the prettiest
crocheted coat in town.*

*Crochet
Sizes 34-40 inch bust.*

33

*Left Double-
breasted closing on
the contrasting front
panels give this crocheted
suit a distinctly naval
flavor.*

*Crochet
Sizes 34-40 inch bust.*

34

*A charming midi
to crochet.
Bell sleeves, a cord
fastening and contrasting
bands of color at the
hem complete the design.*

*Crochet
Sizes 34-42 inch bust.*

35

*A pretty, practical
dressing robe to make
in long or short lengths.*

*Crochet
Sizes 34-42 inch bust.*

36

*Left A glittering
evening smock, to wear
with trousers, over a
long skirt—or even
on its own as a mini.*

*Crochet
Sizes 32-36 inch bust.*

37

*A simple shell
top that's both cool
and comfortable to wear.*

*Crochet
Sizes 34-44 inch bust.*

38

*Soft and warm
in this dainty bed jacket,
crocheted in cozy mohair.*

*Crochet
Sizes 34-40 inch bust.*

39

Pretty to wake up to.
The trimmings and
square motifs on this
crocheted housecoat are
worked separately in a
contrasting color.

Crochet
Sizes 34-38 inch bust.

40

Front zippered vest made of crocheted granny squares.

Crochet
Sizes to fit 36:38 [40:42] inch chest.

41

Crocheted tunic, belted and trimmed in three contrasting colors.

Crochet
Sizes to fit 38 [40:42] inch chest.

42

Crochet a gamekeeper's cap – quick and fun to do. The cap is peaked and earlaps fasten to the top of the crown

Crochet
Sizes to fit an average head

Instructions for designs 1-42

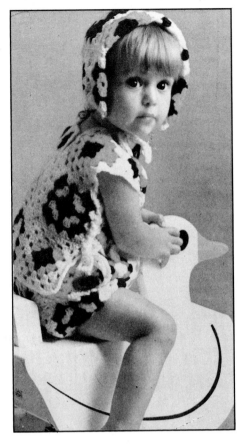

1 Granny squares playsuit and bonnet

Size
Overblouse to fit 20/22in chest
Length to shoulder, 10in
Shorts around widest part, 23½in
Side seam, 7in
Bonnet around face edge, 13½in
Gauge
Each square measures 3½ by3½in worked on
No.E crochet hook
Materials
Spinnerin Wintuk Featherlon, 2oz skeins
3 balls main color, A
1 ball each of contrast colors B and C
No.E crochet hook
1½yds round or narrow elastic

Overblouse

Using No.E hook and C, ch5.
Join with a ss to first ch to form circle.
1st round Using C ch2, 2dc into circle,
ch2, *3dc into circle, ch2, rep from * twice more.
Join with a ss to 2nd of first ch2, leaving last 2
loops on hook. Break off C.
2nd round Using B, draw through 2 loops on
hook, ch2, into ch2 sp work 3dc, ch2, 3dc—called
work corner— *ch1, work corner, rep from *
twice more. Join with a ss to first of first ch2,
leaving last 2 loops on hook. Break off B.
3rd round Using C, draw through 2 loops on
hook, ch2, into ch sp immediately below hook
work 2dc, ch1, *work corner, ch1, 3dc into next
ch sp, ch1, rep from * twice more, work corner,
ch1. Join with a ss to 2nd of first ch2, leaving
last 2 loops on hook. Break off C.
4th round Using A, draw through 2 loops on
hook, ch2, *3dc into next ch sp, ch1, work
corner, ch1, 3dc into next ch sp, ch1, rep from
* 3 times more, skipping ch1 at end of last rep.
Join with a ss to first of first ch2. Fasten off.

Darn in all ends. Work 15 more squares in
same way, varying color sequence on first 3
rounds if required but always working 4th
round with A. Work 2 squares with 2 rounds
only for front and back neck. Fasten off. Darn
in all ends.

Finishing

Press each square on WS under a damp cloth
with a warm iron. Join 2 rows of 3 squares to
form front bodice. Join one square to first square
of 2nd row to form shoulder, setting it in one
complete dc group from side edge to form underarm. Join one square to 3rd square of 2nd row
in same way to form other armhole and shoulder.
Insert small square between 2 shoulder squares
to form center neck. Join squares for back bodice
in same way. Join shoulders. Using No.E
hook, A and with RS of work facing, work
1 round sc around neck edge, working
1sc into each dc, 2sc into each ch sp and 1 sc
into each corner ch sp at either side of seams.
Work all around side and lower edges in same
way, working 3sc into each corner ch sp at
underarm and lower edge. Using No.E
hook and 2 strands of A ch140.
Fasten off. Beg at underarm of back and front
and thread ch through sides of first row of
squares to form lacing. Make another ch in same
way.
Petals Using No.E hook and B ch5. Join with
a ss to first ch to form circle.
1st round Ch2, work 2dc into circle, ss into
circle, *work 3dc into circle, ss into circle, rep
from *twice more, joining last ss to base of first
ch2. Fasten off. Work 1 more petal with B and 2
more with C. Trim each end of lacing·cord with
1 petal. Press seams.

Shorts

Work 15 squares as given for overblouse.

Finishing

Press as for overblouse. Join 2 rows of 7 squares.
Join 2 rows to form circle, marking this seam as
center back. Using No.E hook, A and
with RS of work facing beg at center back,
(2dc into ch2 sp, 1dc into each of next 3dc)
5 times, (2hdc into ch2 sp, 1hdc into each of
next 3dc) 4 times, (2sc into ch2 sp, 1 sc into each
of next 3dc) 10 times, (2hdc into ch2 sp, 1hdc
into each of next 3dc) 4 times, (2dc into ch2 sp,
1dc into each of next 3dc) 5 times. Join with a ss
to top of first dc. Fasten off. Press seams.
Join rem square across center back seam to form
crotch and across center front square. Using
No.E hook, A and with RS of work
facing work 1 round sc around each leg. Thread
elastic through WS at top of waist and around
legs to measurement, securing on WS.

Bonnet

Work 9 squares as given for overblouse.

Finishing

Press as for overblouse. Join 2 rows of 4 squares.
Using last square as a diamond shape, insert
this into edge of 4 squares to form back
crown. Press seams. Fold front edge row of squares
in half to WS and sl st down. Using No.E
hook, A and with RS of work facing;
work 1 row sc along neck edge, working through
double thickness at front edge. Make a cord as
for overblouse. Thread cord through both
thicknesses of squares just in front of sl st seam
to tie under chin. Trim each end of cord with
one petal.

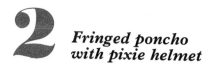

Fringed poncho with pixie helmet

Size
To fit an 18/20in chest.
Length at center back, 10in.
Gauge
5 sts and 2½ rows to 1in over patt worked on No.G crochet hook
Materials
Bernat Nylo Sports
Poncho 4 balls
Pixie helmet 1 ball
Mittens 1 ball
No.G crochet hook
One button

Poncho

Using No.G crochet hook ch 54 and beg at neck edge.
1st row (WS) Into 2nd ch from hook work 1sc, 1sc into each ch to end. Turn. 53 sts.
2nd row Ch2, skip first st, *ch1, skip next st, 1hdc in next st, rep from * to end. Turn.
3rd row 1sc in first st, *1sc in ch sp, 1sc in next st, rep from * ending 1sc in turning ch. Turn.
4th row Ch2, skip 2 sts, *4dc in next st, skip one st, 1dc in next st, skip one st, rep from * to last 3 sts, 4dc in next st, skip one st, 1dc in last st. Turn.
5th row Ch2, *4dc into center sp of 4dc of previous row, skip 2 sts, 1dc in next st, rep from * 5 times more, 8dc into center sp of 4dc of previous row, **skip 2 sts, 1dc in next st, 4dc into center sp of 4dc of previous row, rep from ** to last 3 sts, skip 2 sts, 1dc in last st. Turn.
6th row Ch2, *4dc into center sp of 4dc of previous row, skip 2 sts, 1dc in next st, rep from * 5 times more, 4dc into sp between 2nd and 3rd dc of previous row, 1dc into sp between 4th and 5th dc of previous row, 4dc into sp between 6th and 7th dc of previous row, **skip 2 sts, 1dc in next dc, 4dc into center sp between 4dc of previous row, rep from ** to last 3 sts, skip 2 sts, 1dc in last st. Turn.
7th row Ch2, *4dc into center sp of 4dc of previous row, skip 2 sts, 1dc in next st, rep from * 5 times more, 4dc into center sp of 4dc of previous row, skip 2 sts, 6dc in next st, **4dc into center sp of 4dc of previous row, skip 2 sts, 1dc in next st, rep from ** to end. Turn.
8th row Ch2, *4dc into center sp of 4dc of previous row, skip 2 sts, 1dc in next st, rep from * 6 times more, 4dc into center sp of 6dc of previous row, **skip 2 sts, 1dc in next st, 4dc into center sp of 4dc of previous row, rep from ** to last 3 sts, skip 2 sts, 1dc in last st. Turn.
9th, 10th and 11th rows As 5th, 6th and 7th rows but working patt rep 6 times more instead of 5.
12th, 13th, 14th and 15th rows As 8th, 5th, 6th and 7th rows but working patt rep 7 times more.
16th, 17th, 18th and 19th rows As 8th, 5th, 6th and 7th rows but working patt rep 8 times more.
20th, 21st, 22nd and 23rd rows As 8th, 5th, 6th and 7th rows but working patt rep 9 times more.
24th row As 8th row but working patt rep 10 times more. Fasten off.
Work another piece in same way.

Finishing

Press each piece under a dry cloth with a cool iron. Join side seams. Make a twisted cord and thread through holes at neck and tie at center front. Make 2 pompons and sew to ends of cord. Cut rem yarn into 6in lengths and taking 3 strands tog, knot all round lower edge to form fringe. Trim fringe. Press seams.

Pixie helmet

Using No.G crochet hook ch82.
1st row (RS) Into 2nd ch from hook work 1sc, 1sc into each ch to end. Turn. 81 sts.
2nd row Ch1, *1sc into next sc, rep from * to end. Turn.
3rd row Ch1, *1sc into next sc, rep from * to last 4 sts, ch2, skip 1sc, 1sc into each of next 3sc. Turn.
4th row Ch1, work as 2nd row working 1sc into ch2 sp.
5th row As 2nd.
6th row Ss over 10 sts, ch2, skip first sc, * skip 1sc, 4dc into next sc, skip 1sc, 1 dc into next sc, rep from * 14 times more. Turn.
7th row Ch2, *4dc into center sp of 4dc of previous row, skip 2 sts, 1dc in next st, rep from * to end. Turn.
Rep last row until work measures 5½in from beg, ending with WS row.
Next row Ss over 10 sts, ch2, (4dc into center sp of 4dc of previous row, skip 2 sts, 1dc in next st) 11 times. Turn.
Next row Ss over 10 sts, ch2, (4dc into center sp of 4dc of previous row, skip 2 sts, 1dc in next st) 7 times. Turn.
Next row Ss over 10 sts, ch2, (4dc into center sp of 4dc of previous row, skip 2 sts, 1dc in next st) 3 times. Fasten off.

Finishing

Press as given for poncho. Join back seam. Using No.G crochet hook work 2 rows sc all around neck edge. Sew on button. Press seam.

Mittens

Using No.E crochet hook ch19.
1st row (RS) Into 2nd ch from hook work 1sc, * 1sc into each ch to end. Turn. 18 sts.
2nd row Ch1, 2sc in first sc, 1sc into each of next 7sc, (2sc in next sc) twice, 1sc into each of next 7sc, 2sc into last sc. Turn. 22 sts.
3rd row Ch1, 1sc into each sc to end. Turn.
4th row Ch1, 2sc into first sc, 1sc into each of next 9sc, (2sc into next sc) twice, 1sc into each of next 9sc, 2sc into last sc. Turn. 26 sts.
5th row As 3rd.
6th row Ch1, 2sc into first sc, 1sc into each of next 11sc, (2sc into next sc) twice, 1sc into each of next 11sc, 2sc into last sc. Turn. 30 sts.
7th row As 3rd.
Rep last row until work measures 2½in from beg, ending with a WS row.
Shape top
Next row Ch1, 1sc into each of next 14sc, skip 1sc, *1sc in next st, rep from * to end. Turn. 29 sts.
Next row Ch3, skip first 2sc, 1hdc in next sc, *Ch1, skip 1sc, 1hdc in next sc, rep from * to end. Turn.
Next row Ch1, 1sc into each st to end. Turn.
Next row Ch2, skip first sc, *skip next sc, 4dc in next sc, skip 1sc, 1dc in next sc, rep from * to end. Turn.
Next row Ch2, *4dc into center sp of 4dc of previous row, skip 2 sts, 1dc into next st, rep from * to end. Turn.
Rep last row once more. Fasten off. Work another mitten in same way.

Finishing

Press as given for poncho. Join and press seam. Make a twisted cord and thread through holes at wrist and tie in front. Make 2 small pompons and sew to ends of cord.

Slipper/shoes with ribbon slotted straps

Sizes
Length from heel to toe, 4¾ inches
Gauge
3 shells to 1⅝ inches in width, worked on No.G crochet hook
Materials
1 skein Brunswick Fairhaven Fingering Yarn
No.G crochet hook
One yard narrow ribbon

Shoes

Using No.G crochet hook ch31.
Base row into 3rd ch from hook work 1dc, 1dc into each ch to end. Fasten off.*
Instep
Attach yarn to 11th dc, ch2, 1dc into same dc, (skip 2dc, 3dc into next dc) twice, skip 2dc, 2dc into next dc. Turn. Work in patt over instep.
1st row Ch2, 1dc between 2dc**, 3dc into center 3dc of previous row, rep from ** ending 2dc between last 2dc. Turn.
Rep 1st row 5 times more. Fasten off.
Next row Ss into first dc of base row, ch2, 1dc into each of next 10dc, (2dc into each loop of instep) 7 times, 8dc across instep, (2dc into each loop of instep) 7 times, work in dc to end. Turn.
Shape heel and toe
1st row Ch2, skip 1dc, 1dc into each of next 23dc, skip 1dc, 1dc into each of next 8dc, skip

1dc, work in dc to last 2dc, skip 1dc, 1dc into last dc. Turn.
2nd row Ch2, skip 1dc, 1dc into each of next 21dc, skip 1dc, 1dc into each of next 8dc, skip 1dc, work in dc to last 2dc, skip 1dc, 1dc into last dc. Turn.
Work 1 row dc. Fasten off.
Straps
Work as given for Shoes to *.

Finishing

Press under a damp cloth with a warm iron. Join back and underfoot seams. Sew center of strap to back seam. Thread ribbon through straps.

"Waffle" stitch crib or carriage cover

Size
Overall size 37in long by 21½in wide; with top border turned down, 30in by 21½in
Gauge
9 sts to 2in in width and 12 rows to 2in in depth over patt worked on No.10 needles, using yarn double
Materials
11 balls Bernat Berella Germantown
2-oz balls
No.10 knitting needles
No.F crochet hook
Note
Yarn is used double throughout

Carriage cover

Using No.10 needles and yarn double, cast on 93 sts. Commence patt.
1st row (RS) K to end.
2nd row P to end.
3rd row K2, *P1, yon, K2 tog tbl, rep from * to last st, K1.
4th row P2, *K1 tbl, K1, P1, rep from * to last 4 sts, K1 tbl, K1, P2.
These 4 rows form patt. Rep patt rows 42 times more or until 30 in from beg.
Next row K to end.
Next row (reverse for top border) K to end.
Rep 2nd to 4th rows once, then 1st to 4th rows 8 times more. K 1 row. Bind off as to purl.
Border
Press lightly. Using No.F hook and with RS of work facing, attach double yarn to end of last border row.
1st row Work in sc down first long side working 2sc to every 3 rows ends, 3sc in corner st, cont working in sc along cast on edge working 7sc to every 8 sts, 3sc in corner st, then work in sc up other long side as before, ending at other end of top border row. Turn.
2nd row Ch1, work 1sc into each sc to end, working 3sc into each corner sc. Turn.
3rd row Ch4, skip first 2sc, 1sc in next sc, * ch3, skip 1sc, 1sc in next sc *, rep from * to * down first side, work 1sc, ch3, 1sc all in corner sc, rep from * to * along next edge, work 1sc, ch3, 1sc all in corner sc, rep from * to * up other side to top border row. Turn.
4th row Ch3, 1ss in first sp, * ch3, 1ss in next sp, rep from * all around, working 1ss, ch3, 1ss all in each corner sp, ending ch3, 1ss in base of turning ch. Fasten off.
Work around top border flap edges in same way.

Finishing

Press crochet border only under a dry cloth with a warm iron. Catch-st tog the crochet borders along the top border line.

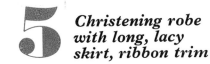

Christening robe with long, lacy skirt, ribbon trim

Size
To fit an 18 to 20in chest
Length to center back, 28in
Sleeve seam, 1in
Gauge
4 patt to 1¾in in width over bodice patt worked on No.G crochet hook; 2 patts to 2¾in in width over skirt patt worked on No.G crochet hook
Materials
9 balls of Bernat Berella Germantown
No.G crochet hook
Six small buttons
4yds 1in wide ribbon
2yds narrow ribbon

Bodice back

Using No.G crochet hook make ch74.
1st row Into 2nd ch from hook work 1sc, *ch2, skip ch2, 1sc in next ch, rep from * to end. Turn. 24 sps.
2nd row Ch1, 1sc in first sc, *ch2, skip ch2 sp, 1sc in next sc, rep from * to end. Turn.
3rd row As 2nd.
Shape armholes
4th row Ch1, skip first sc, 1sc in ch2 sp, ch1, 1sc in next sc, *ch2, skip ch2 sp, 1sc in next sc, rep from * 21 times more, ch1, skip ch2 sp, 1sc in last sc. Turn.
5th row Ch1, skip first sc, skip ch1 sp, 1 sc in next sc, *ch2, skip ch2 sp, 1 sc in next sc, rep from * 21 times more, skip ch1 sp, 1sc in next sc. Turn.
6th row Ch1, skip first sc, 1sc in next sc, *ch2, skip ch2 sp, 1sc in next sc, rep from * 21 times more. Turn.
7th row As 4th row but read 19 times more instead of 21 times more.
8th row As 5th row but read 19 times more instead of 21 times more.
9th row As 6th row but read 19 times more instead of 21 times more.
Rep 2nd row 11 times more.
Shape shoulders
21st row *Ss in first sc, ss in ch sp, ch1, ss in next sc, ss in ch sp, ch1, 1sc in next sc*, **ch2, skip ch2 sp, 1sc in next sc, rep from ** 15 times more, ss in ch sp. Turn.
22nd row Ch1, rep from * to * as given for row 21, **ch2, skip ch2 sp, 1 sc in next sc, rep from ** 11 times more, ss in ch sp. Turn.
23rd row Ch1, rep from * to * as given for row 21, **ch2, skip ch2 sp, 1 sc in next sc, rep from ** 7 times more, ss in ch sp. Fasten off.

Bodice front

Work as given for Bodice back until 9th row has been completed. Rep 2nd row 4 times more.
Shape neck
14th row Ch1, 1sc in first sc, *ch2, skip ch2 sp, 1sc in next sc, rep from * 6 times more. Turn.
15th row Ch1, skip first sc, 1sc in ch sp, ch1, 1sc in next sc, *ch2, skip ch2 sp, 1sc in next sc, rep from * 5 times more. Turn.
16th row Ch1, 1sc in first sc, *ch2, skip ch2 sp, 1sc in next sc, rep from * 5 times more, skip ch1 sp, 1sc in next sc. Turn.
17th row Ch1, skip 1st sc, *ch2, skip ch2 sp, 1sc in next sc, rep from * 5 times more. Turn.
Rep 2nd row 3 times more, ending at inner edge.

Shape shoulder
21st row Ch1, 1sc in first sc, *ch2, skip ch2 sp, 1sc in next sc, rep from * 3 times more, ss in ch sp. Turn.
22nd row Ch1, rep from * to * as given for 21st row on back shoulder, **ch2, skip ch2 sp, 1sc in next sc, rep from ** once. Fasten off. Make a loop and sl on hook, with RS of work facing skip center 6 sps and 5sc, work 1sc in 8th sc from armhole edge, *ch2, skip ch2 sp, 1sc in next sc, rep from * 6 times more. Turn.
15th row Ch1, 1 sc in first sc, *ch2, skip ch2 sp, 1sc in next sc, rep from * 5 times more, ch1, skip ch2 sp, 1sc in last sc. Turn.
16th row Ch1, skip first sc, skip ch1 sp, 1 sc in next sc, *ch2, skip ch2 sp, 1sc in next sc, rep from * 5 times more. Turn.
17th row Ch1, 1sc in first sc, *ch2, skip ch2 sp, 1sc in next sc, rep from * 5 times more. Turn.
Rep 2nd row 3 times more, ending at armhole edge.
Shape shoulder
Next row Ch1, rep from * to * as given for 21st row on back shoulder, **ch2, skip ch2 sp, 1sc in next sc, rep from ** 3 times more. Turn.
Next row Ch1, 1sc in first sc, *ch2, skip ch2 sp, 1sc in next sc, rep from * once, ss in ch sp. Fasten off.

Sleeves

Using No.G crochet hook ch62.
1st row As 1st row of Bodice back. 20sps.
Rep 2nd row as given for Bodice back twice.
4th row As 4th row of back but read 17 times more instead of 21 times more.
5th row As 5th row of back but read 17 times more instead of 21 times more.
6th row As 6th row of back but read 17 times more instead of 21 times more.
Rep 4th-6th rows once but read 15 times more in each row.
Rep 4th-6th rows once but read 13 times more in each row.
Rep 4th-6th rows once but read 11 times more in each row.
Rep 4th-6th row once but read 9 times more in each row.
19th row Ch1, skip first sc, ss in ch2 sp, ch1, 1sc in next sc, *ch2, skip ch2 sp, 1 sc in next sc, rep from * 7 times more, ss in ch sp. Turn.
20th row Ch1, ss in first sc, ss in ch2 sp, ch1, 1sc in next sc, *ch2, skip ch2 sp, 1 sc in next sc, rep from * 5 times more. Turn.
21st row As 20th row but read 3 times more instead of 5 times more.
22nd row As 20th row but read once more instead of 5 times more. Fasten off.

Skirt back

Using No.G crochet hook and with RS work facing, attach yarn to beg of foundation ch of Bodice back.
1st row Ch4, 1sc in ch2 sp *ch4, 1sc in next ch2 sp, rep from * ending ch3, 1sc in last ch. Turn.
2nd row Ch4, 1sc in first ch sp, ch4, 1sc in next ch sp, *ch4, 1sc in next ch sp, ch4, 1sc in same ch sp as last sc, (ch4, 1sc in next ch sp) 6 times, rep from * twice more, ch4, 1sc in next ch sp, ch4, 1sc in same ch sp as last sc, ch4, 1sc in last ch sp, ch4, 1sc in last ch sp. Turn.
3rd row Ch4, 1sc in first ch sp, *ch4, 1 sc in next ch sp, rep from * ending with 1sc in last ch sp. Turn. 30sps.
4th row As 3rd.
5th row Ch4, 1sc in first ch sp, ch4, 1sc in same ch sp as last sc, rep from * as given in

3rd row and end as 3rd row. 31sps.

6th row Ch4, 1sc in first ch sp, 3dc in next sc, 1sc in next ch sp, *ch4, 1sc in next ch sp, 3dc in next sc, 1sc in next ch sp, rep from * ending ch4, 1sc in last ch sp. Turn. (In rep of this row read sc instead of sp).

7th row Ch4, 1sc in first ch sp, *ch4, skip 1sc, skip 1dc, ch4, 1sc in next ch sp, rep from * to end. Turn.

8th row Ch2, 1dc in first sc, 1sc in next ch sp, *ch4, 1sc in next ch sp, 3dc in next sc, 1sc in next ch sp, rep from * ending ch4, 1sc in next ch sp, 2dc in last sc. Turn.

9th row Ch1, 1sc in first dc, *ch4, 1sc in next ch sp, ch4, skip 1sc, skip 1dc, 1sc in next dc rep from * ending ch4, 1sc in next ch sp, ch4, skip 1sc, skip 1dc, 1sc in turning ch. Turn. 30 sps.

Rep 6th-9th rows 19 times more.

Next row Ch3, 2dc in first sc, *ch2, skip ch sp, 1sc in next sc, ch2, skip ch sp, work 2dc, 1tr, 2dc all into next sc, rep from * ending last rep with 2dc, 1tr in last sc. Turn.

Next row Ch2, 1sc in first tr, 1sc in each of next 2dc, *ch1, skip ch sp, ss in sc, ch1, skip ch sp, 1sc in each of next 2dc, work 1sc, 1hdc, 1sc all into next tr, 1sc in each of next 2dc, rep from * ending ch1, skip ch sp, ss in sc, ch1, skip ch sp, 1sc in each of next 2dc, work 1sc, 1hdc in turning ch. Fasten off.

Skirt front

Work as given for Skirt back.

Neck borders

Press each piece under a dry cloth with a warm iron. Using No.G crochet hook and with RS of Bodice front facing, attach yarn to neck edge of left shoulder, (ch3, ss in neck edge) 4 times along shaped neck edge, (ch3, skip ch sp, ss in sc) along center front edge, (ch3, ss in neck edge) 4 times up shaped neck edge. Turn.

2nd row Ch2, ss in first ch sp, ch3, ss in same ch sp as last ss, *ch1, ss in next ch sp, ch3, ss in same ch sp as last ss, rep from * to end. Fasten off.

Work back neck edge to match.

Sleeve borders

Using No.G crochet hook and with RS of work facing, attach yarn to beg of foundation ch.

1st row (RS) ch3, skip 1sc, in next ch sp, *ch3, skip 1sc, in next ch sp, rep from * to last but one ch sp, ch3, ss in end of row. Turn.
Rep 2nd row as given for neck border. Fasten off.

Finishing

Join shoulder seams across 2 sps from armhole edges. Press seams.

Using No.G crochet hook and with WS of work facing, attach yarn to neck edge of back of right shoulder and work 11sc along back edge, then cont along front edge as folls: 2sc, (ch1, 2sc) 3 times, ending at neck edge of front shoulder. Fasten off. Work other shoulder to correspond, working row in reverse. Press shoulders. Sew on buttons. Sew sleeves into armholes, easing in sleeve fullness. Press seams. Join side and sleeve seams. Press seams.

Thread 1in wide ribbon through the 1st row of skirt and tie into a bow leaving very long loops and ends. Cut narrow ribbon into 4 lengths. Thread a length through each sleeve border and tie into a bow.
Thread a length through each neck border and tie into bows on shoulders.

6 Jumpsuit and hooded jacket with ribbon edging

Sizes
To fit 20[22]in chest.
The figures in brackets [] refer to the 22in size
Jacket length to shoulder, 11[12½]in
Sleeve seam, 6[7]in
Jumpsuit side length to underarm, 19[21]in
Gauge
5½ sts to 1in worked on No.D crochet hook
Materials
Reynolds Classique, 50-gram balls
Jacket 5[6] balls
Jumpsuit 6[6] balls
One No.D crochet hook
4yds embroidered ribbon
Four buttons

Jacket back

Using No.D crochet hook ch 61[67].
1st row Skip ch1, *1hdc into each ch to end. Turn.
60[66] sts.
2nd row Ch2, 1hdc into each st to end. Turn.
The 2nd row forms patt and is rep throughout.
Cont in patt until work measures 6[7]in from beg.
Shape armholes
Next row Ss over 1[2] sts, work to within 1[2] sts from end. Turn.
Dec one st at each end of every row in this manner until 20[22] sts rem.
Fasten off.

Jacket left front

Using No.D crochet hook ch 32[35]. Work as given for back until front measures same as back to armholes.
Shape armhole
Next row Ss over 1[2] sts, work to end.
Dec one st at armhole edge on every row until 16[18] sts rem, ending at front edge.
Shape neck
Next row Ss over 5 sts, work to last st. Turn.
Cont to dec at armhole edge as before, *at the same time* dec 2 sts at neck edge on next 2 rows and one st on foll 1[2] rows. Cont dec at armhole edge only until all sts are worked off.

Jacket right front

Work as given for left front, reversing all shapings.

Sleeves

Using No.D crochet hook ch 31[35]. Work as given for back, inc one st at each end of 2nd and every foll 3rd row until there are 44[50]sts. Cont without shaping until sleeve measures 6[7]in from beg.
Shape cap
Next row Ss over 1[2] sts, work to within 1[2] sts of end. Turn.
Dec one st at each end of every row until 4[6] sts rem. Fasten off.

Hood

Using No.D crochet hook ch 82[88] and beg at front. Work as given for back until work measures 6[6½]in from beg. Break yarn.
Shape back
Skip 30[32]sts, attach yarn to next st and work in patt over 21[23]sts. Turn.
Cont in patt over these 21[23] sts, dec one st at each end of 4th and every foll 4th row until 13[15]sts rem. Cont without shaping until back measures 5½[6]in from beg. Fasten off.

Jumpsuit front

** Using No.D crochet hook ch 20[22] for right leg. Work 1 row hdc. Cont in patt, inc one st at beg of next and at same edge on every foll 3rd row until there are 30[33]sts. Cont without shaping until work measures 8¼[9½]in from beg, ending at shaped edge. Fasten off. Work left leg as given for right leg, reversing shaping and ending at straight side edge.
Next row Work across 30[33]sts of left leg, ch8 for crotch, work across 30[33] sts of right leg. Turn.
Cont in patt. Work 2 rows.
Next row Work 32[35]hdc, (work next 2 sts tog) twice, work 32[35]hdc. Turn.
Work 7 rows without shaping.
Next row Work 31[34]hdc, (work next 2 sts tog) twice, work 31[34]hdc. Turn.
Work 7 rows without shaping.
Next row Work 30[33]hdc, (work next 2 sts tog) twice, work 30[33]hdc. Turn.
Work 7 rows without shaping.
Next row Work 29[32]hdc, (work next 2 sts tog) twice, work 29[32]hdc. Turn. 60[66]sts. **
Cont without shaping until side edge measures 19[21]in.
Shape armholes
*** **Next row** Ss over 4 sts, work to within 4 sts of end. Turn.
Next row Ss over 2 sts, work to within 2 sts of end. Turn.
Dec one st at each end of next 3[4] rows. 42[46] sts. Cont without shaping until armholes measure 2½[3]in from beg.
Shape neck
Next row Work 16[18]hdc. Turn.
Next row Ss over 2 sts, work to end.
Next row Work 12[14]hdc. Turn.
Dec one st at neck edge on next 3[4] rows.
Cont without shaping until armhole measures 4¾[5¼]in from beg. Fasten off.
Skip next 10 sts for neck edge, attach yarn to rem sts and work to correspond to other side reversing shaping. Fasten off. ***

Jumpsuit back

Work as given for front from ** to **.
Cont without shaping until side edge measures 16½[18]in from beg.

Shape back
Next row Ss over 5 sts, work to within 5 sts of end. Turn.
Rep last row 4 times more. Break off yarn. Attach yarn at commencement of back shaping and work across all 60[66] sts. Cont without shaping until side edge measures 19[21]in from beg.
Shape armholes
Work as given for front from *** to ***.

Finishing

Press each piece lightly on the WS under a dry cloth with a cool iron for synthetics.
Jacket Sew in sleeves. Join side and sleeve seams. With RS of work facing, attach yarn and work 1 row sc evenly up right front, across top of sleeve, around back of neck, across sleeve top and down left front. Turn.
Next row Ch2, work in hdc to end. Turn.
Next row Ch1, work in sc to end. Fasten off.
Join back seams of hood. Fold 1 in at front edge to RS for border. Join neck edge of hood to neck edge of jacket with the center back of hood to center back of jacket and front edge of hood ½in from front edge of jacket. Thread ribbon through hdc down left front, around lower edge and up right front going over 2 sts and under one st. Thread ribbon in same way round cuffs and hood border. Make a twisted cord and thread through hdc around neck.
Jumpsuit Join side and leg seams
Foot instep Attach yarn and work 10 rows hdc over center 11 sts of front leg. Break yarn and fasten off. Attach yarn to center st of back of leg, work in hdc from center back of leg to instep, working every 2nd and 3rd [3rd and 4th] st tog, work 10hdc up side of instep, 11hdc from instep and 10hdc down side of instep, work in hdc from instep to center back of leg, working every 2nd and 3rd [3rd and 4th] st tog. 49[55] sts. Join with ss to first hdc and work 5[6] rounds hdc.
Fasten off.
Foot sole Skip 19[22] sts at beg and end of round. Work in hdc over center 11 sts, dec one st at each end of foll 9th[10th] row. Work 1[2] rows without shaping. Dec one st at each end of next 2 rows.
Fasten off.
Join foot seams.
Borders With RS of work facing attach yarn and work 1 row sc, 1 row hdc, 1 row sc around shoulder, armhole and neck edges, working 2 small loops on each front shoulder for buttonholes.
Thread ribbon through hdc around neck edge and first row of hdc around instep as given for jacket. Make a twisted cord and thread through waist above back shaping. Make twisted cords and thread round ankles.
Press all seams.
Sew on buttons.

7 Candy stripe maxi-top with pants

Size
To fit an 18/20in chest
Maxi-top length at center back, 10in
Sleeve seam, 5in
Pants length at center front, 9½in
Gauge
6 sts to 1in worked on No.D crochet hook
Materials
Coats and Clarks O.N.T. Pearl Cotton
11 balls main color, A
5 balls of contrast color, B
No.D crochet hook
Eight small buttons
1yd narrow ribbon
Waist length of elastic

Maxi-top

Using No.D crochet hook and A, ch54 loosely and beg at right back edge.
Base row Into 4th ch from hook work 1dc, work 1dc into each of next 40ch, 1sc into each of last 10ch. Turn.
Next row Ch1, 1sc into each of next 20sts, 1dc into each of next 31 sts, 1dc into top of first 3ch. Turn.
Commence patt.
Attach B.
1st row (RS) Using B ch3 to stand as first dc, 1dc into 2nd st, 1dc into each of next 40 sts, 1sc into each of last 10 sts. Turn.
2nd row Using B, ch1, 1sc into each of next 20 sts, 1dc into each of last 32 sts. Turn.
3rd row Using A, as 1st row.
4th row Using A, as 2nd row.
These 4 rows form patt and are rep throughout.
Cont in patt until 8th stripe in A has been completed from beg, then rep 1st row once.
**Divide for sleeve
Next row Using B, ch1, 1sc into each of next 18 sts, ch24. Turn.

Next row Using A work 1dc into 4th ch from hook, 1dc into each of next 20ch, 1dc into each of next 8 sts, 1sc into each of next 10 sts. Turn.
Next row Using A, ch1, 1sc, into each of next 20 sts, 1dc into each of next 14 sts, 1sc into each of last 6 sts. Turn.
Next row Using B ch3, 1dc into 2nd st, 1dc into each of next 28 sts, 1sc into each of last 10 sts. Turn.
Next row Using B, ch1, 1sc into each of next 20 sts, 1dc into each of next 14 sts, 1sc into each of last 6 sts. Turn.
Cont in patt in this way until 8th stripe in A has been completed from beg of sleeve, then rep 1st row again.
Next row Using A, ch1, 1sc into each of next 18 sts, now work across side edge sts, 1sc into each of next 2 sts, 1dc into each of last 32 sts. Turn. ******
Complete front on these sts. Beg with 2 rows in A work 8 rows patt.
Next row Ch3, 1dc into 2nd st, 1dc into each of next 29 sts, skip 1 st, 1dc into each of next 10 sts, 1sc into each of last 10 sts. Turn.
Next row Ch1, 1sc into each of next 20 sts, 1dc into each of last 31 sts. Turn.
Next row Ch3, 1dc into 2nd st, 1dc into each of next 28 sts, skip 1 st, 1dc into each of next 10 sts, 1sc into each of last 10 sts. Turn.
Next row Ch1, 1sc into each of next 20 sts, 1dc into each of last 30 sts. Turn.
Next row Ch3, 1dc into 2nd st, 1dc into each of next 27 sts, skip 1 st, 1dc into each of next 10 sts, 1sc into each of last 10 sts. Turn.
Cont dec in this way every other row until 6 dec in all have been worked. Work 11 rows without shaping, ending with 8th stripe of A from beg of front.
Next row Ch3, 1dc into 2nd st, 1dc into each of next 23 sts, 2dc into next st, 1dc into each of next 10 sts, 1sc into each of last 10 sts. Turn.
Next row Patt as before, working 1 more dc in last group.
Next row Ch3, 1dc into 2nd st, 1 dc into each of next 24 sts, 2dc into next st, 1dc into each of next 10 sts, 1sc into each of last 10 sts. Turn.
Cont inc in this way every other row until 6 inc in all have been worked. Work 9 rows without shaping, ending with 13th stripe in A from beg of front. Rep 1st row once more.
Rep from ** to ** for other sleeve. Work on these sts for left back, beg with 2 rows A until 8th stripe in A has been worked from beg of left back.
Fasten off.

Neck border

Using No.D crochet hook, B and with RS of work facing, work 1sc into top of every stripe around neck edge. Turn. 89sc.
Next row Ch1, 1sc into first sc, *ch2, skip sc, 1 sc into each of next 2sc, rep from * to end. Turn.
Next row Ch1, *1sc into each of next 2sc, 1sc into ch2 sp, rep from * to last st, 1sc into last sc. Turn. 67sc.
Next row Work in sc to end. Fasten off.

Sleeve borders

Using No.D crochet hook, B and with RS of work facing, work 2sc into end of each stripe along sleeve edge. Work 1 row sc. Fasten off.

Lower border

Using No.D crochet hook, B and with RS of work facing, attach yarn to lower corner of right back, work 1sc into corner, 6dc into center of first stripe, *1sc between stripes, 6dc into center of next stripe, rep from * to end, working 1 sc into corner. Fasten off.

Back borders

Using No.D crochet hook, A and with RS of work facing, work 2 rows sc along left back edge. Fasten off. Using A and with RS of work facing work 1 row sc along right back edge, working 1sc into each st along edge.
Next row Ch1, 1sc into each of next 29sc, (ch1, skip 1sc, 1sc into each of next 2sc) 7 times, ch1, skip 1sc, 1sc into last sc. Fasten off.

Finishing

Press work lightly on WS under a damp cloth with a warm iron. Join sleeve seams. Sew on buttons. Cut ribbon in half and sew edge of each piece to back neck edges, thread ribbon through eyelet holes and tie at center front.

Pants back

Using No.D crochet hook and A, ch51 loosely.
1st row Into 2nd ch from hook work 1sc, 1sc into each ch to end. Turn. 50 sts.
2nd row Ch1, 1sc into each sc to end. Turn. Rep 2nd row twice more.
Next row Ch1, 1sc into each of first 2sc, (2sc into next sc, 1sc into each of next 3sc) 12 times. Turn. 62 sts.
Next row Ch3 to stand as first dc, 1dc into 2nd st, 1dc into each st to end. Turn.
Cont in dc until work measures 6in from beg.**
Next row Ss across first 15 sts, ch3, 1dc into 2nd st, 1dc into each of next 30 sts. Turn ***
Next row Ss across first st, ch3, 1dc into 2nd st, 1dc into each st to last st. Turn.
Rep last row until 12 sts rem. Cont in dc without shaping until work measures 9½in from beg. Fasten off.

Pants front

Work as given for back to **.
Next row Ss across first 20 sts, ch3, 1dc into 2nd st, 1dc into each of next 20 sts. Turn.
Complete as given for back from ***.

Leg borders

Join side seams. Using D crochet hook, A and with RS of work facing work 61sc evenly around leg. Work 1 more row sc. Break off A and attach B.
Next row Ch1, 1sc into first sc, *skip 2sc, 6dc into next sc, skip 2sc, 1sc into next sc, rep from * to end. Fasten off.

Finishing

Press as given for maxi-top. Join crotch seam. Sew elastic into circle and sew to WS of waist using casing stitch.

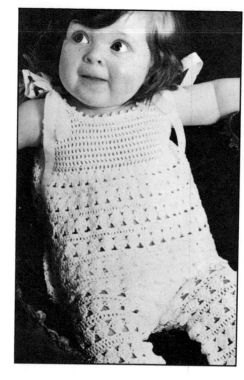

Little girl's lacy pants suit

Sizes
To fit 20[22:24]in chest
The figures in brackets [] refer to the 22in and 24in sizes respectively
Top length from shoulder, 10½[11:11½]in
Trousers inside leg, 6[6:6]in
Gauge
6dc and 3 rows to 1in worked on No.D crochet hook or 4dc groups to 3in
Materials
19[21:23] balls of Coats and Clarks O.N.T. Pearl Cotton
No.E crochet hook
No.D crochet hook
No.B crochet hook
1½yds ribbon
Three small buttons, waist length of elastic

Top front

Using No.D crochet hook ch56[60:64] loosely.
Base row into 3rd ch from hook work 1dc, 1dc into each ch to end. Turn.
Next row Ch3 to stand as 1st dc, 1dc into each dc to end. Turn. Rep last row twice more.
Shape armholes
Next row Ss over 4dc, ch2, work in dc to last 4dc. Turn.
Dec one dc at each end of next 2 rows. Cont without shaping until 8 rows have been worked from beg.
Shape neck
Next row Work in dc over next 10dc. Turn. Complete this shoulder first.
Next row Ss over 2dc, ch2, work in dc to end. Turn.
Next row Ch2, work in dc over 5dc. Turn.
Next row Ch2, skip first dc, work in dc to end. Fasten off.
Attach yarn to 10th dc from other end, ch2, work in dc to end.
Next row Ch2, work in dc over 7dc. Turn.

Next row Ch2, skip first dc, work in dc to end. Turn.
Next row Ch2, work in dc over 4dc. Fasten off.

Top half back

Using No.D crochet hook ch29[33:37] loosely. Work as given for front to armhole.
Shape armhole
Next row Ss over 4dc, ch2, work in dc to end. Turn.
Next row Work in dc to within 1dc from end. Turn.
Cont without shaping until 9 rows have been worked from beg.
Shape neck
Next row Ch2, work in dc over 7dc. Turn.
Next row Ch2, skip first dc, work in dc to end. Turn.
Next row Ch2, work in dc over 4dc. Fasten off.
Work other half back in same way.

Skirt top

Join side seams of front and backs. Using No.B hook and with RS of work facing, beg at center back and work ch3 into first dc.
1st patt row Work 2dc into base of ch3, *skip 1dc, 5dc into next dc, rep from * to end of other side of back, ending with 3dc into last dc. Turn.
2nd patt row Ch3, work 1dc into each of next 2dc leaving last loop of each dc on hook, yrh and draw through all loops on hook, ch1 to fasten, *ch2, 1dc into each of next 5dc leaving last loop of each dc on hook, yrh and draw through all loops on hook, ch1 to fasten, rep from * ending with 1dc into each of last 3dc leaving last loop of each dc on hook, yrh and draw through all loops on hook, ch1 to fasten. Turn.
3rd patt row Ch1, *1sc over dc gr, 3sc under ch2 sp, rep from * to end. Turn.
4th patt row Ch3, 1dc into each sc to end. Turn.
These 4 rows form patt. At the end of 4th patt row join work with a ss into top of ch of first gr, ch3, turn, and change to No.D hook.
1st round 4dc into first dc, *skip 3dc, 5dc into next dc, rep from * ending with skip 3dc, ss into top of ch of first gr, ch3. Turn.
Next round Work as 2nd patt row but working ch3 between gr instead of ch2.
Cont in patt until 8 rounds have been worked. Change to No.E crochet hook and cont in patt until 17 rounds have been worked, or desired length ending with a 1st patt round.
Next round Ch3, *1dc into each dc of gr leaving last loop of each dc on hook, yrh and draw through all loops on hook, ch1 to fasten, ch2, 1sc between gr, ch2, rep from * to end of round. Fasten off.

Neck edging

Using No.B crochet hook and beg at center back neck edge work in sc around neck and armhole edges to other side, turn, ch1, work back in sc.
Next round Ch1, 1sc into next sc, *ch3, ss into top of last sc—called 1 picot—, 1sc into each of next 3sc, rep from * to end. Fasten off.

Center back edging

Using No.B crochet hook work 4 rows of sc along left center back edge. Mark position for 3 buttons on this edge. Beg at neck edge work 2 rows of sc along right center back edge. Work another row sc making buttonholes as markers

re reached by working ch3 and skipping 3sc.
Work another row of sc working 3sc under each ch3 sp.
Fasten off.

Finishing

Press on WS under a damp cloth with a warm iron. Sew on buttons. Divide ribbons into 4 pieces and sew one piece to each shoulder and tie into a bow.

Pants

Using No.D crochet hook beg at waist ch112[128:144] loosely. Join into a circle with a ss.
Base round Ch3 to count as first dc, work 1dc into each ch to end. Join with ss into top of first ch3. Turn.
Next round Ch3, work 1dc into front loop only of each dc to end. Join with ss into top of first ch3. Turn.
1st patt round Ch3, work 4dc into base of ch, *skip 3dc, work 5dc into next dc, rep from * ending with skip 3dc, join with ss into top of first ch3. Turn.
2nd patt round Ch3, work 1dc into next 4dc of first gr leaving last loop of each dc on hook, yrh and draw through all loops on hook, ch1 to fasten, *ch2, 1dc into each dc of next gr leaving last loop of each dc on hook, yrh and draw through all loops on hook, ch1 to fasten, rep from * ending with ch2, ss into top of first ch3. Turn.
3rd patt round Ch1, *1sc over dc gr, 3sc under ch2 sp, rep from * to end. Join with ss into top of first ch. Turn.
4th patt round Ch3, work 1dc into each sc to end. Join with ss to top of first ch3. Turn.
These 4 rounds form patt. Cont in patt until 5 rounds have been worked. On the next round work ch3 between gr instead of ch2. Cont in patt until 16 rounds have been worked, ending with 3rd patt round. Turn. Make ch8 then ss into center back, counting 14[16:18]gr and sp for each leg.
Turn and work 4th patt round, beg over the starting ch.
Work legs
1st leg round Ch3, work 4dc (this gr must be over the gr of previous round), *skip 3dc, work 5dc into next dc, rep from * around leg, ending with ss into top of first ch3.
Turn.
2nd round Ch3, work 1dc into each of next 4dc of gr leaving last loop of each dc on hook, yrh and draw through all loops on hook, ch1 to fasten, *ch2, 1dc into each dc of next gr leaving last loop of each dc on hook, yrh and draw through all loops on hook, ch1 to fasten, rep from * ending with ch2, ss into top of first ch3. Turn. Cont in patt until 18 rounds have been worked from ch8, ending with a 1st patt round.
Last round Ch3, 1dc into each of next 4dc leaving last loop of each dc on hook, yrh and draw through all loops on hook, ch1 to fasten, ch2, 1sc between gr, *ch2, 1dc into each dc of next gr leaving last loop of each dc on hook, yrh and draw through all loops on hook, ch1 to fasten, ch2, 1sc between gr, rep from * ending with ch2, ss into top of first ch3. Fasten off.
Attach yarn at center back and work around in patt ending over the ch8. Complete as given for first leg.

Finishing

Press as given for top. Turn first row of dc at waistline to WS and sl st down. Thread narrow elastic through waistband and secure.

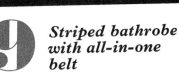

9 *Striped bathrobe with all-in-one belt*

Sizes
To fit a 22[24]in chest
The figures in brackets[] refer to the 24in size
Length to center back, 26[28]in, adjustable
Sleeve seam, 8[10]in, adjustable
Gauge
4½dc to 1in over patt worked on No.E crochet hook
Materials
8[10] balls Bernat Berella Germantown in main color, A
6[8] balls in contrast color, B
One No.E crochet hook

Bodice back

Using No.E crochet hook and A, ch57[61].
Base row Using A work 1dc into 3rd ch from hook, *skip ch1, 2dc into next ch, rep from * to end.
Turn. 28[30] V patts.
1st and 2nd rows Using B, ch3, work 1dc between first 2dc, *2dc between next 2dc of previous row, rep from * to end. Turn.
3rd and 4th rows Using A, as 1st and 2nd rows. These 4 rows form patt and are rep throughout.
Cont in patt until work measures 2[2¾]in from beg.

Shape armholes
Break off yarn.
Next row Skip first 2 V patts, attach yarn to next V patt, ch3, work in patt until 3 V patts rem, 1dc into next V patt. Turn.
Next row Ch3, 1dc into next dc, work in patt until 1 V patt rem, 1dc into next V patt, 1dc into sp between V patt and turning ch. Turn.
22[24] V patts.
Cont in patt without shaping until armholes measure 4¾[5]in from beg.
Shape shoulders
Break off yarn.
Next row Skip first 3 V patts, attach yarn to next V patt, 1sc into this V patt, work across 14[16] V patts, 1sc into next V patt. Turn.
Break off yarn.
Next row Skip 1sc and next 2 V patts, attach yarn to next V patt, 1sc into this V patt, work across 8[10] V patts, 1sc into next V patt.
Fasten off.

Bodice front

Using No.E crochet hook and A, ch29[31].
Work Base row as given for back.
14[15] V patts.
Shape front
Next row (front edge) Using B, work ch3 to form first dc, skip first V patt, patt to end. Turn.
Next row Using B, work in patt until 1 V patt rem, 1dc into this V patt, 1dc into sp between V patt and turning ch. Turn.
Cont in patt, dec at neck edge in this way on every row until work measures 2[2¾]in from beg, ending at armhole edge.
Shape armhole
Break off yarn.
Next row Skip first 2 V patts, attach yarn to next V patt, ch3, work in patt until 1 V patt rem, 1dc into this V patt, 1dc into sp between V patt and turning ch. Turn.
Next row Ch3, skip first V patt, work in patt until 1 V patt rem, 1dc into this V patt, 1dc into sp between dc and turning ch. Turn.
Cont in patt, dec at neck edge as before until 7[7] V patt rem. Cont without shaping until armhole measures same as back to shoulder, ending at armhole edge.
Shape shoulder
Break off yarn.
Next row Skip first 3 V patts, attach yarn to next V patt, 1sc into this V patt, work in patt to end. Fasten off.
Work other front in same way.

Sleeves

Using No.E crochet hook and A, ch39[41].
Work Base row as given for back. 19[20] V patts. Work in patt as given for back, inc 1dc at each end of 4th and every other row until there are 23[24] V patts.
Cont in patt without shaping until sleeve measures 8[10]in from beg, or desired length to underarm, noting that last in of sleeve is set into armhole.
Shape cap
Dec one st at each end of next 4 rows. 21[22] V patts. Fasten off.

Belt

Using No.E crochet hook and A, ch3.
1st row Into 2nd ch from hook work 1sc, 1sc into next ch. Turn.
2nd row Ch1, 1sc into first sc, 1sc into each of next 2sc, 2sc into next sc. Turn.
Cont in this way inc one st at each end of every row until there are 11sc.
Cont in sc without shaping until work measures 44in from beg.

Next row Ch1, skip first sc, (insert hook into next sc and draw loop through) twice, yrh and draw through 3 loops on hook—called dec 1—, 2sc into each sc until 2sc rem, dec 1. Turn. Rep last row until 3sc rem, dec 1. Fasten off.

Skirt

Using No.E crochet hook and A, make ch217[241]. Work Base row as given for Bodice back. 108[120] V patts.
Cont in patt as given for Bodice back until work measures 17[18]in from beg, or desired length.
Next row Using A, ch1, *dec 1 into next 2 V patts, rep from * to end. 56[60]sc.
Next row Work in sc to end. Fasten off.

Finishing

Press each piece lightly under a damp cloth with a warm iron. Join shoulder and side seams of Bodice. Join sleeve seams, leaving last in open. Sew in sleeves, placing last in of sleeve seam to underarm shaping. With RS facing and 9in from end of belt, sew Bodice along one edge of belt from front edge to front edge, leaving 12in of belt free at other end. Sew skirt to other edge of belt to match Bodice top.
Neckband Using No.E crochet hook, A and with RS work facing, beg at lower edge of right bodice front where it joins belt and work a row of sc evenly all around neck edge, ending with ss into belt at other end. Work 2 more rows sc around neck edge, joining each row with ss into belt. Fasten off.

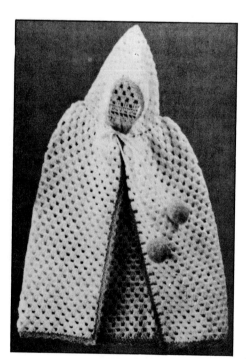

10

Cape with hood and pompon tie

Size
To fit a baby from birth to 6 months

Length of cape, 19in
Length of hood, 7in
Face edge of hood, 13in
Gauge
2 patts to 1½in worked on No.E crochet hook for either yarn.
Materials
Spinnerin Wintuk Featherlon
4 skeins main color, A
1 skein contrast color, B
No.E crochet hook
or
Spinnerin Wintuk Sport
7 skeins main color, A
1 skein contrast color, B

Cape

Using No.E crochet hook and A beg at neck edge and ch77.
1st row Into 3rd ch from hook work 1sc, 1sc into each ch to end.
Turn. 75sc.
2nd row Ch2, *ch1, skip 1sc, 1dc into next sc, rep from * to end.
Turn.
3rd row Ch2, *1sc into ch1 sp, 1sc into next dc, rep from * to end, 1sc into 2nd of 2 turning ch. Turn.
4th row Ch2, 3dc into first sc, *skip 1sc, 3dc into next sc, rep from * to end, 4dc into 2nd of 2 turning ch.
Turn.
5th row Ch2, 3dc into first ch sp between 3dc gr, *ch1, 3dc into next sp, rep from * to end, ch1, 1dc into 2nd of 2 turning ch.
Turn.
6th row Ch2, 3dc into first ch sp, * ch1, 3dc into next sp, rep from * to end, ch1, 1dc into 2nd of 2 turning ch.
Turn.
Rep 5th and 6th rows 15 times more, then 5th row once more.
Fasten off.

Hood

Using No.E crochet hook and A attach yarn to the 6th ch at neck edge.
1st row Ch3, 1dc into each of next ch2, *skip ch1, 1dc into each of next ch3, rep from * to last ch5.
Turn.
2nd row Ch2, 3dc into first sp, *skip next 3dc, 3dc into next sp, rep from * to end, 1dc into 2nd of 2 turning ch.
Turn.
3rd row Ch2, 3dc into first sp, *3dc into next sp, rep from * to last sp, 3dc into last sp, 1dc into 2nd of 2 turning ch.
Turn.
Rep 2nd and 3rd rows 5 times more.
Fasten off.

Finishing

Press over the RS of the garment with a cool iron. Taking a small area at a time, stretch crochet lengthways and sideways, let it relax then pat over with the iron using no pressure.
Join top seam of hood. Using No.E crochet hook and B work 2 rows sc around outer edges of cape and hood.
Next row (picot edge) *Ch3, ss into first ch to form picot, skip 2sc, 1sc into next sc, rep from * around all edges.
Fasten off. Press.
Using 2 strands of A make a ch 48in long. Thread through holes at neck edge.
Using B, make 2 pompons and attach one to each end of ch.

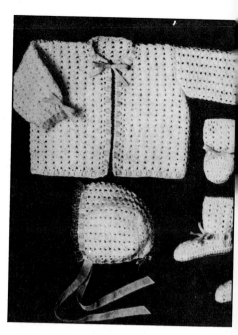

11

Sacque set— bonnet, bootees and mittens

Sizes
Jacket to fit 22[24]in chest.
The figures in brackets [] refer to the 24in size.
Length at center back, 9¼[10½]in
Sleeve seam, 5[6]in
Bootees top of base to heel, 4in.
Heel to toe, 4¼in
Mittens all around hand, 5¼in
Length, 4¼in
Bonnet face edge, 11½in
Front to center back, 5¼in
Gauge
3 shells to 1⅝in in width worked on No.E crochet hook
Materials
Layette 11 skeins of Brunswick Fingering Yarn
No.E crochet hook
4½yds narrow lace
10yds narrow ribbon
¾yd ¼in ribbon for bonnet

Jacket back

Using No.E crochet hook ch66[72].
1st base row Into 3rd ch from hook work 1dc, 1dc into each ch to end.
Turn. 65[71]dc.
2nd base row Ch3, 1dc into base of ch3, *skip 2dc, 3dc into next dc (1 shell completed), rep from * ending 2dc into top of ch3.
Turn.
1st patt row Ch2, 1dc between 2dc, *3dc into center of shell on previous row, rep from * ending 2dc between last 2dc. Turn.
Rep 1st patt row 13[15] times more. ***
Shape armholes
1st row Ss into center of first shell, 1sc and 2dc into shell, work in patt until 1 shell rem, 2dc 1sc into last shell. Turn.
2nd row Ss into center of 2nd shell, 1sc and 2dc into shell, work in patt until 2 shells rem, 2dc, 1sc into next shell. Turn.
3rd row Ss into center of first shell, ch2, 1dc into shell, work in patt ending 2dc into last shell. Turn.
Work 7[8] rows in patt without shaping.
Shape shoulders
Next row Ss over 5[6] shells and into center of next shell, 1sc and 2dc into shell, work in patt

ver 4 shells, 2dc, 1sc into next shell, ss to end. Fasten off.

Jacket front

Using No.E crochet hook ch30[33].
Work as given for Jacket back to ***.
Shape armhole
1st row Ss into center of first shell, 1sc and 2dc into shell, patt to end. Turn.
2nd row Work in patt until 2 shells rem, 2dc and 1sc into next shell. Turn.
3rd row Ss into center of first shell, ch2, 1dc into shell, patt to end. Turn.
Work 2 rows patt without shaping.
Shape neck
1st row Ss into center of first shell, 1sc and 2dc into shell, patt to end. Turn.
2nd row Work in patt until 1 shell rem, 2dc into shell. Turn.
Work 3[4] rows patt without shaping.
Fasten off.
Work other front in same way.

Sleeves

Using No.E crochet hook ch46[51]. Work as given for Jacket back until first 2 rows of armhole shaping have been completed. Work the 2nd row again. Fasten off.

Front and neck edging

Join shoulder seams. Using No.E crochet hook and with RS facing, beg at lower edge of right front, work 2dc into each loop up front until 1 rem, 4dc into last loop, work in dc all around neck edge, 4dc into first loop on left front, 2dc into each loop down left front. Fasten off.

Finishing

Press under a damp cloth with a warm iron. Sew in sleeves. Join side and sleeve seams. Gather lace and sew inside edge of each sleeve. Beg at top of right front, thread ribbon all around Jacket ending at top of left front. Secure ends. Thread ribbon through neck edge and each sleeve and tie in a bow.

Bootees

Using No.E crochet hook ch33. Work as given for Jacket back until 1st patt row has been worked 5 times. *****
Next row (ribbon slots) Work 30dc over last row. Fasten off.
Shape instep
1st row Ss into 11th dc, ch2, 1dc into same dc as ss, (skip 2dc, 3dc into next dc) twice, skip 2dc, 2dc into next dc. Turn.
Work 5 rows patt over instep. Fasten off.
Ss into first dc of ribbon slot row, ch2, 1dc into each of next 10dc, (2dc into each loop of instep) 6 times, 8dc across instep, (2dc into each loop of instep) 6 times, work 11dc to end of row. Turn.
Shape heel and toe
1st row Ch2, skip 1dc, 1dc into each of next 21dc, skip 1dc, 1dc into each of next 8dc, skip 1dc, work in dc to last 2dc, skip 1dc, 1dc in last dc. Turn.
2nd row Ch2, skip 1dc, 1dc into each of next 19dc, skip 1dc, 1dc into each of next 8dc, skip 1dc, work in dc to last 2dc, skip 1dc, 1dc into last dc. Turn.
Work 1 row dc. Fasten off.

Finishing

Press as for Jacket. Join leg and under foot seam. Thread ribbon through slot row.

Bonnet

Using No.E crochet hook beg at face edge and ch63. Work as given for Jacket back until 1st patt row has been worked 10 times.
Next row Ss into center of 6th shell, ch2, 1dc into shell, work in patt over next 7 shells, 2dc into next shell.
Turn.
Bonnet back
Work 5 rows patt.
Shape back
1st row Work in patt over 3 shells, 2dc into next shell, patt to end.
Turn.
2nd row Work in patt over 2 shells, 2dc into center of each of next 3 shells, patt to end.
Turn.
3rd row Work in patt over 1 shell, 2dc into center of each of next 5 shells, patt to end.
Turn.
4th row Ch2, 1dc between 2dc, 2dc into next shell, 2dc between each 2dc, 2dc into last shell, 2dc between 2dc.
Turn.
Work 3 rows of 2dc between 2dc.
Fasten off.

Finishing

Press as for Jacket. Sew row ends of back to main part.
Side and back edging
Ss into first dc, ch2, 1dc into dc, 2dc into each loop at side, 12dc across back, 2dc into each loop at other side, 2dc into side of dc.
Fasten off.
Beg and ending at center back, thread ribbon all around bonnet and tie with a bow at back. Gather lace and sew inside face edge. Sew wide ribbon to each side of bonnet.

Mittens

Work as given for Bootees to *****.
Next row (ribbon slots) Work 30dc over last row. Turn.
Work 3 rows dc.
Shape tip
1st row Ch2, 1dc, *skip 1dc, 1dc into each of next 5dc, rep from * ending 3dc. Turn.
2nd row Ch2, 1dc, *skip 1dc, 1dc into each of next 4dc, rep from * ending 2dc. Turn.
3rd row Ch2, 1dc, *skip 1dc, 1dc into each of next 3dc, rep from * ending 1dc.
Fasten off.

Finishing

Press as for Jacket. Join side and top seams. Thread ribbon through slot row.

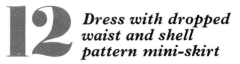

12 Dress with dropped waist and shell pattern mini-skirt

Sizes
To fit 21[23]in chest
The figures in brackets [] refer to the 23in size
Length to center back, 15½[16½]in
Gauge
4sc to 1in worked on No.F crochet hook
Materials
Bernat Berella Germantown
4[5] balls in main color, A
1[1] ball in contrast color, B
No.F crochet hook
Three small buttons

Dress back

Using No.F crochet hook and A, ch54[58].
1st row Into 3rd ch from hook work 1sc, 1sc into each ch to end.
Turn. 52[56]sc.
Work 13[15] rows sc.
1st dec row Work 14[16]sc, dec one st, work in sc until 16[18]sc rem, dec one st, work 14[16]sc. Turn. 50[54]sc.
Work 3 rows sc without shaping.
Rep last 4 rows once more. 48[52]sc.
Cont without shaping until work measures 6½[6¾]in from beg.
Shape armholes
1st row Ss across 4sc, 1sc into each sc until 4sc rem. Turn. 40[44]sc.
2nd row Work in sc to end. Turn.
3rd row Dec one st, work in sc to last 2sc, dec one st. Turn. 38[42]sc.
4th row Work in sc to end. Turn.
5th row Dec one st, work in sc to last 2sc, dec one st. Turn. 36[40]sc.
Work 5 more rows sc without shaping.
Divide for back opening
Next row Work 1sc into each of next 18[20]sc.
Turn.
Complete right shoulder on these sts. Cont without shaping until armhole measures 4½[4¾]in from beg, ending at armhole edge.
Shape shoulder
1st row Ss across 3[4]sc, 1sc into each sc to end. Turn.
2nd row Ch2 to form first sc, 1sc into each of next 10[11]sc, ss into next sc. Turn.
3rd row Ss across 3sc, work in sc to end.
Fasten off.
With RS of work facing, attach yarn to rem sts and work in sc to end. Turn.
Complete left shoulder on these sts. Cont in sc until armhole measures 4½[4¾]in from beg, ending at center edge.
Shape shoulder
1st row Ch2 to form first sc, 1sc into each of next 14[15]sc, ss into next sc. Turn.
2nd row Ss across 4sc, work in sc to end. Turn.
3rd row Ch2 to form first sc, 1sc into each of next 7[8] sc, ss into next sc. Fasten off.

Dress front

Work as given for back until armhole shaping has been completed. 36[40]sc.
Cont in sc without shaping, omitting back opening, until armholes measure 3½[3¾]in from beg.
Shape neck
1st row Ch2 to form first sc, 1sc into each of next 11[12]sc, ss into next sc. Turn.
2nd row Ch2, 1sc into each sc to end. Turn.
3rd row Ch2 to form first sc, 1sc into each of

next 10[11]sc, ss into sp between last sc and ch. Turn.

4th row Ch2, 1sc into each sc to end. Turn.

5th row Ch2 to form first sc, 1sc into each of next 9[10] sc, ss into sp between last sc and ch. Turn.

6th row Ch2, 1sc into each sc to end. Turn.

7th row Ch2 to form first sc, 1sc into each of next 8[9]sc, ss into sp between last sc and ch. Turn.

8th row Ch2 to form first sc, 1sc into each sc to end. Turn. 10[11]sc.

Cont in sc without shaping until armhole measures same as back to shoulder, ending at armhole edge.

Shape shoulder

1st row Ss across 3[4]sc, work in sc to end. Turn.

2nd row Work in sc to end, ss into last ss of previous row. Turn.

3rd row Ss across next 4sc, work in sc to end. Fasten off.

With RS of work facing, skip center 10[12]sc, attach yarn to next sc with ss, work in sc to end. Turn.

Next row Work in sc to end. Turn.

Next row Skip turning ch which forms first sc, work in sc to end. Turn.

Rep last 2 rows until 10[11]sc rem, then cont without shaping until armhole measures same as back to shoulder, ending at center edge.

Shape shoulder

1st row Ch2 to form first sc, 1sc into each of next 6[7]sc, ss into next sc. Turn.

2nd row Ss across 4sc, work in sc to end. Fasten off.

Armbands

Join shoulder and side seams. Using No.F crochet hook, A and with RS facing, beg at side seam and work 1 row sc evenly around armhole. Fasten off.

Back neck borders

Using No.F crochet hook, A and with RS facing, beg at lower edge of left side of back opening and work 2 rows sc. Fasten off.

Using No.F crochet hook, A and with WS facing, beg at lower edge of right side of back opening and work 1 row sc. Turn.

Next row Work 2sc, *skip next 2sc, ch3, work 4sc, rep from * twice more, work in sc to end. Fasten off.

Neckband

Using No.F crochet hook, A and with RS facing, beg at left back neck and work 1 row sc evenly around neck. Fasten off.

Skirt

Using No.F crochet hook, A and with RS facing beg over side seam and work downwards.

1st round *1sc into each of next 3sc, 2sc into next sc, rep from * to end, join with ss to first sc. Break off A and attach B.

2nd round Using B, beg at side seam, ch3, 4dc into next sc, skip 4sc, *5dc into next sc, skip 4sc, rep from * to end, join with ss to 3rd of first ch3. 26[28] shells.

3rd round Using A, *1sc into each of next 5dc, 1sc into sp between shells, rep from * to end, join with ss to first sc.

4th round As 2nd.

5th round Using A, *1sc into each of next 5dc, 2sc into sp between shells, rep from * to end,

join with ss to first sc.

6th round Using B, ch3, 5dc into first sc, skip 5sc, *6dc into next sc, skip 5sc, rep from * to end, join with ss into 3rd of first ch3.

7th round Using A, *1sc into each of next 6dc, 1sc into sp between shells, rep from * to end, join with ss to first sc.

Rep 6th and 7th rounds 1[2] times more. Fasten off.

Finishing

Press lightly under a dry cloth with a warm iron, pressing out shells of skirt gently. Sew on buttons to correspond with buttonholes.

13 *Yellow dress with ribbon trim*

Sizes

To fit 22[24:26] in chest
The figures in brackets [] refer to the 24 and 26in sizes respectively.
Length to shoulder, 11[11¼:11½]in
Sleeve seam, 1[1:1]in

Gauge

6dc and 3 rows to 1in worked on No.B hook.

Materials

11[13:13] balls of Coats and Clark's O.N.T. Pearl Cotton
No.B crochet hook
1½yds narrow ribbon. Six small buttons.

Skirt

Using No.B hook ch 160[160:160].
Beg at waist and work down to hem.

1st row (eyelets) Into 4th ch from hook

work *1dc, ch2, skip ch2, rep from * ending with 1dc into last ch. Turn. 52 eyelet slots.

Base row Ch3, *1dc into first sp, 3dc, ch1, 3dc into next sp, rep from * ending with 1dc into top of turning ch. Turn.

1st patt row Ch3, *3dc, ch1, 3dc into ch1 sp between 6dc, 1dc, ch1, 1dc into next ch1 sp between 2dc, rep from * ending with 1dc into top of turning ch. Turn.

2nd patt row Ch3, *1dc, ch1, 1dc into ch1 sp between 2dc, 3dc, ch1, 3dc into ch1 sp between 6dc, rep from * ending with 1dc into top of turning ch. Turn.

Rep last 2 rows and at the end of the 5th row, join the skirt into a circle, eliminate the 1dc at the end of the row, ss into top of first dc of the 6dc gr, then into the ch1 sp in center of same gr, work as folls:

1st round Ch3, 2dc, ch1, 3dc into 6dc gr, *1dc ch1 1dc into ch1 sp between 2dc, 3dc, ch1, 3dc into ch1 sp between 6dc, rep from * ending with 1dc, ch1, 1dc then ss into top of turning ch and then into ch1 sp between 6dc.

Rep this round until skirt measures 7½[7¾:8]in from beg, or desired length.

Last round *Work 1sc into each st to ch1 between 6dc, 1sc into sp, ch3, and ss into first of these ch to form picot, 1sc into same sp, rep from * around edge of skirt, ss into top of first sc. Fasten off.

Bodice half back

Using No.B hook attach yarn at center back of skirt.

22in size only

1st row Ch3, work 2dc into each of next 13 sp. Turn.

24in size only

1st row Ch3, work 2dc into each of next 5 sp, 3dc into each of next 3 sp and 2dc into each of next 5 sp. Turn.

26in size only

1st row Ch3, 2dc into each of next 3 sp, 3dc into each of next 6 sp, 2dc into each of next 4 sp. Turn.

All sizes

2nd row Ss over first 5dc, work in dc to end of row. Turn.

3rd row Ch3, work over 21[24:27]dc. Turn.

4th row Ch3, work in dc to end.

5th row Ch3, work over 20[23:26]dc. Turn.

Cont without shaping until 9 rows have been worked from beg.

Shape shoulder

Next row Ch2, work over 10[11:12]dc for shoulder. Fasten off.

Bodice front

Attach yarn for front of bodice.

22in size only

1st row Ch3, work 2dc into each of next 26 sp. Turn.

24in size only

1st row Ch3, work 2dc into each of next 6 sp, 3dc into each of next 3 sp, 2dc into each of next 8 sp, 3dc into each of next 3 sp and 2dc into each of next 6 sp. Turn.

26in size only

1st row Ch3, work 2dc into each of next 6 sp, 3dc into each of next 6 sp, 2dc into each of next 2 sp, 3dc into each of next 6 sp and 2dc into each of next 6 sp. Turn.

All sizes

2nd row Ss over 5dc, ch3, work in dc leaving 5dc at other end for underarm. Turn.

3rd row Ch3, work over 40[46:52]dc. Turn.

4th row Ch3, work over 39[45:51]dc. Turn.

5th row Ch3, work over 38[44:50]dc. Turn.

Cont without shaping until 7 rows of dc worked.

Divide for neck and shoulders

Work over 11[13:15]dc, ch2, turn and work back, ch2, turn and work over 10[11:12]dc working the last dc into top of turning ch of previous row. Fasten off.

Attach yarn into the 12th[14th:16th]dc from other end, ch2, work in dc to end, ch2, turn and work over 10[11:12]dc working the last dc into top of turning ch of previous row, ch2, turn and work back. Fasten off.

Bodice half back

Attach yarn into top of first ch3 and work the 1st row as given for half back already completed.
2nd row Ch3, work in dc leaving 5dc at the end for underarm. Turn.
3rd row Ch3, work in dc to end. Turn.
4th row Ch3, work over 21[24:27]dc. Turn.
5th row Ch3, work in dc to end. Turn.
6th row Ch3, work over 20[23:26]dc. Turn.
Cont without shaping until 9 rows have been worked from beg.
Shape shoulder
Next row Ss over 10[12:14]dc, work in dc to end. Fasten off.

Sleeves

Using No.B hook ch 33[37:37] loosely.
Work 1sc into each ch to end.
1st row Ch3, skip 1sc, *2dc, ch1, 2dc into next sc, skip 1sc, 1dc, ch1, 1dc into next sc, skip 1sc, rep from * ending with 2dc, ch1, 2dc, skip 1sc, 1dc into last sc. Turn.
2nd row Ch3, *3dc,ch1,3dc into ch1 sp between 4dc, 1dc, ch1, 1dc into ch1 sp between 2dc, rep from * ending with 3dc, ch1, 3dc into ch1 sp between 4dc and 1dc into turning ch. Turn.
3rd row Ss over 6dc gr and 2dc gr, ch3, 3dc into ch1 sp between 6dc, cont in patt ending with 3dc into 2nd 6dc gr from end and 1dc into first dc on next gr. Turn.
4th row Ch3, 1dc, ch1, 1dc into ch1 sp between 2dc, cont in patt ending with 1dc, ch1, 1dc into ch1 sp between 2dc and 1dc into top of turning ch. Turn.
5th row Ch3, 3dc, ch1, 3dc into ch1 sp between 6dc, cont in patt ending with 3dc, ch1, 3dc into last 6dc gr and 1dc into turning ch. Turn.
6th row Ch3, 1dc, ch1, 3dc into first 6dc gr, cont in patt ending with 3dc, ch1, 1dc into last 6dc gr and 1dc into turning ch. Turn.
7th row Ch3, 2dc into first ch1 sp, cont in patt ending with 2dc into last ch1 sp and 1dc into turning ch. Turn.
8th row Ch3, 1dc over 2dc, cont in patt ending with 1dc over last 2dc. Fasten off.

Finishing

Press pieces under a damp cloth with a warm iron. Join shoulder seams and first row of dc at underarm. Join sleeve seams. Work 2 rows sc around the edge of sleeves. Sew sleeves into armholes, easing sleeves into armhole to give a slightly puffed effect. Work 3 rows sc around neck edge. Work 3 rows sc along right center back edge and mark positions for 6 buttons. Work 2 rows sc along other back edge and on 3rd row sc make button loops as markers are reached by working ch3 and skipping 3sc. Stitch button side of center back opening under the other side at joining of skirt. Thread ribbon through eyelets at waist. Sew on buttons.

Single-breasted coat and hat set

Sizes
To fit 22 [24:26]in chest
The figures in brackets [] refer to the 24 and 26in sizes respectively
Length to shoulder, 15½ [17½:19½]in
Sleeve seam, 9 [10½:12]in
Gauge
11 sts and 10 rows to 3in over hdc worked on No.G crochet hook
Materials
Spinnerin Wintuk Fingering
Coat 4[4:5] skeins
Hat 1 skein
No.G crochet hook
9 buttons

Coat back
Using No.G crochet hook ch77 [85:93].
1st row Into 2nd ch from hook work 1hdc, 1hdc into each ch to end. Turn. 76[84:92] sts.
2nd row Ch1 to count as first hdc, work 1hdc between each st to end. Turn.
Cont working throughout in hdc, working between each st.
3rd row Ch1 to count as first hdc, work 5 [6: 7]hdc, yrh insert hook between next 2 sts and draw up loop, yrh, insert hook between next 2 sts and draw up loop, yrh and draw through all 5 loops on hook – called dec 1 –, work 15 [17:19]hdc, dec 1, work 26 [28:30]hdc, dec 1, work 15 [17:19]hdc, dec 1, work 6 [7:8]hdc. Turn. (4 sts dec).
Work 2 rows without shaping.
6th row Ch1 to count as first hdc, work 5 [6: 7]hdc, dec 1, work 14 [16:18]hdc, dec 1, work 24 [26:28]hdc, dec 1, work 14 [16:18]hdc, dec 1, work 6 [7:8]hdc. Turn.
Cont dec in this way on every foll 3rd row until 44 [48:52] sts rem. Cont without shaping until work measures 11 [12½:14]in from beg.
Shape armholes
Next row Ss over first 2 sts, patt to last 2 sts, turn.
Dec one st at each end of next 3[4:5] rows. 34[36:38] sts. Cont without shaping until armholes measure 4½ [5:5½]in from beg.
Shape shoulders
Next row Ss over first 4 sts, patt to last 4 sts, turn.
Rep last row once more. Fasten off.

Coat left front
Using No.G crochet hook ch42 [46:50].
Work 2 rows patt as given for back. 41 [45:49] sts.
3rd row Ch1 to count as first hdc, work 5 [6: 7]hdc, dec 1, work 15 [17:19]hdc, dec 1, work 16 [17:18]hdc. Turn.
Work 2 rows without shaping.
6th row Ch1 to count as first hdc, work 5 [6: 7]hdc, dec 1, work 14 [16:18]hdc, dec 1, work 15 [16:17]hdc. Turn.
Cont to dec in this way on every foll 3rd row until 25[27:29] st rem. Cont without shaping until work measures same as back to underarm, ending at side edge.
Shape armhole
Next row Ss over first 2 sts, patt to end. Turn.
Dec one st at armhole edge on next 3[4:5] rows. 20[21:22] sts. Cont without shaping until armhole measures 3 [3¼:3½]in from beg, ending at armhole edge.
Shape neck
Next row Patt to within last 5 sts, turn.
Dec one st at neck edge on next 3 rows. Cont without shaping until armhole measures same

as back to shoulder, ending at armhole edge.
Shape shoulder
Next row Ss over first 4 sts, patt to end. Turn.
Next row Patt to last 4 sts, turn. Fasten off.
Mark positions for 5 buttons on left front, first to come 5½ [6:6½]in from beg and last to come in neckband on 3rd row above neck shaping, with 3 more evenly spaced between.

Coat right front
Work to correspond to left front, reversing all shapings and working buttonholes as markers are reached, as foll:
Next row (RS) Ch1 to count as first hdc, work 1hdc between next 2 sts, ch1, skip 1hdc, patt to end. Turn.

Sleeves
Using No.G crochet hook ch27 [28:29].
Work first 2 rows patt as given for back. 26[27: 28] sts. Cont in patt, inc one st at each end of next and every foll 6th row until there are 34[37:40] sts. Cont without shaping until sleeve measures 9 [10½:12]in from beg.
Shape cap
Next row Ss over first 2 sts, patt to last 2 sts, turn.
Dec one st at each end of next 6[7:8] rows, then 2 sts at each end of next 2 rows. 10[11:12] sts. Fasten off.

Neckband
Join shoulder seams, leaving 10 sts in center back for neck. Using No.G crochet hook and with RS of work facing, work 42 [44:46]hdc around neck edge. Work 4 rows hdc, working buttonhole as before on 3rd of these rows. Fasten off.

Pocket flaps (make 2)
Using No.G crochet hook ch13 [14:15].
Work in hdc for 3 rows. 12[13:14] sts. Work 1 row sc. Fasten off.
Shoulder tabs (make 2)
Using No.G crochet hook ch6.
1st row Into 2nd ch from hook work 1sc, work 1sc into each ch to end. Turn. 5 sts.
Work 7 more rows sc.
Next row Ch1 to count as first sc, (insert hook into next st and draw through loop, rep into next st, yrh and draw through all 3 loops on hook) twice, – called dec 2 –. Turn. 3 sts.
Next row Ch1 to count as first sc, dec 2. Fasten off.

Finishing
Press each piece under a damp cloth with a warm iron. Sew in sleeves. Join side and sleeve seams. Work a row of sc along each front edge. Sew on pocket flaps, sewing a button to center of each. Sew on shoulder tabs, sewing a button at shaped end of each. Sew on buttons to left front. Press seams.

Hat
Using No.G crochet hook ch3. Join with a ss into first ch to form circle.
Cont in rounds of hdc, always working between hdc of previous round, and joining each round with a ss.
1st round Work 8hdc into circle.
2nd round Work 2hdc between each st. 16 sts.
3rd round *Work 2hdc between first 2 sts, work 1hdc between next 2 sts, rep from * to end. 24 sts.
4th round *Work 2hdc between first 2 sts, (work 1hdc between next 2 sts) twice, rep from * to end. 32 sts.
5th round Work 32hdc.
6th round *Work 2hdc between first 2 sts, (work 1hdc between next 2 sts) 3 times, rep from * to end. 40 sts.

7th round Work 40hdc.
Cont to inc 8 sts every other round until there are 72 sts. Cont without shaping for a further 12 rounds, or to depth desired.

Work edging
Next round Work 1sc between each st to end. Turn.
Next round With WS of work facing, work 1sc into each st to end. Fasten off.

Finishing
Press lightly if necessary.

Dressing gown with open work panels

Sizes
To fit 22 [24]in chest
The figures in brackets[] refer to the 24in size only
Length to shoulder, 18½ [23½]in
Sleeve seam, 6½ [8½]in

Gauge
20 sts and 11 rows to 4in over dc worked on No.D crochet hook

Materials
8[10] balls Coats & Clark's O.N.T. "Speed-Cro-Sheen"
No. D crochet hook
6[7] buttons

Skirt
Using No.D crochet hook ch155 [177].
1st row Into 3rd ch from hook work 1dc, 1dc into each of next 8 [7]ch, ch1, skip 1ch, *work 1dc into each of next 21 [25]ch, ch1, skip 1ch, rep from * 5 times more, work 1dc into each of next 10 [9]ch. Turn. 153[175] sts.
2nd row Ch3 to count as first dc, work 8 [7]dc, ch1, skip one st, 1dc in ch sp, ch1, skip one st, *work 19 [23]dc, ch1, skip one st, 1dc in ch sp, ch1, skip one st, rep from * 5 times more, work 9 [8]dc. Turn.
3rd row Ch3 to count as first dc, work 7 [6]dc, (ch1, skip one st, 1dc in ch sp) twice, ch1, skip one st, *work 17 [21]dc, ch1, skip one st, 1dc in ch sp) twice, ch1, skip one st, rep from * 5 times more, work 8 [7]de. Turn.
Cont in patt as now set, working 1st, 3rd, 5th and 7th diamonds in patt from chart A and 2nd, 4th and 6th diamonds in patt from chart B, *at the same time* shape skirt, as foll:
4th row Ch3 to count as first dc, work 3 [2]dc, *patt 13 sts from chart A, work 11 [15]dc, yrh, insert hook into next st and draw up a loop, yrh and draw through 2 loops, yrh, insert hook into next st and draw up a loop, yrh and draw through 2 loops, yrh and draw through all 3 loops on hook – called dec 1 –, patt 5 sts from chart B, dec 1, work 11 [15]dc, rep from * twice more, patt 13 sts from chart A, work 4 [3]dc. Turn. 147[169] sts.
5th row Ch3 to count as first dc, work 3 [2]dc, *patt 13 sts, work 12 [16]dc, patt 5 sts, work 12 [16]dc, rep from * twice more, patt 13 sts, work 4 [3]dc. Turn.
Work 2 rows patt.
8th row Ch3 to count as first dc, work 3 [2]dc, *patt 13 sts, work 10 [14]dc, dec 1, patt 5 sts, dec 1, work 10 [14]dc, rep from * twice more, patt 13 sts, work 4 [3]dc. Turn.
Cont dec in this way on every foll 4th row 5[7] times more. 111[121] sts. Cont without shaping until work measures 14 [18½]in from beg.

Divide for armholes
Next row Ch3 to count as first dc, patt 23[25] sts, turn and leave rem sts for time being.
Next row Ss over first 2 sts, patt to end.
Dec one st at armhole edge on next 2 rows. 20[22] sts. Cont without shaping until armhole measures 3 [3½]in from beg, ending at armhole edge.

Shape neck
Next row Patt to last 6[7] sts, turn.
Dec one st at neck edge on next 3 rows. Cont without shaping until armhole measures 4½ [5]in from beg, ending at neck edge.

Shape shoulder
Next row Patt to last 5[6] sts, turn and fasten off.
Return to where work was left, skip first 7[8] sts, attach yarn to rem sts, ch3 to count as first dc, patt 48[52] sts, turn and leave rem sts to be worked later. Complete back on these sts.
Next row Ss over first 2 sts, patt to last 2 sts, turn.
Dec one st at each end of next 2 rows. 41[45] sts. Cont without shaping until armhole measures same as front to shoulder.

Shape shoulders
Next row Ss over first 5[6] sts, patt to last 5[6] sts, turn and fasten off.
Return to where sts were left, skip first 7[8] sts, attach yarn to rem sts, ch3, patt to end.
Complete to correspond to first front.

Sleeves
Using D crochet hook ch36[38].
1st row Into 3rd ch from hook work 1dc, work 1dc into each of next 2 [3]ch, *patt 5 sts from chart B, work 1dc into each of next 2ch, rep from * 3 times more, work 2 [3]dc. Turn. 34[36] sts.

Cont in patt as established, working all panels from chart B and inc one st at each end of 4th and every foll 3rd row until there are 44[50] sts and working increased sts in dc. Cont without shaping until sleeve measures 6½ [8½]in from beg, or desired length to underarm.

Shape cap
Next row Ss over first 4 sts, patt to last 4 sts, turn.
Dec one st at each end of next 6[8] rows. Dec 2 sts at each end of next 3 rows. 12 [14] sts. Fasten off.

Finishing
Press each piece under a damp cloth with a warm iron. Join shoulder seams. Sew in sleeves. Join sleeve seams.
Borders Using D crochet hook and with RS of work facing, beg at lower edge of right front, work 2 sc into every row up front, work 3sc into corner at neck, work in sc around neck, work 3sc in next corner, work in sc down front. Turn.
Next row (buttonhole row) Work in sc up left front and around neck, working 3sc in each corner, work 1sc, ch2, skip 3sc, work 9sc) 6[7] times, work in sc to end. Turn.
Work 1 more row sc, working 2sc into each ch2 sp. Fasten off. Press borders. Make a twisted cord and thread through holes in patt just below beg of armholes.

See chart below

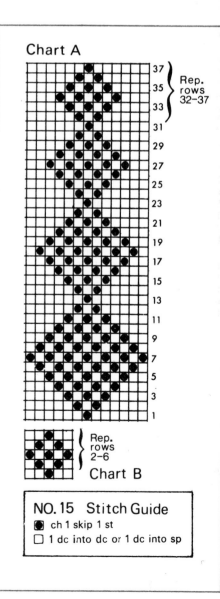

Chart A

37 } Rep. rows 32-37

Chart B

Rep. rows 2-6

NO. 15 Stitch Guide
⬤ ch 1 skip 1 st
☐ 1 dc into dc or 1 dc into sp

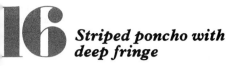

16 Striped poncho with deep fringe

Sizes
To fit 6/8[8/10:10/12] year sizes
The figures in brackets [] refer to the 8/10 and 10/12 year sizes respectively
The poncho is made in two pieces, each measuring about 10 [11:12]in wide by 20 [21:21]in long, excluding fringe

Gauge
5½ sts and 3 rows to 1in over dc worked on No.E crochet hook

Materials
3 skeins of Brunswick Fairhaven Fingering Yarn in main color, A
2 skeins each of contrast colors, B, C, D and E
No.E crochet hook

Half section
Using No.E crochet hook and A, ch55 [60:65].
Base row Into 2nd ch from hook work 1dc, 1dc into each ch to end. Turn.
1st row Ch2 to count as first dc, 1dc into each dc to end. Turn.
The 1st row forms patt and is rep throughout.
Work 1 more row in A then 3 rows each in B, C, D and E. Rep this striped sequence until 20[21:21] stripes in all have been worked.
Fasten off.
Work another section in same manner.

Finishing
Press each piece lightly on WS under a damp cloth with a warm iron. Join commencing ch of one section to left side of second section along 11 stripes, then join the commencing ch of second section to the inside edge of first section along 11 stripes.
Neck border Using No.E crochet hook and A, with RS of work facing work 1 round sc around neck edge. Join with a ss to first sc.
Work 5 more rounds sc, dec one st at center front and back on each round, as foll: insert hook into next sc, yrh and pull through loop, insert hook into next sc, yrh and pull through loop, yrh and pull through all loops on hook. Fasten off.
Fringe Using A, cut lengths of yarn about 9in long. Using 6 strands for each tassel, fold yarn in half, insert hook through the edge of the poncho and pull folded end through for 1in, then pull the ends through the loop and pull up to the edge of the crochet. Rep all around outside edges working into every 3rd sp. Trim fringe evenly.

17 Girl's half-belted coat and pompon hat

Sizes
To fit 24 [26]in chest
The figures in brackets [] refer to the 26in size
Length to shoulder, 14 [17]in
Sleeve seam, 8½ [10]in

Gauge
4 sts and 5 rows to 1in over sc worked on No.F crochet hook

Materials
Bear Brand or Fleisher or Botany Soufflé
Coat 6[7] balls
Hat 2 balls
No.E crochet hook
No.F crochet hook
No.G crochet hook
8 buttons

Coat bodice back
Using No.F crochet hook ch51 [55].
1st row Into 2nd ch from hook work 1sc, 1sc into each ch to end. Turn. 50 [54]sc.
2nd row Ch1 to count as first sc, work 1sc into each sc to end. Turn.
Rep 2nd row until work measures 3½ [4½]in from beg.
Shape armholes
Next row Ss over first 3 sts, patt to last 3 sts, turn.
Next row Ss over first 2 sts, patt to last 2 sts, turn.
Next row Dec 0[1] st, patt to last 0[2] sts, dec 0[1] st. Turn. 40[42] sts.

Cont without shaping until armholes measure 5 [5½]in from beg.
Shape shoulders
Next row Ss over first 3 sts, patt to last 3 sts, turn.
Rep last row 3 times more. 16[18] sts. Fasten off.
Bodice left front
Using No.F crochet hook ch26 [28].
Work as given for back until work measures same as back to underarm. 25 [27]sc.

Shape armhole
Next row Ss over first 3 sts, patt to end. Turn.
Next row Patt to last 2 sts, turn.
Next row Dec 0[1] st, patt to end. Turn. 20[21] sts.
Cont without shaping until armhole measures 3½ [4]in from beg, ending at armhole edge.
Shape neck
Next row Patt to last 4[5] sts, turn.
Dec one st at neck edge on next 4 rows. Cont without shaping until armhole measures same as back to shoulder, ending at armhole edge.
Shape shoulder
Next row Ss over first 3 sts, patt to end. Turn.
Next row Patt to last 3 sts, turn.
Next row Ss over first 3 sts, patt to end.
Fasten off.
Edging
Using No.E crochet hook and with RS of work facing, work 1 row sc down front edge, then turn and work 2 more rows sc. Do not turn at end of last row but work another row of sc from left to right to form crab st edge. Fasten off.
Mark positions for buttons on left front, first to come 2sc from lower edge and last to come 2sc below neck edge, with 2 more evenly spaced between.

Bodice right front
Work as given for left front until shoulder shaping has been completed.
Edging
Using No.E crochet hook and with RS of work facing work 1 row sc along right front edge. Turn.
Next row Ch1 to count as first sc, work 1sc, (ch2, skip 2sc, work in sc to next buttonhole position) 3 times, ch2, skip 2sc, work 2sc. Turn.
Next row Work in sc to end, working 2sc into each ch2 loop. Do not turn work.
Next row Work a row of sc from left to right to form crab st edge. Fasten off.

Sleeves
Using No.F crochet hook ch31 [33].
Work 1½ [2]in sc as given for back. 30[32] sts.
Inc one st at each end of next and every foll 12th row until there are 36[38] sts. Cont without shaping until sleeve measures 8½ [10]in from beg.
Shape cap
Next row Ss over first 3 sts patt to last 3 sts, turn.
Dec one st at each end of every other row until 20 sts rem, then at each end of next 4 rows. 12 sts.
Next row Ss over first 2 sts, patt to last 2 sts. Fasten off.
Cuff
Using No.E crochet hook and with RS of work facing work 1 row crab st along lower edge. Fasten off.

Collar
Using No.F crochet hook ch37 [39].
Work 2 rows sc as given for back. 36[38] sts.
Next row Ch1 to count as first sc, work 5 [6]sc, (work 2sc into next sc, work 5sc) 4 times, work 2sc into next sc, work 5 [6]sc. Turn.
Work 5[6] more rows sc. Fasten off.
Edging
Using No.E crochet hook and with RS of work facing, beg at commencing ch and work 1

row crab st along short sides and outer edge of collar. Fasten off.

Belt (make 2 pieces)
Using No.F crochet hook ch28 [30].
Work 4 rows sc 27[29] sts.

Edging
Using No.E crochet hook and with RS of work facing, work 1 row crab st right around belt. Fasten off.

Skirt
Join side seams of bodice. Using No.G hook and with RS of work facing, attach yarn to 3rd row of sc edging, ch2, work 1sc and 1dc into first st of bodice, *skip one st, work 1sc and 1dc into next st — called gr —, *rep from * to * 7[8] times more, work 1 gr into every st to last 16[18] sts, rep from * to * 8[9] times, work 1dc into 3rd row of sc edging. Turn.
Next row Ch1 to count as first sc, work 1 gr into each sc of previous row to end. Turn.
Rep last row until work measures 14 [17]in from shoulder. Fasten off.

Finishing
Press lightly. Join sleeve seams. Sew in sleeves. Sew on collar. Sew on buttons to left front. Sew 2 halves of belt, one to each side. Sew on button to each end of each piece.

Hat
Using No.G crochet hook ch4. Join with a ss to first ch to form circle.
1st round Work 7sc into circle. Join with a ss to first sc.
2nd round Work 2sc into each sc to end. Join with a ss to first sc. 14 sts.
3rd round *Work 1sc into first sc, work 2sc in next sc, rep from * to end. Join with a ss to first sc. 21 sts.
4th round *Work 1 sc into each of first 2sc, work 2sc into next sc, rep from * to end. Join with a ss to first sc. 28 sts.
Cont to inc 7 sts in this way in each of next 2 rounds. Work 2 rounds without shaping. Inc 7 sts in next round, then inc 3[7] sts in next round. 52[56] sts. Attach a 2nd strand of yarn and use yarn double throughout.
Next round *Skip first st, work 1gr into next st, rep from * to end. Join with a ss to first gr. 26 [28]gr.
Next round Work 1 gr into each sc of previous round to end. Join with a ss to first gr. Rep last round 7[8] times more.
Right earflap
Work 7 gr, then 1sc into next sc. Break off yarn.
Next row Return to beg of last row, skip 1 gr, work 5 gr, work 1 sc into next sc. Break off yarn.
Next row Return to beg of row, skip 1 gr, work 3 gr, work 1sc into next sc. Break off yarn.
Left earflap
Skip 10 [12]gr at center front, attach yarn to next sc, ch1, work 7 gr. Break off yarn.
Next row Return to beg of last row, skip first st, attach yarn to next sc, ch1, work 5 gr. Break off yarn.
Next row Return to beg of row, skip first st, attach yarn to next sc, work 3 gr. Fasten off.
Edging
Using No.G crochet hook, 2 strands of yarn and with WS of work facing, work 4sc across center back sts, turn and work around entire edge in sc. Fasten off.

Finishing
Make a loopy pompon and sew to top of hat. Make 2 smaller pompons and sew one to each earflap.

Boy's striped swim trunks

Sizes
To fit 24 [26:28:30]in hips
The figures in brackets [] refer to the 26, 28 and 30in sizes respectively
Length at side, 6½ [7:7½:8]in
Gauge
11 sts and 10 rows to 2in over hdc worked on No.B crochet hook
Materials
3[3:4:4] balls Coats & Clark's O. N. T. 66 Speed-Cro-Sheen" in main color, A
2 balls each of contrast colors, B and C
No.B crochet hook
2 metal rings 1in diameter

Right half
Using No.B hook and A, ch 75[81:87:93].
1st row Into 2nd ch from hook work 1hdc, work 1hdc into each ch to end. Turn. 74[80:86:92] sts.
2nd row Ch1 to count as first hdc, work 1hdc between each st of previous row, ending with 1 hdc between last st and turning ch. Turn.
Rep 2nd row twice more. Attach B. Cont in patt working throughout in stripes of 2 rows B, 2 rows C and 2 rows A, *at the same time* shape gusset after working 2[2:4:4] rows.
Shape gusset
Next row Ss over first 3 sts, patt to last 3 sts, turn.
Work 3 rows without shaping.
Next row Ch1, work 29 [32:35:38]hdc, yrh, insert hook into next sp and draw up a loop, insert hook into next sp and draw up a loop, yrh and draw through all 4 loops on hook — called dec 1 —, work 1hdc into each of next 4hdc, dec 1, work 30 [33:36:39]hdc. Turn.
Work 7[7:9:9] rows without shaping.
Next row Ch1, work 28 [31:34:37]hdc, dec 1, work 4hdc, dec 1, work 29 [32:35:38]hdc. Turn. 64[70:76:82] sts.
Cont without shaping until work measures 5½ [6:6½:7]in from beg, ending with 2nd row of a stripe. Break off yarn.
Shape back
With RS of work facing, skip first 39[45:46:52] sts, attach yarn to rem sts and patt to end. Turn.
Next row Patt 20[20:24:24] sts, turn. Break off yarn.
Next row Skip 5[5:6:6] sts, attach yarn to rem sts and patt to end. Turn.
Next row Patt 10[10:12:12] sts, turn. Break off yarn.
With RS of work facing, return to beg of row, using A patt to end.
Work 3 more rows with A.
Fasten off.

Left half
Work as given for right half, reversing shaping at top.

Belt
Using No.B crochet hook and A, ch 138 [150:162:174]. Work 4 rows hdc. 137[149:161:173] sts.
Fasten off.

Finishing
Press each piece under a damp cloth with a warm iron.
Join back and front seams. Using A, make a loop at each side of waist for belt. Sew 2 rings to one end of belt. Press seams.

Girl's cotton bikini

Sizes
To fit 24 [26:28:30]in chest
        26 [28:30:32]in hips
The figures in brackets [] refer to the 26, 28 and 30in sizes respectively
Gauge
3 rep of patt to 4in and 10 rows to 4 in worked on No.B crochet hook
Materials
4[5:6:6] balls Coats & Clark's O. N. T. "Speed-Cro-Sheen"
No.B crochet hook
3 metal or plastic rings 1in diameter

Pants front
Using No.B crochet hook ch84 [91:98:104].
1st row Work 1dc into 3rd ch from hook, work 1dc into each of next 3 [2:1:4]ch, *ch2, skip 2ch, 1dc into next ch, skip 2ch, work 5dc into next ch, skip 2ch, 1dc into next ch, rep from * 7[8:9:9] times more, ch2, skip 2ch, work 1dc into each of next 4 [3:2:5] ch. Turn.
2nd row Ch3 to count as first dc, work 3 [2:1:4]dc, *ch2, 1dc into next dc, work 5dc into 3rd of 5dc gr, 1dc in next single dc rep from * 7[8:9:9] times more, ch2, work 4 [3:2:5]dc. Turn.
Rep 2nd row 4[5:6:7] times more. **
Shape legs
Next row Ss over first 14[16:18:20] sts, patt to last 14[16:18:20] sts, turn.
Next row Ss over first 12 sts, patt to last 12 sts, turn.
Next row Ss over first 3[4:4:4] sts, patt to last 3[4:4:4] sts, turn.
Next row Ss over first 3 sts, patt to last 3 sts, turn. 18[19:22:24] sts.
Work 4[5:6:7] rows without shaping. Fasten off.
Pants back
Work as given for front to **.
Shape legs
Next row Ss over first 8 sts, patt to last 8 sts, turn.
Next row Ss over first 6[6:5:4] sts, patt to last 6[6:5:4] sts, turn.
Next row Ss over first 3 sts, patt to last 3 sts, turn.
Rep last row 5[6:7:8] times more. 18[19:22:24] sts. Fasten off.

Belt
Work as given for boy's trunks belt. No. 36.
Finishing
Press as for trunks. Join side and gusset seams.
Waistband Using No.B crochet hook and with RS of work facing, attach yarn at side edge, ch1, *work 1sc into each of next 6 sts,

skip one st, rep from * to last 3[3:3:1] sts, work 1sc into each of last 3[3:3:1] sts, ss to first st. Turn.

Next row Ch3 to count as first dc, work 1dc into each st to end, ss to 3rd of first ch3. Turn.
Next row Ch1 to count as first sc, work 1sc into each st to end, ss to first ch1. Fasten off. With RS of work facing work 1 row sc around legs, turn and work a 2nd row sc. Fasten off. Complete belt as for trunks. Press seams.

Top left front
Using No.B crochet hook ch 40[44:48:52].
1st row Into 3rd ch from hook work 1dc, work 1dc into each of next 7 [9:11:13]ch, *ch2, skip 2ch, 1dc in next ch, skip 2ch, work 5dc in next ch, skip 2ch, 1dc in next ch, 2ch, skip 2ch, *, work 1dc into each of next 19 [21:23:25]ch. Turn.
2nd row Ch3 to count as first dc, work 1dc into each of next 18 [20:22:24] dc, *ch2, 1dc in next dc, work 5dc into 3rd of 5dc gr, 1dc in next single dc, ch2, *, work 1dc into each of next 8 [10 : 12:14]dc. Turn.
Shape front edge and armhole
3rd row Patt to last 5 sts, turn.
4th row Ss over first 2 sts, patt to end. Turn.
5th row Ss over first 6[6:7:7] sts, patt to last 2 sts, turn.
6th row Ss over first 2 sts, patt to last 2[2:3:3] sts, turn.
7th row Ss over first 2 sts, patt to last 2 sts, turn.
Rep 7th row 0[1:1:2] times more. Cont to dec 2 sts at front edge only on next 4[4:5:5] rows. 7 sts. Cont without shaping until work measures 6 [6½:7:7½]in from beg. Fasten off.

Top right front
Using No.B crochet hook ch 40[44:48:52].
1st row Into 3rd ch from hook work 1dc, 1dc into each of next 18 [20:22:24]ch, rep from * to * as given for 1st row of left front, work 1dc into each of next 8 [10:12:14]ch. Turn.
Complete to correspond to left front, reversing all shapings.

Top back
Using No.B crochet hook ch 74[82:88:96].
1st row Into 3rd ch from hook work 1dc, 1dc into each of next 7 [9:11:13]ch, rep from * to * as given for 1st row of left front, work 1dc into each of next 34 [38:40:44] ch, rep from * to * once more, work 1dc into each of next 8 [10:12: 14]ch. Turn.
2nd row Ch3 to count as first dc, work 1dc into each of next 7 [9:11:13]dc, rep from * to * as given for 2nd row of left front, work 1dc into each of next 34[38:40:44]dc, rep from * to * once more, work 1dc into each of next 8 [10:12: 14]dc. Turn.
Rep 2nd row twice more.
Shape armholes
5th row Ss over first 6[6:7:7] sts, patt to last 6[6:7:7] sts, turn.
6th row Ss over first 2[2:3:3] sts, patt to last 2[2:3:3] sts, turn.
7th row Ss over first 2 sts, patt to last 2 sts, turn.
Rep 7th row 0[1:1:2] times more. 52[56:58:62] sts.
Next row Patt 15[17:17:19] sts, turn.
Dec one st at beg of next row, and at same edge on every row until 7 sts rem. Cont without shaping until back neasures same as front from beg. Fasten off.
Return to where sts were left, skip 22[22:24:24] sts in center, attach yarn to rem sts and patt to end. Complete to correspond to first side, reversing shaping.

Finishing
Press as given for pants. Join side and shoulder seams. Using No.B crochet hook and with RS of work facing, work 1 row sc around all edges, turn and work a 2nd row. Fasten off. Press seams. Place a ring at center front and sew to 2 front corners.

Cardigan (in larger sizes too)

Sizes
As given for pullover (design 19)
Length to shoulder, 20½[21:21½:22:22½]in
Sleeve seam, 16[16½:17:17½:18]in
Gauge
As given for pullover (design 19)
Materials
14[16:18:20:21] balls Unger English Crepe in main color, A
2[3:3:4:4] balls in contrast color, B
No.D crochet hook
No.E crochet hook
7 buttons
Back
Using No.E crochet hook and A, ch 114[126:138: 150:162]. Work in patt as given for pullover back. 28[31:34:37:40] gr. Cont in patt until work measures 11½in from beg, or required length to underarm.
Shape armholes
Work as given for pullover back. 22[23:24:25:26]

gr. Cont without shaping until armholes measure 8½[9:9½:10:10½]in from beg. Fasten off.
Left front
Using No.E crochet hook and A, ch 54[62:66: 74:78]. Work in patt as given for back. 13[15:16: 18:19] gr. Cont in patt until work measures same as back to underarm.
Shape armhole
Next row Ss over first 1[1:2:2:3] gr, patt to end. Turn.
Next row Patt to last gr, turn.
Next row Ss over first gr, patt to end. Turn.
Cont to dec 1 gr at armhole edge in this way until 10[11:11:12:12] gr rem. Cont without shaping until armhole measures 4½[5:5½:6:6½]in from beg, ending at armhole edge.
Shape neck
Work as given for pullover front (No.19). Fasten off.
Right front
Work as given for left front, reversing shaping.

Sleeves
Using No.E crochet hook and A, ch 50[54:58: 62:66]. Work in patt as given for back. 12[13:14: 15:16] gr. Cont in patt until work measures 2[2¼:2½: 2¾:3]in from beg.
Shape sleeve

1st row Ch3, work 2dc, ch3, 1sc into first loop, patt to end. Turn.
2nd row Ch3, work 2dc, ch3, 1sc into first loop, patt to end, ending with 2dc in turning ch. Turn.
3rd row As 2nd.
4th row Ch3, work 2dc, ch3, 1sc into first loop, patt to end, ending with 2dc, ch3, 1sc in turning ch. Turn.
5th row Patt to end, ending with 2dc, ch3, 1sc in turning ch. Turn. 1 gr inc at each end.
6th, 7th and 8th rows Work in patt.
Rep last 8 rows 3 times more. 20[21:22:23:24] gr. Cont without shaping until sleeve measures 16[16½:17:17½:18]in from beg. Work 2[2:4:4:6] rows more.

Shape cap
Work as given for pullover (No.19).

Edging
Join shoulder and side seams. Work edging as given for pullover around front edges, neck and lower edges. Work in same way around sleeves.

Finishing
Press as given for pullover. Join sleeve seams leaving last 2[2:4:4:6] rows open. Sew in sleeves, sewing open part to first dec row of armholes of back and front. Press seams. Sew on buttons, using openings in border patt as buttonholes.

21 Pullover (in larger sizes too)

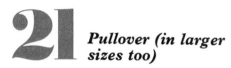

Sizes
To fit 32/34[36/38:40/42:44/46:48/50]in bust
The figures in brackets [] refer to the 36/38, 40/42, 44/46 and 48/50in sizes respectively
Length to shoulder, 19½[20:20½:21:21½]in
Sleeve seam, 2½ [2¾:3:3¼:3½]in
Gauge
3 gr and 5 rows to 2in over patt worked on No.E crochet hook
Materials
10[12:13:15:16] balls Unger English Crepe in main color, A
1[1:2:2:2] balls of contrast color, B
No. D crochet hook
No. E crochet hook
Back
Using No.E crochet hook and A, ch 106[118:130:142:154].
1st row Into 5th ch from hook work 1dc, ch3, 1sc, *skip ch3, work 2dc, ch3, 1sc into next ch, rep from * to last st, 1dc in last st. Turn.
2nd row Ch2, work 2dc, ch3, 1sc into each ch3 loop to end, ending with 1dc in turning ch. Turn. 26[29:32:35:38] gr.
The 2nd row forms patt. Cont in patt until work measures 11in from beg, or desired length to underarm.
Shape armholes
Next row Ss over first 1[1:2:2:3] gr, patt to last 1[1:2:2:3] gr, turn.
Next row Ss over first gr, patt to last gr, turn.
Rep last row 1[2:2:3:3] times more. 20[21:22:23:24] gr.
Cont without shaping until armholes measure 8[8½:9:9½:10]in from beg. Fasten off.
Front
Work as given for back until armhole shaping is completed. Cont without shaping until armholes measure 4[4½:5:5½:6]in from beg.
Shape neck
Next row Patt over first 6[6:7:7:8] gr, turn and

leave rem sts.
Cont on these sts until armhole measures same as back to shoulder. Fasten off.
Skip 8[9:8:9:8] gr in center, attach yarn to rem 6[6:7:7:8] gr and patt to end. Complete to correspond to first side.
Sleeves
Using No.E crochet hook and A, ch 78[82:86:90:94]. Work in patt as given for back. 19[20:21:22:23] gr. Cont in patt until work measures 2[2¼:2½:2¾:3]in from beg. Work a further 2[2:4:4:6] rows.
Shape cap
Dec 1 gr at beg of next 10[10:12:12:14] rows, then at each end of next 2[3:2:3:2] rows.
Fasten off.
Edging
Join right shoulder seam. Using No.D crochet hook and B, attach yarn at neck edge and work 1sc, then work 3dc, ch3, 1sc into each ch3 loop or into turning ch of every other row around neck. Break off B. Using No.D crochet hook and A, return to beg of last row, attach yarn and work 1sc, *ch2, 1sc in ch3 loop of gr, ch1, 1sc between gr, rep from * ending with 1sc in last st, turn.
Next row Ch1, work 1sc, ch3, 1sc into each ch2 loop to end, ending with 1sc in last st. Fasten off. Work edging around sleeves and lower edge in same way.

Finishing
Press each piece under a damp cloth with a cool iron. Join left shoulder seam. Sew in sleeves, sewing the last 2[2:4:4:6] rows of sleeve seams to first dec row at armholes of back and front. Join side and sleeve seams. Press seams.

22 Jacket and beret

Sizes
To fit a 34/36in bust
Length to shoulder, 22in
Sleeve seam, 18in
Gauge
Each square motif measures 2¼in by 2¼in worked on No.D crochet hook
Materials
Jacket 6 skeins Bernat Nylo Baby Yarn

Beret 2 balls
No.D crochet hook

Jacket
Square motif Using No.D crochet hook ch6. Join with a ss into first ch to form circle.
1st round Ch4, (1dc into circle, ch1) 7 times. Join with a ss to 3rd of first ch4.
2nd round Ch4, work 3tr into first ch sp keeping last loop of each st on hook, yrh and draw through all loops on hook, (ch4, work 4tr into next ch sp keeping last loop of each st on hook, yrh and draw through all loops on hook) 7 times, ch4. Join with a ss to 3rd of first ch4.
3rd round (Ch3, 1dc in ch4 loop at corner, ch3, 1sc in top of next tr gr, ch4, 1sc in top of next tr gr) 4 times, working last sc into base of first ch3. Fasten off.
Make 265 more squares in same way.

Gore
Using No.D crochet hook ch6. Join with a ss into first ch to form circle.
1st round As 1st round of square.
2nd round Ch4, gr of 3tr in first ch sp, (ch4, gr of 4tr in next ch sp) 3 times, turn.
3rd round Ch3, 1dc in ch4 loop, ch3, 1sc in top of next gr, ch4, 1sc in top of next gr, ch3, 1dc in ch4 loop, ch4, 1sc in top of next gr – this is the lower edge and 2 corners of the gore –, cont round work with ch4, (gr of 3dc instead of tr in next ch sp, ch3) into each of next 4 one ch sp, ch4. Join with a ss to top of next tr gr, turn.
4th round Ch5, 1dc in loop between first 2 dc gr, (ch3, 1dc in next loop) twice, ch5, 1sc in top of first tr gr, turn.
5th round Ch4, 1sc in first loop, ch3, 1dc in next loop, ch3, 1dc in next dc, ch3, 1dc in next loop, ch3, 1sc in next loop, ch4. Join with a ss to top of tr gr, turn.
6th round Ss along to sc, ch5, skip 1 loop, 1sc in next loop, ch4, 1dc in next dc, ch4, 1sc in loop, ch5, skip next loop. Join with ss into sc.
Fasten off.
Work 1 more gore in same way.

Finishing
Join squares as shown in diagrams for body and sleeves. Join 2 squares at front shoulder to first 2 squares at each back shoulder, leaving 3 squares for back neck. Sew the 6 squares at top of sleeves into armholes, 3 to back armhole and 3 to front armhole. Sew bottom edge of gore to the square at underarm, then sew the sides of the gore to the top part of sleeve seam.
Join rem of sleeve seam.
Edging Using No.D crochet and with RS of work facing, beg at bottom of right front edge, work in sc along first 7 squares ending with 1sc in dc at corner of 7th square, then work across corner with ch3, gr of 4tr in ch4 loop, ch3, gr of 4tr in ch4 loop at side of next square, ch3, 1sc in dc at corner, work across next corner in same way, cont in sc around neck, working in same way across corners, then cont around left side of neck working across corners, and down left front edge and around lower edge. Fasten off. Work a row of sc around sleeve edges. Press work lightly under a damp cloth with a cool iron.

Beret
Make 43 square motifs as given for jacket but working 1st and 2nd rounds only.

Finishing
Join squares as shown in diagram for beret, then join the outside squares thus forming a beret shape.
Edging Using No.D crochet hook and with RS of work facing, work around edge, working 1sc into each loop in the squares and working ch2 and ch3 between sc alternately. Work 4 more rounds sc, working 3sc into each ch loop. Fasten off.

23 *Sleeveless dress*

Sizes
To fit 34[37:40]in bust
　　　36[39:42]in hips
The figures in brackets [] refer to the 37 and 40in
sizes respectively
Length to shoulder, 36[37:38]in

Gauge
5 loops and 10 rows to 4in over patt worked on
No.D crochet hook

Materials
13[14:16] balls Coats & Clarks' O.N.T. "Speed
Cro-Sheen"
No.D crochet hook

Back
Using No.D crochet hook ch 95[103:111].
1st row Into 5th ch from hook work 1dc, ch3, 1dc
into same st, *skip ch3, work 1dc, ch3, 1dc all into
next ch, rep from * ending with ch1, skip ch1, 1dc
in last ch. Turn. 23[25:27] loops.
2nd row Ch3, work 5dc into each ch3 loop, ending
with 1dc in turning ch. Turn.
3rd row *Work 1dc, ch3, 1dc all into 3rd of 5dc gr
on previous row, rep from * ending with 1dc in
turning ch. Turn.
The 2nd and 3rd rows form patt. Cont in patt until
work measures 29[29½:30]in from beg, ending with
a 3rd row.
Shape armholes
Next row Ss over first 2 loops, ch3, patt to last 2
loops, 1dc in sp before next loop, turn.
Next row Patt to end.
Next row Ss over first loop, ch3, patt to last loop,
1dc in sp before next loop, turn. 17[19:21] loops.
Cont without shaping until armholes measure
4½[5:5½]in from beg, ending with a 3rd row.
Shape neck
Next row Patt over 4[4:5] loops, turn and leave
rem sts unworked.
Cont in patt until armhole measures 7[7½:8]in from
beg, ending with a 3rd row. Fasten off. Skip first
9[11:11] loops, attach yarn to rem sts and patt over
last 4[4:5] loops.
Complete to correspond to first side.

Front
Work as given for back.

Belt
Using No.D crochet hook make a ch approx 54in
long. Work 1 row sc along ch. Fasten off.

Finishing
Press each piece under a damp cloth with a warm
iron. Join shoulder and side seams. Work 2 rounds
of sc around neck and armhole edges. Work 2
rounds sc around lower edge working 3sc into each
loop and 1sc between 2dc of first row. Press seams.

Diagrams show how to join squares for beret, sleeves and jacket body. 1 square = 1 square motif

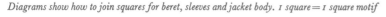

No. 22

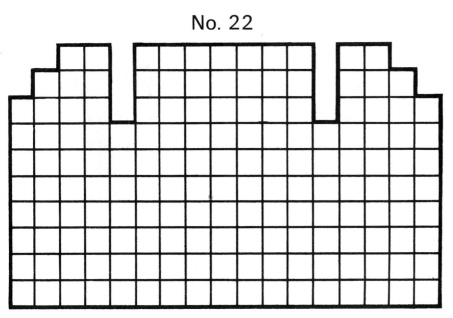

JACKET

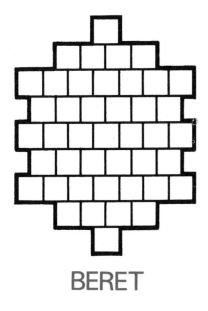

BERET

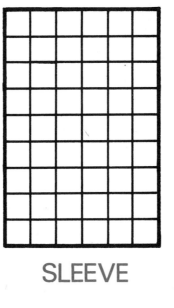

SLEEVE

24 Matching casual jacket

Sizes

To fit 34[37:40]in bust
The figures in brackets [] refer to the 37 and 40in sizes respectively
Length to shoulder, 21[22:23]in
Sleeve seam, 13[13½:14]in

Gauge

As given for dress (design 21)

Materials

10[11:12] balls Coats & Clarks' O.N.T. "Speed Cro-Sheen"
No.D crochet hook

Back

Work as given for dress back (No. 21) until work measures 14[14½:15]in from beg, ending with a 3rd row.

Shape armholes

Next row Ss over first 2 loops, ch3, patt to last 2 loops, 1dc in sp before next loop, turn.

Next row Patt to end.

Next row Ss over first loop, ch3, patt to last loop, 1dc in sp before next loop, turn.

Cont in patt until armholes measure 7[7½:8]in from beg, ending with a 3rd row.

Shape neck and shoulders

Next row Patt over first 5[5:6] loops, turn and work 1 more row on these sts. Fasten off.

Skip 7[9:9] loops in center, attach yarn to rem sts and patt over last 5[5:6] loops, turn and work 1 more row. Fasten off.

Left front

Using No.D crochet hook ch 47[51:55].
Work in patt as given for back (No. 21). 11[12:13] loops. Cont in patt until work measures same as back to underarm, ending with a 3rd row.

Shape armhole

Next row Ss over first 2 loops, ch3, patt to end.

Turn.

Next row Patt to end. Turn.

Next row Ss over first loop, ch3, patt to end. Turn. 8[9:10] loops.

Cont without shaping until armhole measures 4½[5:5½]in from beg, ending at armhole edge.

Shape neck

Next row Patt to last 2 loops, 1dc in sp before next loop, turn.

Next row Patt to end. Turn.

Next row Patt to last loop, 1dc in sp before last loop, turn.

Rep last 2 rows 0[1:1] times more. Cont without shaping until armhole measures same as back to shoulder, ending with a 3rd row. Fasten off.

Right front

Work as given for left front, reversing all shaping.

Sleeves

Using No.D crochet hook ch 47[51:55].
Work 9 rows patt.

Next row Ch3, 2dc in same place, work 5dc in each loop to end, 3dc in turning ch. Turn.

Next row Ch3, 1dc on next 2dc, work 1dc, ch3, 1dc all into 3rd of next 5dc gr, patt to end, ending with 2dc, then 1dc in turning ch. Turn.

Next row Ch3, 2dc in each of next 2dc, work 5dc in each loop, ending with 2dc in each of last 2dc, 1dc in turning ch. Turn.

Next row Ch3, work 1dc, ch3, 1dc all into 2nd dc, patt to last 5dc, work 1dc, ch3, 1dc all into 3rd dc, 1dc in turning ch. Turn. (1 loop inc at each side).

Work 2 rows without shaping.

Rep last 6 rows more. 17[18:19] loops. Cont without shaping until sleeve measures 13[13½:14]in from beg, ending with a 3rd row.

Shape cap

Dec 2 loops at each end of next row. Work 3 rows without shaping. Dec one loop at each end of next and foll 4th row, then dec one loop each end every other row 3[4:4] times. 5[4:5] loops.
Fasten off.

Finishing

Press as given for dress (No. 21). Join shoulder seams. Sew in sleeves. Join side and sleeve seams. Work 2 rows sc around lower edge and sleeves as given for dress hem. Work 1 row sc up right front, around neck and down left front, turn and work 2 patt rows around these edges.
Fasten off. Press seams.

25 Bikini and long jacket

Sizes

To fit 32[35:38]in bust
      34[37:40]in hips
The figures in brackets [] refer to the 35 and 38in and 37 and 40in sizes respectively
Jacket length to shoulder, 43[44:45]in
Gauge

21 sts and 12 rows to 4in over dc worked on No.C crochet hook
Materials

Bikini 5[6:6] balls Coats & Clarks' O.N.T. "Speed Cro-Sheen"
Jacket 16[17:19] balls
No.B crochet hook

No.C crochet hook
Spool of shirring elastic
One hook and eye; 12 buttons

Bikini top

Using No.C hook ch 133[137:141].

1st row Into 4th ch from hook work 1dc, 1dc into each of next 46[47:48] ch, work 3dc into next ch – called inc 2 –, 1dc into each of next 16[17:18] ch, ch3, skip ch1, 1sc in next ch, ch3, skip ch1, 1dc into each of next 16[17:18] ch, inc 2, 1dc into each of next 48[49:50] ch. Turn.

2nd row Ss over first 5 sts, ch3 to count as next dc, work 43[44:45] dc, inc 2, work 17[18:19] dc, ch4, skip (ch3, 1sc, ch3), work 17[18:19] dc, inc 2, work 44[45:46] dc, turn.

3rd row Ss over first 5 sts, ch3, work 39[40:41] dc, inc 2, work 18[19:20] dc, ch3, work 1sc into ch4 loop, ch3 – called V –, work 18[19:20] dc, inc 2, work 40[41:42] dc, turn.

4th row Ss over first 5 sts, ch3, work 35[36:37] dc, inc 2, work 19[20:21] dc, ch4, skip V, work 19[20:21] dc, inc 2, work 36[37:38] dc, turn.

5th row Ss over first 4 sts, ch3, work 32[33:34] dc, inc 2, work 20[21:22] dc, work V, work 20[21:22] dc, inc 2, work 33[34:35] dc, turn.

6th row Ss over first 4 sts, ch3, work 29[30:31] dc, inc 2, work 21[22:23] dc, ch4, skip V, work 21[22:23] dc, inc 2, work 30[31:32] dc, turn.

7th row Ss over first 4 sts, ch3, work 49[27:28] dc, 0[inc 2: inc 2], work 0[23:24] dc, turn. 50[54:56] dc

8th row Ss over first 2 sts, ch3, work in dc to last 4 sts, turn.

9th row Ss over first 4[4:2] sts, ch3, work in dc to last 2dc, turn. 38[42:46] dc.

10th row Ss over first 2dc, ch3, work in dc to last 2dc, turn.

Rep 10th row 8[9:10] times more. 2dc. Fasten off.

Return to where work was left on 7th row, skip ch4 in center, attach yarn to next st, ch3 to count as first dc, on 32in size only work in dc to last 4dc, turn, and on 35 and 38in sizes work 22[23] dc, inc 2, work in dc to last 4dc, turn.

Complete to correspond to first side, reversing shaping.

Edging

Using No.B crochet hook and with WS of work facing, attach yarn to point at top and work edging for front part between shoulder straps, as foll: *ch4, 1sc into next row, rep from * to center, work V into center, 1sc in next st, then work up other side in same way, ending with 1sc at top.

Next row Ch1, work (2sc, ch2, 2sc) into each ch4 loop to center, ch4, skip V, then work up other side in same way, ending with 1sc at top. Do not fasten off but cont with rest of edging and shoulder straps as foll: Using No.B crochet hook and with RS of work facing, ss down other side of point working approx 62[64:66] sts, then cont around lower edge and up other side to point, turn.

Next row (WS) Ch 68[72:76] for shoulder strap, skip first ch, work 1sc into each of rem 67[71:75] ch, cont in sc down side of point to back, ch 20[22:24] for strap to fasten, turn work and skip first ch, work 1sc into each of rem 19[20:21] ch, then cont in sc around lower edge and up point to top, ch 68[72:76] for other shoulder strap, turn and skip first ch, work 1sc into each rem 67[71:75] ch. Fasten off.

Next row Using No.B crochet hook and with WS of work facing, attach yarn to inside edge of left shoulder strap and work in sc from left to right – called crab st –, around strap, around to other strap and around strap. Fasten off.

Finishing

Press work under a damp cloth with a warm iron. Sew on hook and eye to back. If desired, thread shirring elastic through all edges.

Bikini pants back

Using No.C crochet hook ch 16[18:20].

1st row Into 2nd ch from hook work 1sc, 1sc into each ch to end. Turn. 15[17:19] sc.

2nd row Ch3 to count as first dc, work 1dc into each st to end. Turn.

3rd row Ch3, inc 2, work in dc to last 2 sts, inc 2 work 1dc. Turn.

Rep 3rd row until there are 91[97:103] dc. Turn. Break off yarn.

Shape seat

1st row Skip 12[13:14] dc, attach yarn to next dc, ch2, work in dc to last 13[14:15] sts, work 1sc in next st, turn. Break off yarn.

Rep this row twice more, working 24[26:28] sts less each time, Break off yarn.

4th row Attach yarn at beg of row, ch3, work in dc to end. Turn.

**5th row Ch3, work 3[6:5] dc, *ch3, skip next st, 1sc in next st, ch3, skip next st, work 5 dc, rep from * 9[9:10] times more, ch3, skip next st, 1sc in next st, ch3, skip next st, work 4[7:6] dc. Turn.

6th row Ch3, work 3[6:5] dc, *ch4, skip V, work 5dc rep from * 9[9:10] times more, ch4, skip V, work 4[7:6] dc. Turn.

7th row Ch3, work 3[6:5] dc, *work V, work 5dc, rep from * 9[9:10] times more, work V, work 4[7:6] dc. Turn.

Rep 6th and 7th rows once more, then 6th row once. Fasten off. ******

Bikini pants front

Using No.C crochet hook ch 16[18:20] and work 1st row as given for back. 15[17:19] sc. Work 5 rows in dc.

Next row Ch3 to count as first dc, work 2dc in next dc – called inc 1 –, work in dc to last 2 sts, inc 1, 1dc in turning ch. Turn.

Rep last rows 7 times more, then inc 2 as given for back at end of next 6[7:8] rows. Turn. Break off yarn. Ch16, work dc into first st of last row, inc 2, patt to last 2 sts, inc 2, work 1dc, ch19. Turn.

Next row Into 3rd ch from hook work 1dc, work 1dc into each of next ch15, patt across work and across ch16. Turn. 91[97:103] sts. Work as given for back from ** to **. Fasten off.

Edging

Join 7 rows for side seams. Using No.B hook and with RS of work facing, ss around leg working one ss into each st and 2ss into each row end, turn and work 1 row sc, turn and with RS of work facing work 1 row of crab st. Work 1 row sc, 1 row crab st around top edge. Join gusset seam. Press under a damp cloth with a warm iron. If desired thread shirring elastic through all edges.

Jacket back

Using No.C crochet hook ch 161[169:177].

1st row (RS) Into 3rd ch from hook work 1dc, work 1dc into each ch to end. Turn. 159[167:175] dc.

2nd row Ch3 to count as first dc, 1dc in next dc, *ch3, skip 1dc, 1sc in next dc, ch3, skip 1dc, 1dc in next dc – called V –, rep from * ending with 1dc in turning ch. Turn. 39[41:43] V patt.

3rd row Ch3, 1dc in next dc, *ch4, skip V, 1dc in next dc – called 1 bar –, rep from * ending with 1dc in turning ch. Turn.

4th row Ch3, 1dc in next dc, *ch3, 1sc in bar, ch3, 1dc in dc – also called V –, rep from * ending with 1dc in turning ch. Turn.

5th row As 3rd.

6th row Ch3, 1dc in next dc, work 10[11:12] V, 3dc in bar, 1dc in next dc – called gr –, 3 V, 1 gr, 9 V, 1 gr, 3 V, 1 gr, 10[11:12] V, 1dc in turning ch. Turn.

7th row Ch3, 1dc in next dc, work 10[11:12] bars, (1dc in each of next 4dc – also called gr), 3 bars, 1 gr, 9 bars, 1 gr, 3 bars, 1 gr, 10[11:12] bars, 1dc in turning ch. Turn.

8th row Ch3, 1dc in next dc, work 10[11:12] V, 2 gr, 1 V, 2 gr, 9 V, 2 gr, 1 V, 2 gr, 10[11:12] V, 1 dc in turning ch. Turn.

Cont in patt from chart, working 1[5:5] more rows.

Next row Ch3, 1dc in next dc, work ch2, 1sc, ch2 in next bar, patt to last bar, work ch2, 1sc, ch2 in last bar, 1dc in turning ch. Turn.

Next row Ch3, 1dc in next dc, ch2, 1dc in next dc, patt to last V, ch2, 1dc in next dc, 1dc in turning ch. Turn.

Next row Ch3, 1dc in next dc, ch2, 1dc in next dc, patt to last bar, ch2, 1dc in next dc, 1dc in turning ch. Turn.

Next row Ch3, 1dc in next dc, skip bar, 1dc in next dc, patt to last bar, skip bar, 1dc in next dc, 1dc in turning ch. Turn.

Next row Ch3, 1dc into sp between 2dc, patt to last 3 sts, 1dc into sp between 2dc, 1dc in turning ch. Turn. 1 V dec at each end.

Keeping patt correct throughout, (work 8 rows without shaping, then rep 4 dec rows) 6 times. 7 V dec at each side. Cont without shaping until work measures 36[36½:37] in from beg, ending with a RS row.

Shape armholes

Next row Ss over first 2 bars, patt to last 2 bars, turn.

Next row Ss over 1 bar, patt to last bar, turn.

Next row Ch3, 1dc in next dc, work ch2, 1sc, ch2 in next bar, patt to last 2 bars, work ch2, 1sc, ch2 in next bar, 1 V, 1dc in turning ch. Turn.

Next row Ch3, 1dc in next dc, 1 bar, ch2, 1dc in next dc, patt to last 2 V, ch2, 1dc in next dc, 1 bar, 1dc in turning ch. Turn.

Next row Ch3, 1dc in next dc, 1 V, skip bar, 1dc in next dc, patt to last 2 bars, skip next bar, 1dc in next dc, 1 V, 1dc in turning ch. Turn.

Next row Ch3, 1dc in next dc, 1 bar, working the dc into sp between 2dc, patt to last bar, working last dc into sp between 2dc, 1 bar, 1dc in turning ch. Turn.

Rep these last 4 rows 1[2:2] times more. Cont without shaping until armholes measure 7[7½:8]in from beg, ending with a RS row.

Shape neck and shoulders

Next row Mark 5[5:7] bars in center and leave for back neck, patt to neck sts, turn.

Next row Patt to end. Turn.

Next row Ss over first bar, patt to last bar, turn.

Next row Patt to end. Turn.

Rep last 2 rows once more. Fasten off. Skip 5[5:7] bars in center, attach yarn to rem sts and complete to correspond to first side.

Jacket right front

Using No.C crochet hook ch 81[85:89]. Work first 5 rows as given for back. 19[20:21] V patts.

6th row Ch3 to count as first dc, 1dc in next dc, work 10[11:12] V, 1 gr, 3 V, 1 gr, 4 V, ending with 1dc in turning ch. Turn.

7th row Ch3, 1dc in next dc, 4 bars, 1 gr, 3 bars, 1 gr, work 10[11:12] bars, ending with 1dc in turning ch. Turn.

8th row Ch3, 1dc in next dc, work 10[11:12] V, 2 gr, 1 V, 2 gr, 4 V, ending with 1dc in turning ch. Turn. Cont in patt, dec at side edge as given for back, beg on 10th[14th:14th] row, until 7 V have been dec. Cont without shaping until work measures 34[34½:35]in from beg; end with RS row.

Shape front edge

Dec inside 1 V as given for back armhole, and rep 4 dec rows until work measures same as back to underarm, ending at armhole edge.

Shape armhole

Still dec at front edge, shape armhole as given for back. Cont to dec at front edge only until 4[4:5] V have been dec at this edge. Cont without shaping until armhole measures same as back to shoulder, ending at armhole edge.

Shape shoulder

Next row Ss over first bar, patt to end. Turn.

Next row Patt to end. Turn.

Rep these 2 rows once more. Fasten off.

Jacket left front

Work as given for right front, reversing patt and all shaping.

Finishing

Press each piece under a damp cloth with a warm iron. Join shoulder and side seams.

Front border Using No.B crochet hook and with RS of work facing, beg at lower edge of right front and work 2sc into each row end up right front, work 44sc around neck, then 2sc into end of each row down left front. Turn.

Mark positions for 12 buttons on left front, first to come ½in below beg of front shaping and last 3in from lower edge, with 10 more evenly spaced between.

Next row Work in sc to end, dec one st at each side of back neck and making buttonholes as markers are reached on right front by working (ch2, skipping 2sc, work in sc to next marker) 11 times, ch2, skip 2sc, work in sc to end. Turn.

Next row Work in sc to end, dec one st at each side of back neck and working 2sc into each ch2 buttonhole of previous row. Do not turn.

Next row With RS of work facing work in crab st to end. Fasten off.

Armbands Using No.B crochet hook and with RS of work facing, work 3 rows sc around armholes, then with RS of work facing work 1 row crab st. Fasten off.

Press seams and borders Sew on buttons.

26 *Bikini and short jacket*

Sizes

To fit 32[34:36]in bust
34[36:38]in hips
The figures in brackets [] refer to the 34 and 36 and 38in sizes respectively

Jacket length to shoulder, 26[27:28]in

Gauge

23 sts and 18 rows to 4in over hdc worked on No.C crochet hook

Materials

Bikini 5[5:6] balls Coats & Clarks' O.N.T. "Speed Cro-Sheen"

Jacket 12[13:14] balls
No.C crochet hook
No.D crochet hook
Three small buttons
Spool shirring elastic

Bikini top

Using No.C crochet hook ch 42[46:50].

1st row Into 2nd ch from hook work 1hdc, 1hdc into each ch to end. Turn. 41[45:49] sts.

2nd row Ch2 to count as first hdc, yrh, insert hook into next st and pull through loop, insert hook into next st and pull through loop, yrh and draw through all 4 loops on hook – called dec 1 –, work 17[19:21] hdc, work 3hdc into next st – called inc 2 –, work 17[19:21] hdc, dec 1, 1hdc in turning ch. Turn.

3rd row Ch2, work in hdc to last 3 sts, dec 1, 1hdc in turning ch. Turn.

4th row Ch2, dec 1, work 17[19:21] hdc, inc 2, work 16[18:20] hdc, dec 1, 1hdc in turning ch. Turn.

5th row As 3rd.

6th row Ch2, dec 1, work 17[19:21] hdc, inc 2, work 15[17:19] hdc, dec 1, 1hdc in turning ch. Turn.

7th row As 3rd.

8th row Ch2, dec 1, work 17[19:21] hdc, inc 2, work 14[16:18] hdc, dec 1, 1hdc in turning ch. Turn.

9th row As 3rd.

10th row Ch2, dec 1, work 17[19:21] hdc, inc 2, work 13[15:17] hdc, dec 1, 1hdc in turning ch. Turn.
11th row As 3rd.
12th row Ch2, dec 1, work 30[34:38] hdc, dec 1, 1hdc in turning ch. Turn.
13th row As 3rd.
14th row Ch2, dec 1, work 27[31:35] hdc, dec 1, 1hdc in turning ch. Turn.
15th row As 3rd.
16th row Ch2, dec 1, work 11[13:15] hdc, (dec 1) twice, work 9[11:13] hdc, dec 1, 1hdc in turning ch. Turn.
17th row As 3rd.
18th row Ch2, dec 1, work 8[10:12] hdc, (dec 1) twice, work 7[9:11] hdc, dec 1, 1hdc in turning ch. Turn.
19th row As 3rd.
20th row Ch2, dec 1, work 5[7:9] hdc, (dec 1) twice, work 5[7:9] hdc, dec; hdc in turning ch. Turn.
21st row Ch2, dec 1, work in hdc to last 3 sts, dec 1, 1hdc in turning ch. Turn.
Cont to dec in center of row 0[1:2] times more, *at the same time* cont to dec at each end of every row until 6 sts rem.
Next row Ch2, (dec 1) twice, 1hdc in turning ch. Turn.
Next row Ch2, dec 1, 1hdc in turning ch. Turn.

Next row Ch2, dec 1, ch 40[44:48] for shoulder strap, turn.
Next row (1dc, ch3, 1dc) into 4th ch and every foll 4th ch, then cont in same way down front edge which is the edge dec on every row, working into every 3rd row, turn.
Next row (RS) Work (1sc, 3dc, 1sc) into every ch3 loop up front edge and along shoulder strap, then along other side of shoulder strap, then work in sc down other edge. Fasten off.
Make second piece in same way, reversing shaping.
Join cups
Using No. C crochet hook ch 41[45:49] work 41[45:49] hdc along lower edge of cup, 3sc along picot edging, skip edging of 2nd cup, work 41[45:49] hdc along edge, then ch 42[46:50] Turn.
Next row Beg in 2nd ch from hook and work in hdc along ch, lower edge and ch at other end, working over length of shirring elastic. Work a 2nd row of hdc over shirring elastic, then at end of row ch3 and ss to end of strap to make loop for button, turn and work 3sc over the ch3 loop. Fasten off.

Finishing
Press lightly under a damp cloth with a warm iron. Sew button to end of strap at back and to end of one shoulder strap, using the opening in other strap to fasten.

Bikini pants back
Using No. C crochet hook ch 16[18:20]
1st row Into 2nd ch from hook work 1hdc, 1hdc into each ch to end.
2nd row Ch3, insert hook into first of these ch3 a[?] make 2hdc, work in hdc to last st, 2hdc in last st. Turn. 3 sts inc.
Rep 2nd row 21[23:25] times more. 81[89:97] sts.[?]
Next row Ch5, work hdc into 3rd of these ch5 a[?] rem ch2, work in hdc to end of row. Turn.
Rep last row once more. Work 9[11:13] rows without shaping. Fasten off.

Bikini pants front
Beg at cast on edge of back and work 1hdc into ea[?] st. Turn. 15[17:19] sts. Work 6 rows in hdc. Inc o[?] st by working 2hdc into st at each end of next and[?] foll 2[3:3] alt rows, then at each end of next 8[8:1[?]] rows. 37[41:47] sts. Break off yarn.
Next row Ch 28[29:29] for leg, work across 37[41:47] sts of front, ch 29[30:30] turn.
Next row Into 2nd ch from hook work 1hdc, 1hd[?] into each st to end. Turn. 93[99:105] sts. Work 9[11:13] rows hdc. Fasten off.

NO.25

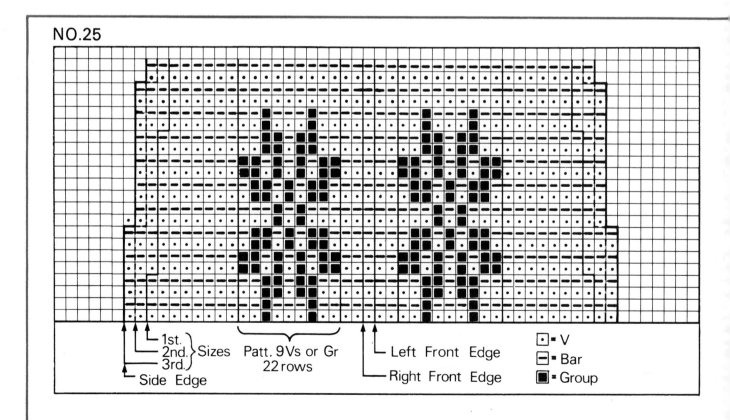

1st. ⎫
2nd. ⎬ Sizes
3rd. ⎭
Side Edge

Patt. 9 Vs or Gr
22 rows

Left Front Edge
Right Front Edge

⊡ = V
⊟ = Bar
▣ = Group

Finishing
[Pre]ss as given for top. Join side seams. Using
[No].C crochet hook and with RS of work facing,
[wo]rk 1 row sc around top edge working over
[sh]irring elastic. Turn.
[N]ext row Ch6, work 1dc into first st, * skip 3 sts,
[wo]rk 1dc, ch3, 1dc into next st, rep from * to end.
[Jo]in with a ss to 3rd of first ch6. Turn.
[N]ext row Work 1sc, 3dc, 1sc into every ch3 loop
[to] end. Fasten off.
[U]sing No.C crochet hook and with RS of work
[fa]cing work 1 row sc around each leg working over
[sh]irring elastic. Fasten off.

Jacket back
[U]sing No.D crochet hook ch 102[110:118]
1st row Into 2nd ch from hook work 1sc, *ch2,
[sk]ip ch1, 1sc into each of next ch3, rep from * to
[la]st ch3, ch2, skip ch1, 1sc into each of next
[ch]2. Turn.
2nd row Ch3, *work 1dc, ch3, 1dc into ch2 sp, rep
[fr]om* ending with 1dc in turning ch. Turn.
3rd row Ch3, *work 3sc into ch3 loop, ch2, rep
[fr]om * ending with 1sc in turning ch. Turn.
4th row Ch5, 1dc into first ch2 sp, *work 1dc, ch3,
[1]dc into next ch2 sp, rep from * ending with 1dc in
[la]st ch2 sp, ch2, 1dc in turning ch. Turn.
5th row Ch1, 1sc into first ch2 loop, *ch2, work
[1]sc into ch3 loop, rep from * ending with ch2, 2sc
[in]to last ch2 loop. Turn.
[R]ep 2nd to 5th rows until work measures 19[19½:
[20]]in from beg, ending with a 3rd row. Break off
[y]arn.
Shape armholes
[A]ttach yarn to third ch2 sp, ch3, work 1dc,
[ch]3, 1dc into each ch2 sp to last three ch2 sp, 1dc in
[ne]xt ch2 sp, turn.
[N]ext row As 5th patt row. 3 gr dec each end.
[C]ont in patt without shaping until armholes
[m]easure 7[7½:8]in from beg, ending with a 2nd or
[4t]h row.
Shape neck
[N]ext row Patt over 5 gr, turn and patt to end.
[B]reak off yarn.
[A]ttach yarn to 5th gr from other end and work to
[c]orrespond to first side.

Jacket left front
[U]sing No.D crochet hook ch 50[54:58].
[W]ork in patt as given for back until front measures
[sa]me as back to underarm, ending with a 3rd row.
[B]reak off yarn.
Shape armhole
[A]ttach yarn to third ch2 sp, ch3, work 1dc,
[ch]3, 1dc into each ch2 sp to end. Turn.
[C]ont without shaping until armhole measures
[5[5½:6]]in from beg, ending with a 2nd patt row.
[B]reak off yarn.
Shape neck
[A]ttach yarn to 4th[5th:6th] loop, ch3, patt to end.
[T]urn. Cont without shaping until armhole
[m]easures same as back to shoulder. Fasten off.

Jacket right front
[W]ork as given for left front, reversing all shaping.

Finishing
[P]ress as given for bikini. Join shoulder and side
[se]ams. Using No.C crochet hook and with RS of
[w]ork facing, work 1 row sc around armholes.
[U]sing No. C crochet hook and with RS of work
[fa]cing, work in sc up front edge as far as back neck.
[B]reak off yarn. Attach yarn at other side of back
[ne]ck and cont in sc down left front. Break off yarn.
[B]eg at right side seam, work 1dc ch3, 1dc into each
[lo]op along lower edge, into every 4th st up front
[ed]ge, into each loop across back neck and into every
[4t]h st down left front, then into each loop along
[lo]wer edge to right side seam. Work 1sc, 3dc, 1sc
[in]to each ch3 loop all around edges. Fasten off. Press
[se]ams and edging. Sew on button to left neck, using
[op]ening in patt at opposite corner for fastening.

27 Beach hat and bag

Size
Hat to fit an average head
Gauge
4 sts and 2 rows to 1in over dc worked on No.H
crochet hook
Materials
Hat 5 skeins Columbia-Minerva Hi-Straw in
main color, A
4 skeins in contrast color, B
Bag 6 skeins in main color, A
5 skeins in contrast color, B
No.H crochet hook
No.G crochet hook
6in diameter ring for base of bag
Hat
Using No.H crochet hook and A, ch5. Join
with a ss to first ch to form circle.
1st round Using A work ch2 to count as first dc,
work 21dc into circle. Using B join with a ss to 2nd
of first ch2. 22dc.
2nd round Using B work ch3 to count as first dc
and ch1, *work 1dc into next dc, ch1, rep from * to
end. Using A join with a ss to 2nd of first ch3. 22dc.
3rd round Using A work ch2, 1dc into same ch, *
work 2dc into next ch sp, rep from * to end. Using
B join with a ss to 2nd of first ch2. 44dc.
4th round Using B work ch3, *skip 2dc, work 1dc
into next sp between dc, ch1, skip 1dc, work 1dc
into next sp, ch1, rep from * to end.
Using A join with a ss to 2nd of first ch3. 29dc.
5th round Using A work ch2, 1dc into same ch,
*work 2dc into next ch sp, rep from * to end. Using
B join with a ss to 2nd of first ch2. 58dc.
6th round Using B work ch3, *skip 1dc, work 1dc
into next sp between dc, ch1, skip 2dc, work 1dc into
next sp between dc, ch1, skip 2dc, work 1dc into next
sp between dc, ch1, rep from * to end. Using A join
with a ss to 2nd of first ch3. 35dc.
7th round As 5th.
8th round As 6th.
9th round As 5th.
10th round Using B work ch3, *skip 2dc, work 1dc
into sp between next dc, ch1, rep from * to end.
Using A join with a ss to 2nd of first ch3.
11th round As 5th.
12th round As 10th.
13th round As 5th.
14th round As 10th.
15th round As 5th, working only 1dc into each of
last ch2. 82dc.
16th round As 10th.
17th round Using A work ch2, work 1dc into same
ch, *work 3dc into next ch sp, work 2dc into next ch
sp, rep from * ending with 2dc into last ch sp. Using
B join with a ss in 2nd of first ch2. 102dc.

18th round As 10th. 51dc.
19th round Using A work ch2, 2dc into same ch,
*work 3dc into next ch sp, rep from * to end. Using
B join with a ss in 2nd of first ch2. 153dc.
20th round As 10th, skipping 1dc instead of 2 at
end of round. 77dc.
21st round As 5th.
22nd round As 10th.
Change to No.G crochet hook.
23rd round Using A ch2, work 1dc into same ch
until 2 loops rem on hook, using B complete dc
and make 2 more dc into same ch, using A make
2dc in next ch sp, cont in this way working alt
4dc and 2dc into ch; change colors after 2dc.
24th round Work alternately 2dc in A above B and
2dc in B above A.
25th round Work alternately 2sc in A above B and
2sc in B above A. Make 2ss at end of round.
Fasten off.

Bag
Using No.G hook and A, ch5. Join with a ss to first
ch to form circle. Work first 3 rounds as given for hat.
44dc.
4th round Using B work ch3, skip 2dc, work 1dc
into next sp between dc, *ch2, skip 2dc, work 1dc
into next sp between dc, ch1, skip 2dc, work 1dc into
next between dc, rep from * to end. Using A join
with a ss to 2nd of first ch3. 22dc.
5th round Using A work ch2, work 1dc into same
ch, *work 3dc into next ch sp, work 2dc into next
ch sp, rep from* to end. Using B join with a ss into
2nd of first ch2. 55dc.
Change to No.H hook.
6th round Take a ring with a diameter of 6in,
using B attach ring by making 1sc into each dc, inc
1sc into each 3rd dc. When 2 loops of last sc rem on
hook, change colors. 74sc.
7th round Using A work in dc to end, inc 12 sts
evenly around by working 2dc into one st. Using B
join with a ss. 86dc.
8th round Using B work ch3, *skip 2dc, work, 1dc
into next sp between dc, ch1, rep from * to end.
Using A join with a ss into 2nd of first ch3. 43dc.
9th round As 3rd.
10th round As 4th.
11th round Using A work ch2, work 1dc into same
ch, *work 3dc in next ch sp, work 2dc in next ch sp,
rep from *ending with 3dc in last ch sp. Using B
join with a ss in 2nd of first ch2. 108dc.
12th round Using B work ch3, *skip 2dc, work 1dc
in next sp between dc, ch1, rep from * to end. Using
A join with a ss in 2nd of first ch3. 54dc.
13th round Using A work ch2, work 1dc in same ch,
*work 2dc in next ch sp, rep from * to end. Using B
join with a ss to 2nd of first ch2. 108dc.
14th round As 12th.
15th round As 13th.
16th round As 12th.
17th round As 11th.
18th round As 12th.
19th round As 13th.
20th round As 12th.
21st round As 13th.
22nd round As 12th.
23rd round As 11th.
24th round As 12th.
25th round As 13th.
26th round As 12th.
Change to No.G crochet hook.
27th round As 23rd round of hat.
28th round As 24th round of hat.
29th round As 25th round of hat.

Handles
Using No.H crochet hook and 3 strands of A, make a
ch 8in long. Attach this chain to side having 28dc
between each end. Using No.H crochet hook and 2
strands of B, join with a ss to where handle is
attached and work 3sc, then cont working
in sc all around handle. Join with a ss at other end.
Work another handle in same way.

28 Toreador bolero

Sizes
To fit 34/36in bust
Length to shoulder, 22in
Gauge
Small flower motif measures 2in across worked on
No.G crochet hook
Materials
5 balls Reynolds Sonata in main color, A
1 ball each in contrast colors B, C and D
No.G crochet hook

Small flower
Using No.G crochet hook and A, ch8. Join
with a ss into first ch to form circle.
1st round Ch2, work 13sc into circle. Join with a
ss into 2nd of first ch2.
2nd round Ch1, *work 3dc into next st, 1sc into
next st, rep from * to end, ending with 3dc in last
st. Join with a ss to first ch1. Fasten off. Make
approx 149 more small flowers in A, 8 in B, 8 in C
and 2 in D.

Small rose
Using No. G crochet hook and D, ch6. Join
with a ss into first ch to form circle.
1st round Ch2, work 9sc into circle. Join with a ss
to 2nd of first ch2.
2nd round As 2nd round of small flower.
3rd round *Ch3, insert hook from back of work
around stem of sc and work 1sc – called 1scB –, rep
from * 4 times more, working last 1scB into ss at end
of previous round.
4th round Into each ch3 loop work 5dc and 1sc.
5th round *Ch4, 1scB, rep from * 4 times more,
working last 1scB into last 1scB of 3rd round.
6th round Into each ch4 loop work 4dc, ch2, 3dc
and 1sc. Fasten off.
Make another small rose in same way.

Large rose
Using No. G crochet hook and D, ch8. Join with a
ss into first ch to form circle. Work first 2 rounds
as given for small flower.
3rd round (ch3, 1scB) 7 times, working last 1scB
into ss at end of previous round.
4th round As 4th round of small rose.
5th round (ch4, 1scB) 7 times, working last 1scB
into last 1scB of 3rd round.
6th round Into each ch4 loop work 7dc and 1sc.
7th round (ch6, 1scB) 7 times, working last 1scB

into last 1scB of 5th round.
8th round Into each ch6 loop work 6dc, ch2, 5dc
and 1sc. Fasten off.
Make another large rose in same way.

Small rings
Using No.G crochet hook and A, ch6. Join with a
ss to first ch to form circle.
1st round As 1st round of small flower. Fasten off.
Make approx 11 more in same way.

Finishing
Pin out flowers and press under a damp cloth with
a warm iron. Make a paper patt from diagram.
Lay flowers onto patt, as foll: make an outline with
flowers in A having 11 up each front edge, 2 at
shoulder and 4 down each side of armhole, 1 at
bottom edge of armhole and 7 across top of back.
Fill in whole of back with flowers in A, having 7 li
of 11 flowers. Place 1 large and 1 small rose on ea
front and fill rem of fronts with flowers in A, B, C
and D, using small rings to fill out spaces, as
desired. Join flowers with a short stem by making
2 sts into each flower, leaving about ⅛in between
them, then working 2 buttonhole sts over the stem
Join shoulder seams. If desired, work around
armhole edges, working sc into each flower and ch
between them. Press.

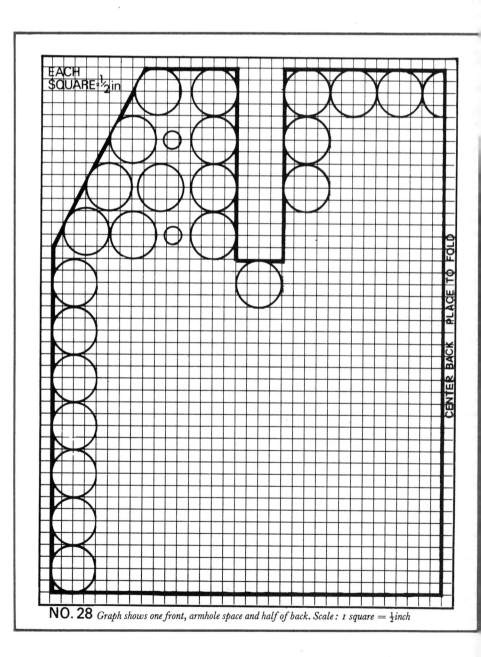

EACH SQUARE = ½in

CENTER BACK   PLACE TO FOLD

NO. 28 *Graph shows one front, armhole space and half of back. Scale: 1 square = ½inch*

29 Triangular shawl

Size
Approx 63in by 33in plus fringe

Gauge
Each square motif measures 3in by 3in worked on No.E crochet hook

Materials
? balls Bernat Nylo Sports in main color, A
? balls Bernat Nylo Sports in contrast, B
? balls Bernat Nylo Sports in contrast, C
No.E crochet hook

Square motif
Using No.E crochet hook and A, ch6. Join with a ss to first ch to form circle.
1st round Ch2, work 9sc into circle. Join with a ss to 2nd of first ch2 10 sts.
2nd round Ch3, work 1dc in same place, 2 dc into each st to end. Join with a ss to 3rd of first ch3. 20 sts.
3rd round Ch7, *skip 4 sts, work 6dc into next st, ch4, rep from * twice more, skip 4 sts, work 5dc into last st. Join with a ss to 3rd of first ch7.
4th round Ch1, *work 4sc into ch4 loop, work 8dc between 3rd and 4th dc of 6dc gr, rep from * 3 times more. Join with a ss to first ch.
5th round Ch1, *1sc into each of next 4sc, ch5, work 1sc into 4th dc, ch1, work 1sc into next dc, ch5, rep from * 3 times more. Join with a ss to first ch. Fasten off. Darn in ends.
Work 120 more square motifs in same way, making 41 more in A, 44 in B and 35 in C, or varying colors as desired.

Finishing
Join square motifs tog in desired color sequence, making one strip of 21 squares, one of 19 squares, one of 17 squares, and so on, ending with one square.

Work border
Using No.E crochet hook, A and with RS of work facing, attach yarn to ch1 at front corner and work along two short sides, as foll:
1st row *Ch12, work 1sc into 2nd of 4sc at side of square, ch1, work 1sc into next sc, ch12, work 1sc into ch1 at corner, ch12, work 1sc into 2nd of next 4sc, ch1, work 1sc into next sc, ch1, work 1sc into ch1 at corner, ch1, work 1sc into ch1 at corner of next square, rep from * around the 2 sides of each square along one edge, work in same way around 3 sides of square at center, then work in same way along other edge.
Fasten off. Turn.
2nd row (WS) Attach yarn into first ch12 loop, work 1sc to this loop, (ch12, work 1sc into next ch12 loop) 3 times, ch2, work 1sc into first ch12 loop of next square, cont in this way along both edges working 5 loops around square at center.
Fasten off. Turn.
3rd row (RS) Attach yarn into first ch12 loop, work 1sc into this loop, *(ch12, work 1sc into next ch12 loop) twice, ch12 to stretch across angle between 2 squares, work 1sc into next ch12 loop, rep from * along both edges working 4 loops around square at center. Fasten off. Turn.
4th row Attach yarn into first ch12 loop, work 1sc into this loop, *ch12, work 1sc into next ch12 loop, rep from * along both edges working 3 loops around square at center. Fasten off. Turn.
5th row As 4th row working 3 loops around square at center by working twice into the center loop. Fasten off.
Pin out and press under a damp cloth with a warm iron.
Fringe Cut B and C into 16in lengths. Taking 3 strands of each color tog at a time, knot into each loop along border, using alt colors.
Trim fringe.

30 Fashionably styled pants suit

Sizes
Directions are for 32in bust.
The figures in brackets [ ] refer to the 35in bust size.
Jacket. Length, 27[27½]in. Sleeve seam, 15in.
Pants. Inside leg, 30in adjustable.

Gauge
10dc to 3in worked on No.G hook.
15 bean sts to 8in and 3 bean st rows to 2in.

Materials
Bernat Berella 4 (Knitting Worsted) 8[9] skeins
One No.G crochet hook
8 buttons
¾yd elastic

Pants left leg
Begin at waistline and using No G hook, ch52[56].
1st row 1dc into 4th ch from hook, 1dc into each ch to end. 50[54] sts.
2nd row Ch3 to count as first dc, 1dc into each dc to end. Continue in dc, inc one st at each end of 5th and every following 5th row until there are 56[60] sts.
Continue without shaping until work measures 10in.

Shape crotch
Next row Ch8, turn, 1dc into 4th ch from hook, 1dc into each of next 4ch, 1dc into each st to end, attach a separate length of yarn to the end of the row, ch5 and break off, then with original yarn work 1dc into each of 5ch. 67[71] sts
Work 2 rows.
Next row Patt to within last st. Turn.
Rep the last row twice more. 64[68] sts.

Continue without shaping until leg measures 27½in from beg of crotch shaping, or 2½in less than desired length.
Next row Ch3 to count as first hdc, 1hdc into next st, *(yoh, insert hook into next st and draw through loop, yoh and draw through 2 loops) 3 times into the same st, yoh and draw through all loops on hook—called bean st—, skip one st, rep from * to last 2 sts, 1hdc into each of last st. 30[32] bean sts with 2hdc at each end.
Next row Ch3 to count as first hdc, 1hdc into next st, 1 bean st into each bean st, 1hdc into each of last 2 sts.
Rep last row once more.
Next row Ch3 to count as first hdc, 1hdc into next st, 2hdc into each bean st, 1hdc into each of last 2 sts. Fasten off.

Right leg
Work to correspond to left Leg, reversing shaping.

Jacket back
Ch67[71].
1st row 1hdc into 3rd ch from hook, *skip 1ch, 1 bean st into next ch, rep from * to last 2 sts, 1hdc into each of last 2 sts. 31[33] bean sts with 2hdc at each end.
2nd row Ch3 to count as first hdc, 1hdc into next st, 1 bean st into each bean st, 1hdc into each of last 2 sts.
Rep the 2nd row until work measures 20in from beg or length desired to armhole.

Shape armholes
Next row Ss over first 2hdc and first bean st, ch3, 1hdc into next bean st, patt to within last 2 bean sts, 2hdc into next bean st. Turn.

Next row Ch3 to count as first hdc, 1hdc into next hdc, 1hdc into bean st, patt to within last bean st, 1hdc into bean st, 1hdc into each of last 2 sts.
Next row Ch3 to count as first hdc, yoh, insert hook into next st and draw through loop, insert hook into next st and draw through all 4 loops—called dec 1—, patt to within last 3 sts, dec 1, 1hdc into last st. 25[27] bean sts with 2hdc at each end.
Continue without shaping until armholes measure 7[7¾]in.

Shape shoulders
Next row Ss over 2hdc and 3[4] bean sts, ch3, 1hdc into next bean st, 1 bean st into each of next 4 bean sts Fasten off. Skip 9 bean sts in center, attach yarn, ch3, 1 bean st into each of next 4 bean sts, 2hdc into next bean st. Fasten off.

Left front
Ch39[43] and work in patt as given for Back until work measures the same as Back to armholes. 17[19] bean sts.

Shape armhole
Next row Ss over 2hdc and 1 bean st, ch3, 1hdc into next bean st, patt to end.
Next row Patt to within last bean st, 1hdc into bean st, 1hdc into each of last 2 sts.
Next row Ch3 to count as first hdc, dec 1, patt to end. 14[16] bean sts.
Continue without shaping until armhole measures 5in, ending at front edge.

Shape neck
Next row Ss over 2hdc and 4[5] bean sts, ch3, 1hdc into next bean st, patt to end.
Next row Patt to within last bean st, 1hdc into bean st, 1hdc into each of last 2 sts.
Next row Ch3 to count as first hdc, dec 1, patt to end. 8[9] bean sts.
Continue without shaping until armhole measures the same as on Back, ending at armhole edge.

Shape shoulder
Next row Ss over hdc and 3[4] bean sts, ch3, 1hdc into next bean st, patt to end.

Right front
Work to correspond to left Front, reversing shaping.

Sleeves
Ch41[45] and work in patt as given for Back for 10 rows. 18[20] bean sts.
Next row Ch3 to count as first hdc, 2hdc into the next st, patt to within last 2 sts, 2hdc into next st, 1hdc into last st.
Rep last row once more.
Next row Ch3 to count as first hdc, 1hdc into next st, 1 bean st into next st, patt to end, ending with 2hdc. 20[22] bean sts.
Work 3 rows without shaping. Rep the inc rows once more. 22[24] bean sts.
Continue without shaping until work measures 15in from beg.

Shape cap
Next row Ss over 2hdc and 1 bean st, ch3, 1hdc into next st, patt to within last 2 bean sts, 2hdc into next bean st. Turn.

Next row Ch3 to count as first hdc, 1hdc into next st, 1hdc into bean st, patt to within last bean st, 1hdc into bean st, 1hdc into each of last 2 sts.
Next row Ch3 to count as first hdc, dec 1, patt to within last 3 sts, dec 1, 1hdc into last st. Rep last 2 rows 2[3] times more. Fasten off.

Collar
Join shoulder seams. With WS facing, work 42[46]hdc around neck edge.
Next row Ch2 to count as first hdc, 1hdc into

each st to end.
Next row Ch2 to count as first hdc, 1hdc into each of next 3[5]hdc, *2hdc into next st, 1hdc into each of next 2hdc, rep from * 11 times more, 1hdc into each of next 2[4]hdc. 54[58] sts.
Continue in hdc until collar measures 3in.
Fasten off.

Belt
Ch8.
Next row 1hdc into 3rd ch from hook, 1hdc into each ch to end.
Continue in hdc until work measures 30[32]in or desired length.
Dec one st at each end of every row until 3 sts rem.
Fasten off.

Finishing
Press pieces under a dry cloth using a cool iron.
Pants. Join Back and Front seams. Join leg seams.
Fold over first row at waist and slip stitch in place.
Thread elastic through.
Jacket. Sew in sleeves. Join side and sleeve seams.
With RS facing, attach yarn at lower corner of right Front and work 1 row of hdc along front edge, around collar working 2hdc into each corner, then down left front edge, turn.

Mark position of 8 buttonholes on right front edge placing bottom one 2in from lower edge, top one just below neck edge, then 6 more evenly spaced between.
Next row Work in hdc to position of first buttonhole, (ch2, skip 2 sts, 1hdc to next buttonhole) 7 times, ch2, skip 2 sts, 1hdc in each st to end.
Next row Work in hdc with 2hdc into each ch2 sp. Work 1 more row in hdc. Fasten off.
Work 1 row hdc around lower edge of jacket and sleeves.
Press all seams lightly. Sew on buttons.
Sew buckle to straight end of belt.

31 *Classic sports jacket*

Sizes
Directions are for 34in bust.
The figures in brackets [] refer to the 37 and 40in sizes respectively.
Length from shoulder, 33in.
Sleeve seam, 17[17½:18]in.

Gauge
4hdc and 3 rows to 1in worked on No.G crochet hook.

Materials
Spinnerin Wintuk Sports
5[6:6] skeins main color, A
4[4:4] skeins contrast, B
One No.F crochet hook; one No.G crochet hook

Main section
NB The coat is worked from the top downward, the back and fronts in one, starting at the neck edge. Using No.G hook and A, ch49 loosely.
1st row 1hdc in 3rd ch from hook, 2hdc in each of next 2ch, 4hdc, 2hdc in each of next 2ch, 28hdc, 2hdc in each of next 2ch, 4hdc, 2hdc in each of next 2ch, 2hdc. Place a marker thread between each pair of 2hdc for raglans.
2nd row Ch2 to count as first hdc, hdc in same place, 2hdc, 2hdc in each of next 2hdc (1 inc made at each side of marker thread), 6hdc, 2hdc in each of next 2hdc, 30hdc, 2hdc in each of next 2hdc, 6hdc, 2hdc in each of next 2hdc, 2hdc, 2hdc in last st.
Continue in this way, inc at each side of markers and each end of row for 3 rows more.

6th row Ch12[14:16], 1hdc in 3rd and following 9[11:13] ch, 11hdc, 2hdc in each of next 2hdc, 14hdc, 2hdc in each of next 2hdc, 38hdc, 2hdc in each of next 2hdc, 14hdc, 2hdc in each of next 2hdc, 11hdc. With a separate length of yarn join to top turning ch of 5th row and ch11[13:15] and fasten off, then continuing from 6th row work 1hdc into each of these ch.
7th row Ch2 to count as first hdc, 22[24:26]hdc, 2hdc in each of next 2hdc, 16hdc, 2hdc in each of next 2hdc, 40hdc, 2hdc in each of next 2hdc, 16hdc, 2hdc in each of next 2hdc, 23[25:27]hdc. 134[138:142] sts.
Continue inc at each side of each marker but not at each end of row for 15[17:19] rows more *at the same time* working in stripe patt rows as follows: (beg 8th row) 1A, 6B, 8A[1A, 6B, 8A, 2B: 1A, 6B, 8A, 2B, 2A]. 254[274:294] sts.

Armholes
Next row With B[A:B], ch2, 39[43:47]hdc, ch5, skip next 50[54:58] sts for armhole and continue without breaking yarn, 74[78:82]hdc, ch5, skip next 50[54:58] sts for second armhole, 40[44:48]hdc. 164[176:188] sts.
Continue without further shaping in hdc working stripe patt rows as follows: 1B, 2A, 2B[1A, 2B, *6A, 4B, 6A, 2B, 2A, 2B*, 8A, 6B, 8A, 2B, 2A, 2B, rep from * to * once more. 100 rows.
Fasten off.

Sleeves
Using color to correspond to main section and with RS facing, attach yarn in center of 5ch at underarm.
Ch2, 1hdc in each of next 2ch, 1hdc in each of next 50[54:58] sts of armhole, 1hdc in each of next 2ch at underarm. 55[59:63]hdc.
Continue in stripe patt to correspond to main section dec one st at each end of every 4th row until 12 have been worked.
Continue without further shaping until 52[54:56] rows have been worked on sleeve from beg.
Fasten off. Work second sleeve to correspond.

Finishing
Lightly press all pieces on wrong side under a damp cloth using a warm iron.
Join sleeve seams

Edging
Using No.G hook and B, work 2 rows sc around neck edge. Break off yarn.
Attach A and work 2 rows more. Break off yarn.
Using No.F hook and B, starting at bottom of right front edge work 2 rows sc around all edges working 3sc into each corner st, Work a 3rd row sc from left to right in crab stitch
Fasten off.
Work around sleeve edges in same manner.
Press all seams.

61[65:69:73] sts rem. Cont as given for back until 8th line of openwork st has been worked, ending at front edge.

Shape dart

Next row Patt to last 7[7:8:8] sts, turn and patt to end. Turn.

Next row Patt to last 14[14:16:16] sts, turn and patt to end. Turn.

Next row Patt to last 21[21:24:24] sts, turn and patt to end. Turn.

Next row Patt to last 28[28:32:32] sts, turn and patt to end. Turn.

Cont without shaping until work measures same as back to underarm, ending at armhole edge.

Shape armhole

Next row Ss over first 4 sts, patt to end. Turn. Dec one st at armhole edge on every row until 31[33:35:37] sts rem, ending at front edge.

Shape neck

Next row Ss over first 10[12:12:14] sts, patt to last 2 sts, dec one st. Turn.

Next row Dec one st, patt to last 2[2:3:3] sts, turn.

Next row Ss over first 2[2:3:3] sts, patt to last 2 sts, dec one st. Turn.

Dec one st at each end of next 5 rows, then cont dec at armhole edge only twice more. 2 sts. Fasten off.

Right front

Work as given for left front, reversing all shaping.

Sleeves

Using No.D crochet hook ch 55[59:63:67]. Work 4 rows hdc as given for back. 53[57:61:65] sts.

Next row Ch3, skip first hdc, *1dc in next st, ch1, skip one st, rep from * ending with 1dc in turning ch. Turn.

Work 3 rows hdc.

Rep patt row, then work 3 rows hdc, inc one st at each end of 2nd row of hdc. Rep patt row once more. Cont in hdc, inc one st at each end of next and every foll 3rd row until there are 79[83:87:91] sts. Cont without shaping until sleeve measures 14in from beg. Mark each end of last row with colored thread. Work 4 more rows.

Shape cap

Dec one st at each end of every row until 7 sts rem. Fasten off.

Pockets (make 2)

Using No.D crochet hook ch 33. Work 15 rows hdc as given for back. (Work openwork patt row, then work 3 rows hdc) twice, then work patt row once more and 2 rows of hdc. Fasten off.

Finishing

Press each piece under a damp cloth with a warm iron. Join raglan seams, sewing last 4 rows of sleeve from markers to bound-off sts at underarm. Join side and sleeve seams. Using No.D crochet hook and with RS of work facing, work 5 rows sc along right and left front edges.

Collar Using No.D crochet hook and with WS of work facing, attach yarn to beg of neck, ch2, work 90[92:94:96] hdc around neck edge. Turn. Work 2 rows hdc.

Next row Ch2, work 20[20:21:21] hdc, *2hdc in next st, 1hdc in next st, 2hdc in next st, work 20[21:21:22] hdc, rep from * once more, 2hdc in next st, 1hdc in next st, 2hdc in next st, work 21[21:22:22] hdc. Turn.

Work 2 rows without shaping.

Next row Ch2, work 21[21:22:22] hdc, *2hdc in next st, 1hdc in next st, 2hdc in next st, work 22[23:23:24] hdc, rep from * once more, 2hdc in next st, 1hdc in next st, 2hdc in next st, work 22[22:23:23] hdc. Turn.

Work 2 rows without shaping.

Cont inc in this way on next and foll 3rd row. Work 2 rows without shaping. Fasten off. With RS of collar facing work a row sc around edges, turn and work a 2nd row. Fasten off. Sew on pockets. Press all seams.

32 *Elegant town coat*

Sizes

To fit 34[36:38:40]in bust
36[38:40:42]in hips

The figures in brackets [] refer to the 36, 38 and 40in bust sizes and 38, 40, 42in hip sizes respectively

Length to shoulder, 35[35½:36:36½]in

Sleeve seam, 14in

Gauge

5 sts and 4 rows to 1in over hdc worked on No.D crochet hook

Materials

12[13:14:16] balls Bear Brand or Fleisher Winsport. No.D crochet hook

Back

Using No.D crochet hook ch 125[131:137:143].

1st row Into 3rd ch from hook work 1hdc, 1hdc in each ch to end. Turn. 123[129:135:141] sts.

2nd row Ch2 to count as first hdc, 1hdc into each hdc to end.

The 2nd row forms patt. Cont in patt until work measures 9in from beg.

Shape sides

Dec one st at each end of next and every foll 8th row until 113[119:125:131] sts rem. Cont without shaping until work measures 18in from beg.

**Next row Ch3, skip first hdc, *1 dc in next st, ch1, skip one st, rep from * ending with 1dc in turning ch. Turn.

Work 3 rows in hdc. **

Rep from ** to ** 7 times more, then cont in hdc until work measures 27in from beg.

Shape armholes

Next row Ss over first 4 sts, patt to last 4 sts, turn. Dec one st at each end of every row until 33[35:37:39] sts rem. Fasten off.

Left front

Using No.D crochet hook ch 68[72:76:80]. Work in patt as given for back until work measures 9in from beg. 66[70:74:78] sts.

Shape side

Dec one st at beg of next and every foll 8th row until

Sizes

To fit 34[36:38:40]in bust
36[38:40:42]in hips

The figures in brackets [] refer to the 36, 38, 40 and 42in sizes respectively

Jacket length to shoulder, 21½[22:22½:23]in

Sleeve seam, 17in

Skirt length, 21½[22:22½:23]in

Gauge

5 sts and 5½ rows to 1in over patt worked on No.F crochet hook

Materials

11[12:13:14] skeins Columbia-Minerva Nantuk Sports Yarn in main color, A

2[2:2:3] skeins in contrast color, B

No.F crochet hook

12 buttons

Waist length of elastic

One 8in zipper

Skirt back

Using No.F crochet hook and A, ch 66[72:78:84] and beg at waist.

1st row Into 3rd ch from hook work 1sc, *ch1, skip ch1, 1sc in next ch, rep from * to end. Turn. 65[71:77:83] sts.

2nd row Ch3, *1sc in next sc, ch1, rep from * ending with 1sc in turning ch. Turn.

The 2nd row forms patt and is rep throughout. Work 2 more rows in patt. Place colored marker at each side of center 27[29:31:33] sts.

Shape darts

Next row Ch3, work 1sc in same st to inc 2 sts, *ch1, 1sc in next sc,*, rep from * to first marker, (ch1, 1sc) twice into next st, rep from * to * to st before next marker, (ch1, 1sc) twice into next st, patt to end, ending with 1sc, ch1, 1sc into turning ch. Turn.

Cont to inc in this way on every foll 10th row 3 times more. 97[103:109:115] sts. Cont without shaping until work measures 21½[22:22½:23]in from beg.

Fasten off.

Skirt front

Work as given for back.

Finishing

Press each piece under a damp cloth with a warm iron. Join side seams leaving 8in open at top of left seam for zipper. Sew in zipper. Sew elastic inside waist edge with casing st.

Press seams.

Jacket back

Using No.F crochet hook and A, ch 90[96:102:108]. Work in patt as given for skirt until work measures 14in from beg. 89[95:101:107] sts.

Shape armholes

Next row Ss over first 6[6:8:8] sts, ch3, patt to last 6[6:8:8] sts, turn.

Dec 2 sts at each end every other row 3[4:4:5] times. 65[67:69:71] sts. Cont without shaping until armholes measure 7½[8:8½:9]in from beg.

Shape neck and shoulders

Next row Ss over first 7[7:7:8] sts, patt 17[18:18:18] sts, turn.

Next row Ss over first 2 sts, patt to last 7[8:8:8] sts. Fasten off.

Skip first 17[17:19:19] sts, attach yarn to rem sts, patt to last 7[7:7:8] sts, turn.

Next row Ss over first 7[8:8:8] sts, patt to last 2 sts. Fasten off.

Jacket left front

Using No.F crochet hook and A, ch 36[38:42:

44]. Work in patt as given for skirt until work measures same as jacket back to underarm. 35[37:41:43] sts.

Shape armhole

Next row Ss over first 6[6:8:8] sts, patt to end. Turn. Work 1 row. Dec 2 sts at armhole edge every other row 3[4:4:5] times. 23[23:25:25] sts. Cont without shaping until armhole measures same as back to shoulder, ending at armhole edge.

Shape shoulder

Next row Ss over first 7[7:7:8] sts, patt to end. Turn.

Next row Patt to last 7[8:8:8] sts. Fasten off.

Left front band

Using No.F crochet hook and B, with RS of work facing beg at neck edge, skip first 6[6:7:7] row ends, attach yarn to next row end, ch3, *skip 1 row end, 1sc in next row end, ch1, rep from * to end, ending with 1sc in last row end. Turn. Cont in patt, dec 2 sts at neck edge every other row 4 times. Cont without shaping until 18[20:20:22] rows have been worked, then inc 2 sts at neck edge every other row 3 times. Fasten off. Mark positions for 10 buttons, the first 2 buttons ¾in above lower edge and the last 2 buttons 3in below neck edge, with 3 more sets of 2 buttons evenly spaced between.

Jacket right front

Work as given for left front reversing all shapings.

Right front band

Work as given for left front band, beg at lower edge and making buttonholes on 4th and foll 20th[22nd:22nd:24th] row as foll: work in patt until marker is reached, ch2, skip ch1, 1sc, ch1.

Next row Patt to end, working 1sc into each ch2 loop on previous row.

Sleeves

Using No.F crochet hook and A, ch 44[46:48:50]. Work 2 in patt as given for back. 43[45:47:49] sts. Inc 2 sts at each end of next and every foll 10th row until there are 67[69:71:73] sts. Cont without shaping until sleeve measures 17in from beg.

Shape cap

Next row Ss over first 6[6:8:8] sts, patt to last 6[6:8:8] sts, turn.

Work 3 rows without shaping. Dec 2 sts at beg of every row until 11 sts rem. Fasten off.

Collar

Using No.F crochet hook and B, ch 86[88:90:92]. Work 4 rows patt. 85[87:89:91] sts.

Next row Patt 14 sts, work 1sc, ch1, 1sc all into next st, patt to last 15 sts, work 1sc, ch1, 1sc all into next st, patt to end.

Work 2 rows patt.

Rep last 3 rows 4 times more. Fasten off.

Cuffs

Using No.F crochet hook and B, ch 44[46:48:50]. Work 4 rows patt. Inc 2 sts at each end of next and every foll 3rd row 3 times in all. Work 2 rows after last inc row. Fasten off.

Finishing

Press as given for skirt. Join shoulder seams. Sew in sleeves. Join side and sleeve seams. Sew on collar and cuffs. Turn cuffs back over sleeves, sew one button to center of outer side and make button loop on inner side to correspond. Press all seams. Sew on buttons to left front. Sew snap to top corner of right front under collar if desired.

 Midi dress with bell sleeves

Sizes

To fit 34[36:38:40:42]in bust
36[38:40:42:44]in hips
The figures in brackets [] refer to the 36, 38, 40 and 42in sizes respectively
Length to shoulder, 43[43½:44:44½:45]in
Sleeve seam, 6in

Gauge

5 sts and 2 rows to 1in over patt worked on No.F crochet hook

Materials

7[8:8:8:9] balls Spinnerin Wintuk Sport in main color, A
1 ball in contrast color, B
1 ball in contrast color, C
No.F crochet hook
No.E crochet hook

Back

Using No.F crochet hook and B, ch 147[151:157:161:167].

1st row Work 1dc into 5th ch from hook, *ch1, skip ch1, 1dc into next ch, rep from * to end. Turn. 145[149:155:159:165] sts.

2nd row Ch4 to count as first dc and ch1, *work 1dc into next dc, ch1, rep from * to end, 1dc in turning ch. Turn.

The 2nd row forms patt and is rep throughout.

Work 2 more rows with B, 3 rows A, 2 rows C, 3 rows B, then 1 row A. Cont with A only, dec 2 sts at each end of next and every foll 6th row until 113[117:123:127:133] sts rem. Cont without shaping, if necessary, until work measures 25in from beg. Change to No.E crochet hook.

Next row Ch3, 1dc in ch sp, 1dc into next dc, * skip next ch sp, 1dc into next dc, 1dc in next ch sp, 1dc into next dc, rep from * to last 2[2:0:0:2] sts, 1dc in

ch sp, 1dc in last dc [1dc in ch sp, 1dc in last dc :0 : 1dc in ch sp, 1dc in last dc]. 86[89:93:96:101] sts.

Next row Ch3, work 1dc into each dc to end, dec one st at end of row on 32in size only, and inc one st at end of row on 38in size only. 85[89:93:97:101] sts. Work in dc as set for 5in. Change to No.F crochet hook. Cont in patt as at beg until work measures 36in from beg.

Shape armholes

Next row Ss over first 6 sts, ch3, patt to last 6 sts, turn.

Next row Ss over first 2 sts, ch3, patt to last 2 sts, turn.

Next row Patt to end.

Rep last 2 rows 1[2:2:3:3] times more. 65[65:69:69:73] sts. Cont without shaping until armholes measure 7[7½:8:8½:9]in from beg.

Shape shoulders

Next row Ss over first 6 sts, ch3, patt to last 6 sts, turn.

Next row Ss over first 6[6:8:8:10] sts, ch3, patt to last 6[6:8:8:10] sts. Fasten off.

Front

Work as given for back until armhole shaping is completed. 65[65:69:69:73] sts.

Divide for opening

Next row Patt 31[31:33:33:35] sts, turn and complete this side first.

Cont until armhole measures 5[5½:6:6½:7]in from beg, ending at neck edge.

Shape neck

Next row Ss over first 15 sts, ch3, patt to end. Turn

Next row Patt to last 2 sts, turn.

Next row Ss over first 2 sts, ch3, patt to end. Turn. 12[12:14:14:16] sts.

Cont without shaping until armhole measures same as back to shoulder, ending at armhole edge.

Shape shoulder

Next row Ss over first 6 sts, ch3, patt to end. Turn.

Next row Ss over rem sts. Fasten off.

Skip ch1, 1dc, ch1 at center front, attach yarn to rem sts and patt to end. Complete to correspond to first side, reversing shaping.

Sleeves

Using No.F crochet hook and A, ch 99[101:103:105:107]. Work 5 rows patt as given for back. 97[99:101:103:105] sts.

Next row Ch4, *1dc into next dc, ch1, 1dc into next dc, ch1, skip next ch, dc and ch, rep from * 14[15:15:15:16] times more, 1dc into next dc, patt to end. 67[67:69:71:71] sts.

Cont in patt until sleeve measures 6in from beg.

Shape cap

Next row Ss over first 6 sts, ch3, patt to last 6 sts, turn.

Next row Ss over first 2 sts, ch3, patt to last 2 sts, turn.

Rep last row 8[8:8:9:9] times more.

Next row Ss over first 3 sts, ch3, patt to last 3 sts, turn.

Rep last row once more. Fasten off.

Finishing

Press each piece under a damp cloth with a warm iron. Join shoulder seams. Sew in sleeves. Join side and sleeve seams.

Edgings Using No.F crochet hook, B, and with RS of work facing, work a row of sc around lower edge, working into each dc and ch sp. Do not turn work but work a 2nd row of sc from left to right to form crab edging. Work around sleeves and front opening and neck in same way. Using 3 strands of A make a ch cord and thread through holes in front opening. Using 3 strands of yarn make a ch cord in A, B and C. Thread cord in C through first row at beg of skirt, cord in A through 3rd row and cord in B through 2nd row of stripe in A. Press all seams.

Change to No.D hook. Commence lace patt.

1st round (Ch9, skip next st, 1sc in next st) 4 times, *ch4, skip next st, work 1tr into each of next 3 sts, ch4, skip next st, 1sc in next st, (ch9, skip next st, 1sc in next st) 8 times, rep from * 10 times more, ch4, skip next st, work 1tr into each of next 3 sts, ch4, skip next st, 1sc in next st, (ch9, skip next st, 1sc in next st) 4 times, thus ending last sc in first st of round.

2nd round (Ch9, 1sc into 5th of next ch9) 4 times, *ch4, work 3tr in next ch4 sp, ch3, work 1dtr in center of 3tr, ch3, work 3tr in next ch4 sp, ch4, 1sc into 5th of ch9, (ch9, 1sc into 5th of next ch9) 7 times, rep from * 10 times more, ch4, work 3tr in next ch4 sp, ch3, work 1dtr in center of 3tr, ch3, work 3tr in next ch4 sp, ch4, 1sc into 5th of ch9, (ch9, 1sc into 5th of next ch9) 3 times, ch5, 1sc into 5th of first ch9.

3rd round (Ch9, 1sc into 5th of next ch9) 3 times, *ch4, work 3tr into next ch4 sp, ch3, work 2hdc into next ch3 sp, 1hdc in next dtr, work 2hdc into next ch3 sp, ch3, work 3tr into next ch4 sp, ch4, 1sc into 5th of ch9, (ch9, 1sc into 5th of next ch9) 6 times, rep from * 10 times more, ch4, work 3tr into next ch4 sp, ch3, work 2hdc into next ch3 sp, 1hdc in dtr, work 2hdc into next ch3 sp, ch3, work 3tr into next ch4 sp, ch4, 1sc into 5th of ch9, (ch9, 1sc into 5th of next ch9) 3 times, thus ending last sc in first st of round.

4th round (Ch9, 1sc into 5th of next ch9) 3 times, *ch9, 1tr into each of next 3tr, ch3, 1hdc into each of next 5hdc, ch3, 1tr into each of next 3tr, (ch9, 1sc into 5th of next ch9) 6 times, rep from * 10 times more, ch9, 1tr into each of next 3tr, ch3, 1hdc into each of next 5hdc, ch3, 1tr into each of next 3tr, (ch9, 1sc into 5th of next ch9) 3 times, ch5, 1sc into 5th of first ch9.

5th round (Ch9, 1sc into 5th of next ch9) 3 times, *ch9, work 3tr into next ch3 sp, work 1dtr into 3rd of 5hdc, work 3tr into next ch3 sp, (ch9, 1sc into 5th of next ch9) 7 times, rep from * 10 times more, ch9, work 3tr into next ch3 sp, work 1dtr into 3rd of 5hdc, work 3tr into next ch3 sp, (ch9, 1sc into 5th of next ch9) 4 times, thus ending last sc in first st of round.

6th round (Ch9, 1sc into 5th of next ch9) 4 times, *ch8, skip 2tr, work 1tr into each of next 3 sts, ch8, 1sc into 5th of ch9, (ch9 1sc into 5th of next ch9) 7 times, rep from * 10 times more, ch8, skip 2tr, work 1tr into each of next 3 sts, ch8, 1sc into 5th of ch9, (ch9, 1sc into 5th of next ch9) 3 times, ch5, 1sc into 5th of first ch9.

7th round *Ch9, 1sc into 5th of next ch sp, rep from * to end noting that the 5th ch of ch8 sp are worked into, ending last sc in first st of round.

8th round As 7th, ending ch5, 1sc into 5th of first ch9.

9th round (Ch9, 1sc into 5th of next ch9) 4 times, *ch4, 1tr into 9th of ch9, 1tr into next sc, 1tr into next ch, ch4, 1sc into 5th of next ch9, (ch9, 1sc into 5th of next ch9) 8 times, rep from * 10 times more, ch4, 1tr into 9th of ch9, 1tr into next sc, 1tr into next ch, ch4, 1sc into 5th of next ch9, (ch9, 1sc into 5th of next ch9) 4 times, thus ending last sc in first st of round.

Rounds 2 to 9 form patt and are rep throughout. Work 2nd and 3rd rounds once more.

Divide for back, front and sleeves

Next round Work as 4th round of patt, rep from * twice, ch9, 1tr into each of next 3tr, ch3, 1hdc into each of next 5hdc, ch3, 1tr into each of next 3tr, (ch9, 1sc into 5th of next ch9) 3 times, skip 3 flower motifs, now work 1sc in center of the 4th ch9 after this 3rd flower, this completes back, now work across front in same way thus joining with ch9 to 5th of first ch9.

Next round Work as 5th round, rep from * 4 times instead of 10, join to 5th st of ch9 across underarm.

Cont until 5 complete patts have been worked from beg.

Evening smock

Size
To fit 32/36in bust
Length to shoulder, 21in
Sleeve seam, 2in.

Gauge
7 sts and 4 rows to 1in over dc worked on No.C crochet hook

Materials
8 balls Bucilla Brocade
No.C crochet hook
No.D crochet hook

Smock
Using No.C crochet hook, beg at yoke and ch153.
Join with ss to first ch to form circle.
Base row Work 1sc into each ch, ss in first st.
152 sts.
Commence dc edging.
1st round Ch3, work 3dc into next st, (work 1dc into each of next 36 sts, work 3dc into each of next 2 sts) 3 times, work 1dc into each of next 36 sts, work 2 dc into base of ch3, ss in top of ch3.

168 sts.
2nd round Ch3, work 3dc into next st, (work 1dc into each of next 40 sts, work 3dc into each of next 2 sts) 3 times, work 1dc into each of next 40 sts, work 2dc into base of ch3, ss in top of ch3.
184 sts.
3rd round Ch3, work 3dc into next st, (work 1dc into each of next 44 sts, work 3dc into each of next 2 sts) 3 times, work 1dc into each of next 44 sts, work 2dc into base of ch3, ss in top of ch3.
200 sts.
4th round Ch3, work 3dc into next st, (work 1dc into each of next 48 sts, work 3dc into each of next 2 sts) 3 times, work 1dc into each of next 48 sts, work 2dc into base of ch3, ss in top of ch3.
216 sts.
5th round Ch3, work 3dc into next st, (work 1dc into each of next 52 sts, work 3dc into each of next 2 sts) 3 times, work 1dc into each of next 52 sts, work 2dc into base of ch3, ss in top of ch3. 232 sts.
6th round Ch3, work 3dc into next st, (work 1dc into each of next 56 sts, work 3dc into each of next 2 sts) 3 times, work 1dc into each of next 56 sts, work 2dc into base of ch3, ss in top of ch3. 248 sts.
7th round Ch3, work 3dc into next st, (work 1dc into each of next 60 sts, work 3dc into each of next 2 sts) 3 times, work 1dc into each of next 60 sts, work 2dc into base of ch3, ss in top of ch3. 264 sts.

Work picot edge
Next round Turn work so that WS is facing, *1sc into next st, ch3, 1sc into 3rd of these ch3 to form picot, skip next st, 1sc into next st, rep from * to end. Fasten off.

Sleeves
Using No.D crochet hook and with RS of work facing, attach yarn to where sts were left before start of main part, ch9, ss to next st of round.
Next round As 4th round of patt, rep from * once. Cont in patt until 8th round has been worked.
Work picot edge
As given for smock.

Finishing
Do not press. Run in all ends.

36 *Long or short dressing robe*

Sizes
To fit 34[36:38:40:42]in bust
The figures in brackets [] refer to the 36, 38, 40 and 42in sizes respectively
Length to shoulder, 52[52½:53:53½:54]in for long version; 37[37½:38:38½:39]in for short version
Sleeve seam, 12½in
Gauge
4½ sts and 3 rows to 1in over sc worked on No.G crochet hook
Materials
Long version 19[20:20:21:22] balls Spinnerin Mona
Short version 14[15:15:16:16] balls of same
No.E crochet hook
No.G crochet hook
Four buttons

Back
Using No.G crochet hook ch 71[75:79:83:87].
1st row Work 1sc into 2nd ch from hook, 1sc into each ch to end. Turn. 70[74:78:82:86] sts.
Next row Ch2 to count as first sc, work 1sc into each sc to end. Turn.
The last row forms patt. Rep this row 9 times more.

Shape armholes
Next row Ss over first 3 sts, ch2, patt to last 3 sts, turn.
Dec one st at each end of next 4[5:6:7:8] rows. 56[58:60:62:64] sts. Cont without shaping until armholes measure 7½[8:8½:9:9½]in from beg.
Shape shoulders
Next row Ss over first 6 sts, ch2, work 10[10:11:11:12] sc, turn.
Next row Patt to last 6 sts. Fasten off.
Leave first 22[24:24:26:26] sts in center, attach yarn to rem sts, patt to last 6 sts, turn.
Next row Ss over first 6 sts, ch2, patt to end. Fasten off.

Left front
Using No.G crochet hook ch 35[37:39:41:43]. Work 11 rows sc as given for back. 34[36:38:40:42] sts.

Shape armhole
Next row Ss over first 3 sts, ch2, patt to end.
Dec one st at armhole edge on next 4[5:6:7:8] rows. 27[28:29:30:31] sts. Cont without shaping until armhole measures 5[5½:6:6½:7]in from beg, ending at armhole edge.
Shape neck

Next row Patt to last 4[5:5:6:6] sts, turn.
Next row Ss over first 2 sts, ch2, patt to end.
Dec one st at neck edge on next 4 rows. Cont without shaping until armhole measures same as back to shoulder, ending at armhole edge.
Shape shoulder
Next row Ss over first 6 sts, ch2, patt to end.
Next row Patt to last 6 sts. Fasten off.

Right front
Work as given for left front, reversing all shaping.

Skirt
Join side seams. Using No.G crochet hook and with RS of work facing, attach yarn with ss at front edge, ch3 to count as first dc, work 1dc into each of next 4[5:6:7:8] sts, *skip 2 sts, work 3dc, ch1, 3dc all into next st – called GrA–, skip 2 sts, work 1dc, ch2, 1dc all into next st – called GrB –, (skip 2 sts, GrA, skip 2 sts, GrB) twice more, skip 2 sts, GrA, **, work 1dc into each of next 12[14:16:18:20] sts, *, rep from * to * twice more, then from * to ** once, skip 2 sts, work 1dc into each of next 5[6:7:8:9] sts. Turn.
Next row Ch3 to count as first dc, dc into each of next 4[5:6:7:8] dc, *(GrB into ch1 of GrA, GrA into ch2 of GrB) 3 times, GrB into ch1 of GrA,**, 1dc into each of next 12[14:16:18:20] dc, *, rep from * to * twice more, then from * to ** once, 1dc into each of next 5[6:7:8:9] dc. Turn.
Next row Ch3 to count as first dc, 1dc into each of next 4[5:6:7:8] dc, *(GrA into ch2 of GrB, GrB into ch1 of GrA) 3 times, GrA into ch2 of GrB,**, 1dc into each of next 12[14:16:18:20] dc,*, rep from * to * twice more, then from * to ** once, 1dc into each of next 5[6:8:7:9] dc. Turn.
Rep last 2 rows twice more.
Shape skirt
Next row Ch3, work 2[3:4:5:6] dc, 2dc in next dc, 1dc, (work patt panel, 1dc, 2dc in next dc, work 8[10:12:14:16] dc, 2dc in next dc, 1dc) 3 times, work patt panel, 1dc, 2dc in next dc, work 3[4:5:6:7] dc. Turn.
Work 7 rows patt as now set without shaping.
Next row Ch3, work 3[4:5:6:7] dc, 2dc in next dc, 1dc (work patt panel, 1dc, 2dc in next dc, work 10[12:14:16:18] dc, 2dc in next dc, 1dc) 3 times, work patt panel, 1dc, 2dc in next dc, work 4[5:6:7:8] dc. Turn.
Work 7 rows patt as now set without shaping.
Cont to inc in this way on next and every foll 8th row until work measures 37[37½:38:38½:39]in from beg for short version, or 52[52½:53:53½:54]in from beg for long version. Fasten off.

Sleeves
Using No.G crochet hook ch 50[52:54:56:58]. Work in sc as given for back for 8in. 49[51:53:55:57] sts.
Shape cap
Next row Ss over first 3 sts, ch2, patt to last 3 sts, turn.
Dec one st at each end of next 4[5:6:7:8] rows. 35 sts. Dec one st at each end of every other row until 19 sts rem, then at each end of next 6 rows. Fasten off.
Work frill
Using No.G crochet hook and with RS of work facing, attach yarn wth ss to lower edge, ch3, work 0[1:2:0:1] dc, (skip 2 sts, GrA, skip 2 sts, GrB) 7[7:7:8:8] times, skip 2 sts, GrA, skip 2 sts, work 1[2:3:1:2] dc. Turn.
Next row Ch3, work 0[1:2:0:1] dc, (GrB in GrA, GrA in GrB) 7[7:7:8:8] times, GrB in GrA, work 1[2:3:1:2] dc. Turn.
Cont in patt as set until frill measures 4½in from beg. Fasten off.

Front edging
Join shoulder seams. Using No.E crochet hook and with RS of work facing, beg at lower edge of right front, work in sc up front edge, work 3sc in

corner, work around neck, work 3sc in corner, work in sc down left front. Turn. Work 2 more rows sc, working 3sc into each corner st at neck. Mark positions for 4 buttons on left front, first to come 3sts before neck edge with 3 more evenly spaced at 5in intervals.
Next row Work in sc to first buttonhole position, (ch3, skip 3sc, work to next buttonhole position) 3 times, ch3, skip 3sc, work in sc to end, working 3sc into each corner st at neck. Turn.
Work 2 more rows sc working 3sc into each ch3 buttonhole on last row and working 3sc into each corner st at neck. Fasten off.

Finishing
Do not press. Join sleeve seams. Sew in sleeves. Sew on buttons.

37 *Sleeveless shell top*

Sizes
To fit 34[36:38:40:42:44]in bust
The figures in brackets [] refer to the 36, 38, 40, 42 and 44in sizes respectively
Length to shoulder, 19[19½:20:20½:21:21½]in
Gauge
11 sts and 9 rows to 2in over patt worked on No.D crochet hook
Materials
5[5:5:6:6:6] balls Bernat Berella Sportspun
No.D crochet hook

Back

Using No.D crochet hook ch 98[104:110:116:122:128]

1st row Work 1 sc into 2nd ch from hook, 1sc into each ch to end. Turn. 97[103:109:115:121:127] sc.

2nd row Ch2 as first sc, 1 sc into each sc to end. Turn.

3rd row *Ch3, skip 2sc, 1sc into next st, rep from * to end. Turn.

4th row *Ch3, 1sc into next ch loop, rep from * to end. Turn. 32[34:36:38:40:42] loops.

The 4th row forms patt and is rep throughout.

Cont in patt until work measures 12½in from beg.

Shape armholes

Next row Ss over first 2[2:3:3:4:4] ch loops, patt to last 2[2:3:3:4:4] ch loops, turn.

Next row Ss over first ch loop, patt to last ch loop, turn. 26[28:28:30:30:32] loops.

Cont without shaping until armholes measure 4½[4¾:5:5¼:5½:5¾]in from beg.

Shape neck

Next row Patt over first ch4 loops, turn and slip rem sts.

Next row Patt to end.

Next row Patt over ch3 loops, turn and cont in patt on these 3 loops until armhole measures 6½[7:7½:8:8½:9]in from beg. Fasten off.

With RS of work facing attach yarn to 4th loop from other end, patt to end. Complete to correspond to reversing shaping.

Front

Work as given for back.

Finishing

Press lightly. Join shoulder and side seams. Using No.D crochet hook and with RS of work facing, work 2 rounds sc around neck and armholes.

38

Mohair bed jacket

Size
To fit 34/40in bust. Length, 17in

Gauge
1 complete patt to 2in width and 1¼in depth worked on No.K crochet hook

Materials
5 balls Bear Brand or Fleisher or Botany Supra Mohair
No.K crochet hook
No.I crochet hook
1½yd 1in wide ribbon

Cape

Using No.I crochet hook ch52.

1st row Into 4th ch from hook work 1hdc, *ch1, skip ch1, 1hdc in next ch, rep from * to end. Turn. 51 sts.

2nd row Ch3, work 1hdc, ch1, 1hdc all into first ch sp, *(ch1, 1hdc) in next ch sp 3 times, (ch1, 1hdc) twice in next ch sp, rep from * ending with 1hdc in turning ch. Turn.

3rd row Ch3, skip first hdc, (1hdc, ch1, 1hdc) in next ch sp above inc on previous row, *(ch1, 1hdc) in ch sp 4 times, (ch1, 1hdc) twice in next ch sp; rep from * ending with 1hdc in turning ch. Turn.

Cont to inc in this way on next 5 rows.

9th row Ch3, skip next hdc, 1hdc in ch sp, (ch1, 1hdc) in each ch sp to end, working (ch1, 1hdc) twice into center ch sp only. Turn.

Change to No.K crochet hook.

10th row Ch4, *skip next ch sp, (2tr, ch1, 2tr) in next ch sp, ch1, skip next ch sp, inserting hook from right to left around stem of hdc from front of work, work 1tr around stem of next hdc, ch1, rep from * to last 2 ch sps, (2tr, ch1, 2tr) in next ch sp, ch1, 1tr in turning ch. Turn.

11th row Ch4, *(2tr, ch1, 2tr) in ch sp of gr, ch1, inserting hook from right to left from back of work, work 1tr around stem of single tr, ch1, rep from * to last gr, (2tr, ch1, 2tr) into ch sp of gr, ch1, 1tr in turning ch. Turn.

12th row As 11th row but working single tr around stem of tr from front of work.

Rep 11th and 12th rows 3 times more, then 11th row once. Fasten off.

Edging

Using No.K crochet hook beg at neck edge of left front, work in sc down front edge, then work along lower edge as foll: ch4, 1tr in first ch sp, *(ch3, ss into first of these ch3 – called 1 picot –, 2tr) twice into ch sp of gr, (1 picot, 2tr) into each of next 2 ch sps, rep from * to last gr, (1 picot, 2tr) twice into ch sp, 1 picot, 2tr in last ch sp, cont in sc up left front edge, then work around neck edge, as foll: (1 picot, 2tr) into each ch sp to end. Join with ss to 4th of first ch4. Fasten off.

Finishing

Press lightly under a damp cloth with a warm iron. Thread ribbon through first row of openings at neck edge.

39

Cotton housecoat

Sizes
To fit 34[36:38]in bust
36[38:40]in hips
The figures in brackets [] refer to the 36, 38 and 40in sizes respectively
Length to shoulder, 37[37½:38]in
Sleeve seam, 17in

Gauge
6 sts and 3 rows to 1in over patt worked on No.D crochet hook

Materials
24[26:28] balls Coats & Clarks' O.N.T. Speed Cro-Sheen in main color A, 2 balls in contrast color, B; No.D crochet hook

Back

Using No.D crochet hook and A, ch 151[157:163].

1st row Into 3rd ch from hook work 1dc, 1dc in each ch to end. Turn. 149[155:161] sts.

2nd row Ch3 to count as first dc, 1dc in next dc, *ch1, skip 1dc, 1dc into each of next 2dc, rep from* to end. Turn.

3rd row Ch3, work 1dc into each dc and ch sp to end. Turn.

The 2nd and 3rd rows form patt. Rep these 2 rows 3 times more, then 2nd row once. Keeping patt correct, dec one st at each end of next and every

To alter the length of a garment

If you like a garment shown, but want to alter the length to make it either longer or shorter, here is a simplified method of calculating the yarn required.

Take, for example, a skirt that is given as 23 inches long, and you want a finished length of 26 inches.

1. If the skirt is worked in two sections, draw a small diagram of both halves of the skirt as given in the directions (sometimes the front is wider than the back).

2. Find out the hem measurement by dividing the number of stitches in the directions for each section by the number of stitches to one inch given in the gauge.

$$\left.\begin{array}{l}\text{(eg front } 144 \div 6 = 24 \text{ inches}\\ \text{back } 144 \div 6 = 24 \text{ inches}\end{array}\right\} = 48 \text{ inches)}$$

3. Draw the additional length required on to your skirt diagram with a dotted line, taking any flare into account.

4. Multiply the sum of the approximate new hem measurements by the length to be added (48 inches +4 inches flare allowance = 52 inches wide × 3 inches deep = 156 square inches).

The actual area to be added will, in fact, be slightly smaller than the area calculated, because the shaded triangles will not be made. But this extra area allows you a small margin of extra yarn when the calculation is complete, and it's always better to have enough yarn of the same dye lot.

5. Work a gauge square 2 inches by 2 inches (ie 4 square inches) in the yarn needles and stitch to be used. When unravelled, this square will give you the length of yarn required to work four square inches (eg 5 yards).

6. Divide the area arrived at in step 4 by 4 to find out how many times the length of the yarn must be multiplied for the total area (156 ÷ 4 = 38 × 5 yards = 190 yards of yarn).

You now know how many yards of extra yarn you will need to lengthen the skirt.

7. Check how many yards are in one ball of the chosen yarn and divide this into the total length arrived at in Step 6. This gives the total number of extra balls you will need.

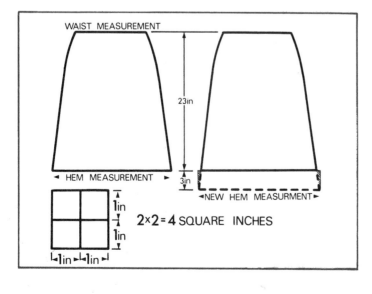

WAIST MEASUREMENT

23in

HEM MEASUREMENT

3in

NEW HEM MEASURMENT

1in

1in

1in

1in

2×2 = 4 SQUARE INCHES

---

foll 4th row until 113[119:125] sts rem. Cont without shaping until work measures 29in from beg

Shape armholes
Next row Ss over first 5 sts, patt to last 5 sts, turn. Dec 3 sts at each end of next row, then 2 sts at each end of foll row. Cont without shaping until armholes measure 6½[7:7½]in from beg.
Shape shoulders
Next row Ss over first 7[8:9] sts, patt to last 7[8:9] sts, turn.
Rep last row once more.
Next row Ss over first 9 sts, patt to last 9 sts. Fasten off.

Left front
Using No.D crochet hook and A, ch 76[82:88]. Work first 10 rows as given for back. 74[80:86] sts. Dec one st at beg of next and every foll 4th row until 56[62:68] sts rem. Cont without shaping until work measures same as back to underarm.
Shape armhole
Next row Ss over first 5 sts, patt to end. Turn. Work 1 row. Dec 3 sts at armhole edge on next row and 2 sts on foll row. 46[52:58] sts. Cont without shaping until armhole measures 5[5½:6]in from beg, ending at armhole edge.
Shape neck and shoulder
Next row Patt to last 12[13:14] sts, turn.
Next row Ss over first 3[5:7] sts, patt to end. Turn.
Next row Patt to last 6[7:8] sts, turn.
Next row Ss over first 2 sts, patt to last 7[8:9] sts, turn.
Next row Ss over first 7[8:9] sts, patt to end. 9 sts. Fasten off.

Right front
Work as given for left front, reversing all shaping.

Sleeves
Make 20 square motifs, as foll: Using No.D crochet hook and B, * ch10, ss into first ch, rep from * 3 times more, ss into first loop. 4 loops.
Next round Using B, work 16sc into each loop. Join with ss to first sc. Fasten off.
Next round Using A, join to 3rd sc of one loop, work ch4 to count as first tr, 1tr into next st, 1dc into each of next 3 sts, skip 2 sts, ch3, 1dc into each of next 3 sts, 1tr into each of next 2 sts, *beg in 3rd sc of next loop, work 2tr, 3dc, skip 2 sts, ch3, 3dc, 2tr, rep from * twice more. Join with ss to 4th of first ch4.
Next round Ch3 as first dc, 4dc, *(work 2dc, ch3, 2dc) into loop at corner, 10dc, rep from * twice more, (2dc, ch3, 2dc) into loop, 5dc. Join with ss to 3rd of first ch3. Fasten off.
Using No.D crochet hook and A, ch 31[34:37] and work main part of sleeve. Work first 10 rows as given for back. 29[32:35] sts.
Next row Ch3, work 12[13:15] dc, 2dc into each of next 3 sts, work in dc to end. 32[35:38] sts.
Cont in patt, inc 3 sts in center of every foll 6th row 5 times more, then in center of every foll 4th row 3 times. 56[59:62] sts. Cont without shaping until sleeve measures 17in from beg.
Shape underarm
Next row Ch3, work 22[23:24] dc, turn and leave rem sts.
Dec one st at beg of next row and at same edge on foll 8[9:10] rows, then dec 2 sts at same edge on every row until 4 sts rem. Fasten off. Skip first 10[11:12] sts, attach yarn to rem sts and patt to end. Complete to correspond to first side, reversing shaping.

Finishing
Press each piece under a damp cloth with a warm iron. Join square motifs into 2 strips of 10. Sew strip of squares into each sleeve, leaving last 2 squares for saddle shoulder. Sew these 2 squares to front and back shoulders. Sew in sleeves. Join side seams.
Edging Using No.D crochet hook and B, beg at

ottom of right front edge and work 12sc, (ch10, 1sc in next st, ch10, 1sc in each of next 12 sts) up front edge, working loops at corners, around neck edge in same way but working only 10sc between loops, then cont down left front.
Next row Work 1sc into each st and 14sc into each ch10 loop.
Using No.D crochet hook and B, make a ch about 10in long, then work 1 row hdc along this ch. Fasten off. Make another cord in same way. Sew on cords. Press seams.

Granny squares vest

Sizes
To fit 36/38 [40/42]in chest
The figures in brackets [] refer to the 40/42in size only
Length to shoulder, 27¼ [29]in
Gauge
Each square measures 3¾ by 3¾in worked on No.E crochet hook; 4 by 4in worked on No.F Crochet hook

Materials
Bear Brand, Fleisher or Botany Shamrock
5[6] balls of main color, A
4[4] balls each of contrasting colors, B, C and D
One No. E[F] crochet hook
One 20[21]in open end zipper

Square motif
Using No.E[F] hook and A,
ch5. Join with a ss to first ch to form circle.
1st round Using A ch2, 2dc into circle, ch2, *3dc into circle, ch2, rep from * twice more. Join with a ss to 2nd of first ch2, leaving last 2 loops on hook. Break off A.
2nd round Using B, draw through 2 loops on hook, ch2, into 2ch sp work 3dc, ch2, 3dc – called work corner –, *ch1, work corner, rep from * twice more. Join with a ss to first of first 2ch, leaving last 2 loops on hook. Break off B.
3rd round Using C, draw through 2 loops on hook, ch2, into ch sp immediately below hook work 2dc, ch1, *work corner, ch1, 3dc into next ch sp, ch1, rep from * twice more, work corner, ch1. Join with a ss to 2nd of first ch2, leaving last 2 loops on hook. Break off C.
4th round Using D, draw through 2 loops on hook, ch2, *3dc into next ch sp, ch1, work corner, ch1, 3dc into next ch sp, ch1, rep from * 3 times more skipping 1ch at end of last rep. Join with a ss to first of first ch2. Fasten off. Make 61 more squares in this manner, varying color combination by using one, two, three or four colors in different sequence.

Corner motif
Using No.E[F] hook and A,
ch32.
1st row Using A, work 1dc into 3rd ch from hook, 1dc into next ch, skip 1ch, (work 1dc into each of next 3ch, ch1, skip 1ch) twice, work 1dc into each of next 3ch leaving last loop of each dc on hook, skip 1ch, work 1dc into each of next 3ch leaving last loop of each dc on hook, yrh and draw through all 7 loops on hook, (ch1, skip 1ch, work 1dc into each of next 3ch) 3 times. Turn.
2nd row Using A ch3, into first ch loop work 3dc, ch1, skip 3dc, work 3dc into next ch loop, ch1, skip 3dc, work 3dc into next ch loop leaving last loop of each dc on hook, skip corner cluster, work 3dc into next ch loop leaving last loop of each dc on hook, yrh and draw through all 7 loops on hook, (ch1, skip 3dc, work 3dc into next ch loop) twice, 1dc in turning ch. Turn.

Break off A.
3rd row Using B ch3, into first ch loop work 3dc, ch1, skip 3dc, 3dc into next ch loop leaving last loop of each dc on hook, skip corner cluster, work 3dc into next ch loop leaving last loop of each dc on hook, yrh and draw through all 7 loops on hook, ch1, skip 3dc, 3dc into next ch loop. 1dc in turning ch. Turn.
4th row Using B ch3, work 3dc into first ch loop leaving last loop of each dc on hook, skip corner cluster, work 3dc into next ch loop leaving last loop of each dc on hook, yrh and draw through all 7 loops on hook, 1dc in turning ch. Fasten off.
Make one more corner motif in same manner using C and D.

Finishing
Run in all ends. Press each motif under a damp cloth with a warm iron. Sew or crochet 10 squares tog to form one row and join 5 rows in same manner. 50 squares. To 4 center squares of last row join 2 rows of 4 squares for center back. 58 squares. Skip first and last square at end of last row and join 2 rows of one square to 2nd and 9th squares, leaving 3rd and 8th squares on last row to form underarm. Join corner motifs to first and 10th squares of last row to form neck shaping. Join 2nd square to first of 4 center back squares and 9th square to 4th of 4 center back squares to form shoulders. Press all seams.

Borders. Using No.E[F] hook and A, with RS of work facing beg at underarm square of lower edge and work one round of sc along lower edge, up front, around neck, down front and around lower edge. Join with a ss to first st. Work 3 more rounds sc, working 3sc into each corner st at lower edge and bottom edge of corner motifs, and dec 2sc at top edge of corner motifs and back neck corners, on each round. Fasten off. Work 2 rounds sc around armholes in same manner, dec 2sc at underarm corners, and 10 sts evenly across 2 shoulder squares on 2nd round. Press borders. Sew zipper to center front.

Belted tunic

Sizes
To fit 38[40:42]in chest
The figures in brackets [] refer to the 40 and 42in sizes respectively
Length to shoulder, 31[31½:32]in, adjustable
Gauge
4 sts and 2¼ rows to 1in over dc worked on No.F crochet hook
Materials
5[5:5] skeins Columbia-Minerva
Nantuk Sports in main color, A
1 skein each of contrasting colors, B, C and D
1 extra skein of D for belt if desired
One No.F crochet hook
One buckle for belt if desired

Back
Using No.F hook and A, ch72
[76:80].
Base row Into 3rd ch from hook work 1dc, 1dc in to each of next ch4, *1dc in next ch, ch1, skip 1ch, 1dc in next ch, work 1dc into each of next 11[12:13]ch, rep from * 3 times more, 1dc in next ch, ch1, skip 1ch, 1dc in next ch, work 1dc into each of next 6ch. Turn. 71[75:79] sts.

1st row Ch3 to count as first dc, 1dc into each of next 3dc, *(1dc in next dc, ch1, skip one st) 3 times, 1dc in next dc, work 1dc into each of next 7[8:9]dc, rep from * 3 times more, (1dc in next dc, ch1, skip one st) 3 times, 1dc in next dc, work 1dc into each of last 4 sts. Turn.
2nd row Ch3 to count as first dc, work 1dc into each of next 5 sts, *1dc in next st, ch1, skip one st, 1dc in next st, work 1dc into each of next 11 [12:13] sts, rep from * 3 times more, 1dc in next st, ch1, skip one st, 1dc in next st, work 1dc into each of last 6 sts, Turn.
The last 2 rows form patt and are rep throughout. Cont in patt until work measures 6in from beg.
Shape side slits
Next row Using separate length of A, ch4. Break yarn and leave for later. Work ch5, into 3rd ch from hook work 1dc, 1dc into each of next ch2, work in patt to end, work 1dc into each of separate ch4. Turn. 79[83:87] sts. Keeping extra sts in dc at each end, cont in patt until work measures 21in from beg, or 1in less than required length to underarm, ending with a 1st patt row.
Shape armholes
Next row Ss over first 9[10:11] sts, patt to last 9[10:11] sts, turn.
Working in patt, dec 2 sts at each end of next 3 rows. 49[51:53] sts. Dec one st at each end of next 3 rows. 43[45:47] sts. Work 1 row without shaping.
Shape neck
Next row Ch3, dec one st, patt 11[12:13] sts, turn.
Dec one st at beg of next 6[7:8] rows. 7 sts. Cont on these sts until armhole measures 9 [9½:10]in from beg. Fasten off.
With RS of work facing, skip first 15 sts, attach yarn to rem sts, patt to last 3 sts, dec one st, 1dc in turning ch. Turn.
Complete to correspond to first side, reversing shaping by dec one st at end of rows.

Front
Work as given for back

Lower edging
Using No.F hook, B, and with RS of back facing, beg at top of side slit and work 1 row sc down slit, working 3sc into corner, along lower edge, work 3sc into corner, work up other side slit, working 2sc into last st of each row and 1sc into each commencing ch. Break off B.
** Attach C and start at beg of row again, work 1 row sc working 2sc into each corner st. Break off C. Attach D and rep from ** twice more. Fasten off. Work lower edge of front in same way,

Armbands
Join shoulder seams. Work as given for lower edging, omitting inc at corners.

Neckband
Work as given for armbands all around neck edge.

Belt
Using No.F hook nad B, ch151 [159:167].
1st row Into 2nd ch from hook work 1sc, 1sc into each ch to last ch, work 2sc in later ch, do not turn work but cont in sc along other side of commencing ch to end. Break off B.
Using C, rep 1st row once more. Using D, rep 1st row twice more. Fasten off.

Finishing
Press each piece under a damp cloth with a warm iron. Join side and armband seams to top of slit. Press seams. Sew on buckle to unshaped short edge of belt.

 *Gamekeeper's cap*

Size
Average size
Gauge
6 clusters and 4½ rounds to 2in over patt worked on No.F crochet hook
Materials
3 skeins Bear Brand or Fleisher Winsom
One No.F crochet hook
One button

Cap
Using No.F hook beg at center ch6. Join with a ss to first ch to form circle.
1st round Ch1, work 6sc into circle. Join with a ss to first sc.
2nd round Ch1, work 2sc into each sc. Join with a ss to first sc. 12 sts.
3rd round Ch2, yrh, insert hook into first st and draw up a loop approx ½in long, yrh, insert hook into same st and draw up another loop, yrh and draw through all loops on hook – called 1cl –, work 1cl into each st to end. Join with a ss to 2nd of first ch2. 12 cl plus the ch, which is not counted as a st.
4th round Ch2, work 2cl into each st to end. Join with a ss to 2nd of first ch2. 24 cl.
5th round Ch2, *1cl in first st, 2cl in next st, rep from * to end. Join with a ss to 2nd of first ch2. 36 cl.
6th round Ch2, *1cl in each of next 2 sts, 2cl in next st, rep from * to end. Join with a ss to 2nd of first ch2. 48 cl.
7th round Ch2, *1cl in each of next 3 sts, 2cl in next st, rep from * to end. Join with a ss to 2nd of first ch2. 60 cl.
8th round Ch2, 1cl into each st to end. Join with a ss to 2nd of first ch2. 60 cl.
9th round Ch2, *1cl in each of next 5 sts, 2cl in

next st, rep from * to end. Join with a ss to 2nd of first ch2. 70 cl.
10th round Ch2, *1cl in each of next 6 sts, 2cl in next st, rep from * to end. Join with a ss to 2nd of first ch2. 80 cl.
Work 9 rounds in patt without shaping. Attach a 2nd strand of yarn and cont working using yarn double.
20th round Ch1, work 1sc into each 1cl to end. Join with a ss to first ch.
Work 3 more rounds sc. Break off yarn.

Peak
Using No.F hook, 2 strands of yarn and with RS of work facing, skip first 30 sts from joining, attach yarn and work over next 20 sts, as foll:
1st row Working into front loop only of sts, (work 1sc into each of next 2 sts, work 2sc into next st) 6 times, work 1sc into each of next 2 sts, turn. 26 sts.
2nd row Ch1, work 1sc into each st to end, inserting hook through both loops, then work 1sc into each of next 3 sts of band, inserting hook into back loop only, turn. 29 sts.
3rd row Ch1, inserting hook into both loops work 1sc into each of first 6 sts, (2sc in next st, 1sc into each of next 3 sts) 5 times, 2sc into next st, 1sc into each of next 2 sts, then 1sc into each of next 3 sts of band, inserting hook into front loop only, turn. 38 sts.
4th row Ch1, work 1sc into each st to end, inserting hook through both loops, then work 1sc into each of next 2 sts of band, inserting hook into back loops, turn. 40 sts.
5th row As 4th row but inserting hook into front loops for last 2 sts, turn. 42 sts.
6th row Ch1, work 1sc into each st to end,

inserting hook through both loops, then work 1sc into each of next 2 sts of band, inserting hook into back loops, ss into next st, turn. 45 sts.
7th row Ch1, skip ss, work 1sc into each of next 44 sts, inserting hook into both loops, 1sc into next st of band, inserting hook into front loop, ss into next st. 46 sts. Fasten off. Fold band to RS on first sc round, (20th round of cap), using No.F hook and 1 strand of yarn, work 1 round sc on the inside of this round, working into every other st.
Fasten off.

Earflaps
Using No.F hook, 2 strands of yarn and with RS of work facing, skip one st next to peak, attach yarn and work 1sc into each of next 12 sts, inserting hook into front loops only, turn.
Next row Ch1, work 1sc into each st, inserting hook into both loops. Turn.
Rep last row until earflap measures approx 4½in from beg, ending with a WS row. Dec one st at each end of next 2 rows. 8 sts.
Next row Ss into first 2 sts, work 1sc into each of next 4sc, ss into next st, turn.
Next row Ch1, skip ss, work 1sc into each of next 4sc, turn.
Cont on these 4 sts until earflap measures 7½in from beg. Make a button loop by working ch6, ss to last st. Fasten off. Work 2nd earflap in same manner.

Finishing
Using No.F hook, 2 strands of yarn and with RS of work facing, attach yarn to st before left earflap, work 1 row sc around earflap, along back of cap and around right earflap. Fasten off. Press. Sew button to top of crown to fasten earflaps.

43

A classic buttoned cardigan worked in crochet. It has two patch pockets and a V-neck

Crochet
Sizes to fit 38(40:42. 44) inch chest

44

A V-necked, raglan sleeved crocheted pullover, worked in panels of doubles and crossed triple crochet stitches

*Crochet
Sizes to fit 38(40:42) inch chest*

45-47

Three ties, two entirely crocheted and one knitted and crocheted. One of the crochet ties is wide and handsome, the other is in random colors. The knit and crochet tie is slim and basic

Crochet and knit

Designs for your home

48

*Have fun with hexagons
—and make a single
place mat or a rug for
the floor.*

*Crochet
Rug diameter: 52 inches.*

49

To make this unusual
rounds-and-bands rug,
start with the center
circle, sew on the small
circles and then crochet
them into the outer band.
Finally sew on the
outer circles.

Crochet
Diameter: 50 inches.

50

Cuddle up in a colorful afghan, made on the ultra-simple Granny Squares principle. The jewel-like effect is created by keeping all the bright colors to the center of each motif and using dark brown, black or navy to frame them.

Crochet
Size: 40 × 60 inches.

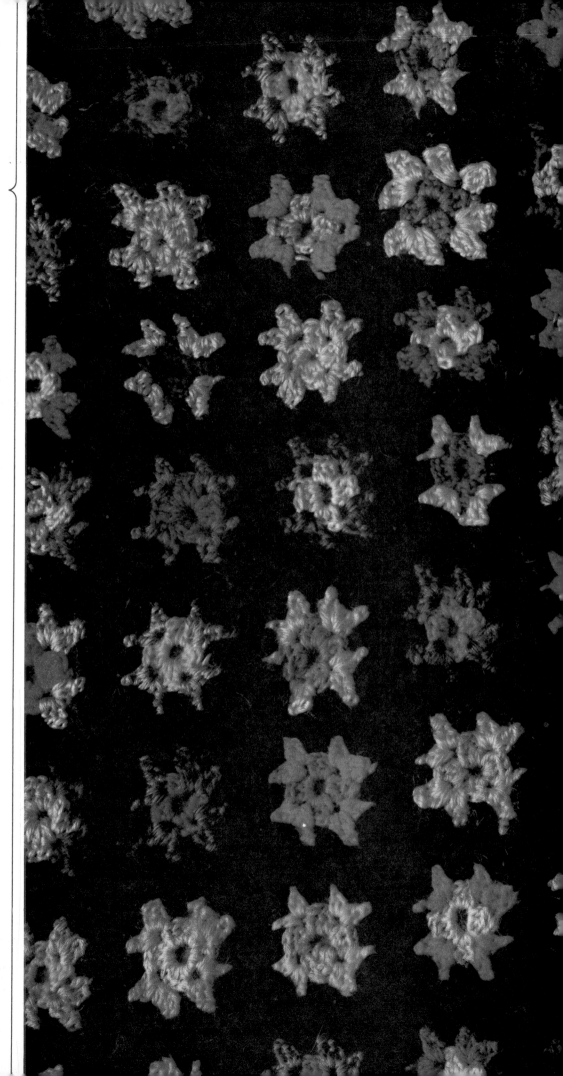

51, 52

Large comforting
pillows to lounge by
the fire with. The
stripes and checks of
tufts can be worked to
match the background
or to contrast.

Crochet
Striped pillow: 24 ×
32 inches.
Checkered pillow: 26
inches square.

53

Get out of bed on the
right side with this
soft, pretty bedside rug.
It's easy and extra-
quick to make.

Crochet
Size: 24 × 14 inches.

54

Machine washable
rug is just the thing
for babies to romp on.
And to show that this
star spangled motif
looks as good from the
back as the front, we've
mixed right and
wrong sides.

Crochet
Rug size: 32½ × 45½
inches.

55

Bored with your old cotton curtains? Tear them up into strips and crochet a rag rug with a giant hook—the more multi-colored the better.

Crochet
Diameter: as required.

56

This rings-of-color pillow may look round, but in reality has 12 'sides'.

Crochet
Diameter: 16 inches.

57

Diamond-patterned pillow, given texture interest with rows of nobbly bobbles.

Crochet
Size: 16 inches square.

58

Zigzag-patterned pillow gives a smart, modern look to a long, plain sofa.

Crochet
Size: 16 inches square

Patchwork afghan with a
knitted rib look, but
made with the extra
firmness of crochet. An
excellent way of using
leftover yarn.

Crochet
Each square is 4 × 4
inches.

60

Handsome floral wall
panel, with the flowers
worked separately and
applied to the
background. Choose the
colors for flowers and
background to enhance
your own room.

Crochet
Size: 29½ × 19½
inches.

61

This beautiful tablecloth has the romantic name 'Moon and Stars'—the moons being the large circles, and the stars the little eight-pointed motifs in between. Make it up in Chalky white for summer, or deep blue for winter.

Crochet
Size: 40 inches square.

62

Put out more flags!
Six basic flag-like
designs cleverly
staggered to add up to
a magnificent throw
which looks as
much at home on a
sofa in a living room
as on a big brass four
poster bed. If you like
the pattern but haven't
time for a whole
bedspread, just use some
of the motifs to make a
pillow.

Crochet
Size: 57 × 90 inches.

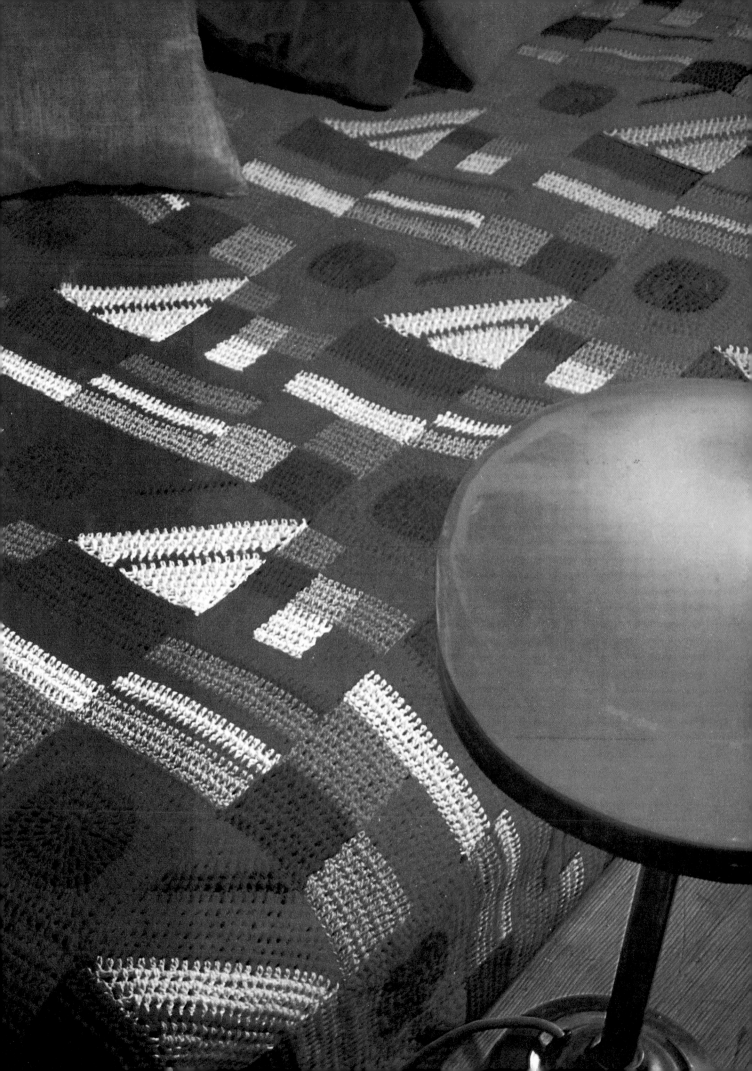

63

Left: these spinning wheel place mats are generously sized to look well with 10 inch dinner plates.

Crochet
Diameter: 14 inches.

64

To wrap around the knees or hug around the shoulders—a chevron striped blanket trimmed with pompons.

Crochet
Size: 36 × 52 inches.

65

Lacy curtains filter the light prettily, and show up the intricate pattern.

Crochet
Size: 38 × 41 inches.

66

Crochet at its most glamorous, worked in a large, repeating design made up of lacy and solid sections that add up to an even bigger and grander overall design. The perfect pattern for a bedspread for a double bed.

Crochet
Size: 80 × 96 inches.

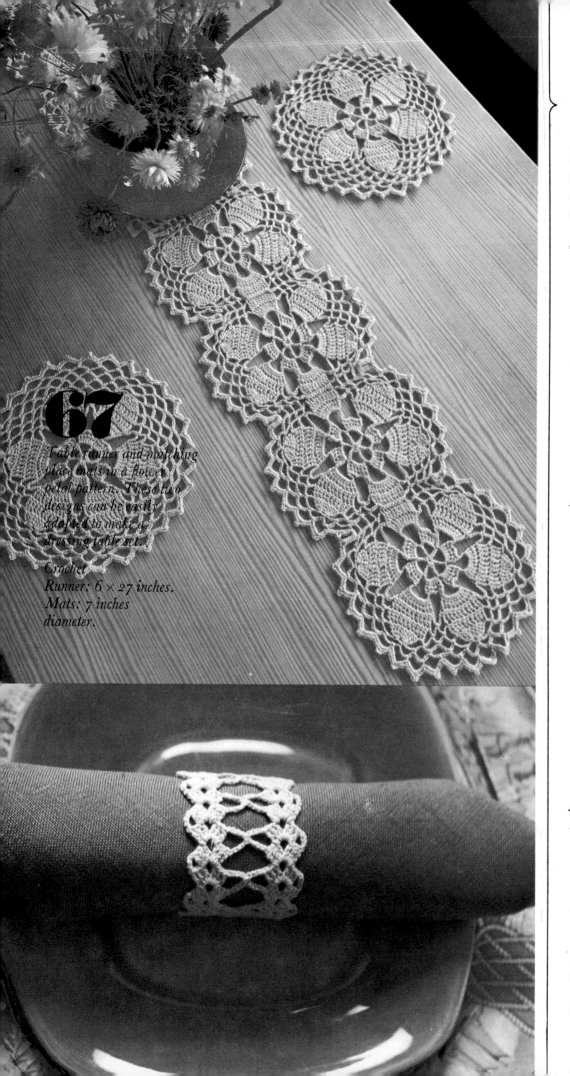

68

Make a set of lacy table napkin rings—white to contrast with colored napkins, or in different colors for each member of the family.

Crochet
Width: 1½ inches.

69

Right: Rajah lampshade in a spectacular, lacy pattern trimmed with a deep fringe. Slip it over a wire lampshade frame covered with a plain cotton lining.

Crochet
Diameter of frame: 14 inches.

70-73

Far right: braids and fringes to trim curtains, pillows, turn into tie-backs or edge a window shade (useful as fashion trims too).

From the top:
Knit. Depth: 3 × 21 inches, plus fringe.
Knit. 4 × 25 inches.
Crochet. Depth: 4½ inches.
Crochet. Depth: 3 inches.

67

Table runner and matching place mats in a flower petal pattern. These two designs can be easily adapted to make a dressing table set.

Crochet
Runner: 6 × 27 inches.
Mats: 7 inches diameter.

74

Double-thickness pot
holder insures that the
hottest dishes can't burn.
One side is solid, the
other patterned.

Crochet
Size: 7¼ inches square.

75

The kind of shopping
bag that folds up small
enough to tuck in a
pocket, then stretches and
stretches to hold
a morning's shopping.

Crochet and knit
Size (unstretched): 16
inches, excluding handles.

76

No home should be
without one—a pretty,
useful cotton dishcloth.

Knit
Size: 18 inches square.

77

The kind of bedspread
that becomes an heirloom,
worked in a crisp
openwork lattice motif
which shows up well
against a subtle
background color.

Crochet
Size: 52 × 80 inches.

Instructions for designs 43-77

Back

Using No.G hook, ch75[77:80:82].

1st row Into 3rd ch from hook work 1sc, 1sc into each ch to end. Turn. 74[76:79:81]sc.

2nd row Ch2 to count as first sc, 1sc into each sc to end. Turn.

Commence patt.

38 and 42in sizes only

1st row Ch4, 1dc into sc on which ch4 stands, * skip 2sc, 1dc, ch1, 1dc into next sc – called 1gr–, skip 1sc, 1gr into next sc, rep from * to last 3sc, skip 2sc, 1gr into top of turning ch. Turn. 30[32]gr. Note that first ch4 counts as 1dc, ch1 throughout.

40 and 44in sizes only

1st row Ch4, 1dc into sc on which ch4 stands, * skip 2sc, 1dc, ch1, 1dc into next sc – called 1gr –, skip 1sc, 1gr into next sc, rep from * to end. Turn. 31[33]gr. Note that first ch4 counts as 1dc, ch1 throughout.

All sizes

2nd row Ch4, 1dc into ch1 sp, *1gr into next ch1 sp, rep from * to end. Turn.

The 2nd row forms patt. Cont in patt until work measures 17in from beg, ending with a WS row.

Shape armholes

Next row Ss across first 4gr, ch4, 1dc into next gr patt to last 4gr, turn. 22[23:24:25]gr.

Cont in patt without shaping until armholes measure 8½in from beg, ending with a WS row.

Shape shoulders

Next row Ss across first 4gr, ch2, 1dc into next gr, patt to last 5gr, 1dc into next gr, ch2, 1ss into same gr. Fasten off.

Left front

Using No.G hook ch35[37:40:42].

1st row Into 3rd ch from hook work 1sc, 1sc into each ch to end. Turn. 34[36:39:41]sc.

2nd row Ch2, 1sc into each sc to end. Turn.**

Commence patt.

38 and 42in sizes only

1st row Ch4, 1dc into sc on which ch4 stands, * skip 2sc, 1gr into next sc, skip 1sc, 1gr into next sc, rep from * to last 3sc, skip 2sc, 1gr into top of turning ch. Turn. 14[16] gr.

40 and 44in sizes only

1st row Ch4, 1dc into sc on which ch4 stands, * skip 2sc, 1gr into next sc, skip 1sc, 1gr into next sc, rep from * to end. Turn. 15[17]gr.

All sizes

2nd row Ch4, 1dc into ch1 sp, *1gr into next ch1 sp, rep from * to end, Turn.

Cont in patt until work measures same as back to underm, ending with a WS row.

Shape armhole and front edge

1st row Ss across first 4gr, ch4, 1dc into next gr, patt to last gr, 1dc into 3rd of first ch4. Turn.

2nd row Ch4, 1dc into first ch1 sp, patt to end. Turn.

3rd row Ch4, patt to last gr, 1gr into last gr, 1dc into 3rd of first ch4. Turn.

Rep 2nd and 3rd rows twice more, then 2nd row once more. Cont in patt without shaping until work measures same as back to shoulder, ending with a WS row.

Shape shoulder

Next row Ss across first 4gr, ch2, 1dc into next gr, patt to end. Fasten off.

Right front

Using No.G hook, ch35[37:40:42].
Work as given for left front to **. Commence patt.

38 and 42in sizes only

1st row Ch4, 1dc into sc on which ch4 stands, * skip 2sc, 1gr into next sc, skip 1sc, 1gr into next sc, rep from * to last 3sc, skip 2sc, 1gr into top of turning ch. Turn. 14[16]gr.

40 and 44in sizes only

1st row Ch4, 1dc into sc on which ch4 stands, * skip 2sc, 1gr into next sc, skip 1sc, 1gr into

next sc, rep from * to end. Turn. 15[17]gr.

All sizes

2nd row Ch4, 1dc into ch1 sp, *1gr into next ch1 sp, rep from * to end. Turn.

Cont in patt until work measures same as back to underarm, ending with a WS row.

Shape armhole and front edge

1st row Ch3, 1gr into 2nd ch1 sp, patt to last 4gr, turn.

2nd row Ch4, patt to last gr, 1dc into ch1 sp, ch1, 1dc into top of turning ch. Turn.

3rd row Ch3, 1gr into 2nd ch1 sp, patt to end. Turn.

Rep 2nd and 3rd rows twice more, then 2nd row once more. Cont in patt until work measures same as back to shoulder, ending with a WS row.

Shape shoulder

Next row Patt to 5th gr from end, 1dc into 5th gr, ch2, ss into same gr. Fasten off.

Sleeves

Using No.G hook, ch35[35:37:37],
Work as given for left front to **. 34[34:36:36]sc. Rep 2nd row 4 times more. Commence patt.

38 and 40in sizes only

7th row Ch4, 1dc into sc on which ch4 stands, * skip 2sc, 1gr into next sc, skip 1sc, 1gr into next sc, rep from * to last 3sc, skip 2sc, 1gr into top of turning ch. Turn. 14[14]gr.

42 and 44in sizes only

7th row Ch4, 1dc into sc on which ch4 stands, * skip 2sc, 1gr into next sc, skip 1sc, 1gr into next sc, rep from * to end, working last gr into top of turning ch. Turn. 15[15]gr.

All sizes

8th row Ch4, 1dc into ch1 sp, *1gr into next ch1 sp, rep from * to end. Turn.

9th row Ch3, 1gr into first ch1 sp, patt to last gr, 1gr into last gr, 1dc into top of turning ch. Turn.

10th row Ch3, 1gr into first ch1 sp, patt to last gr, 1gr into last gr, 1dc into top of turning ch. Turn.

11th row Ch4, 1dc into dc on which ch4 stands, patt to last dc, 1gr into top of turning ch. Turn.

12th row Ch4, patt to end. Turn.

Rep from 9th to 12th rows inclusive 4 times more. 24[24:25:25]gr. *** Rep 9th row twice then 10th and 11th rows once more.

Next row Patt to end. Turn. ***

Next row Patt to end. Turn.

Rep from *** to *** once more. 28[28:29:29]gr. Cont in patt without shaping until work measures 21½ in from beg, ending with a WS row. Fasten off.

Pockets (make 2)

Using No.G hook, ch25.

1st row Into 5th ch from hook work 1dc, *skip 2ch, 1gr into next ch, skip 1ch, 1gr into next ch, rep from * to end. Turn. 9gr.

2nd row Ch4, 1dc into ch1 sp, *1gr into next ch1 sp, rep from * to end. Turn.

Rep 2nd row 8 times more.

Next row Ch2, work 1sc into each dc and ch1 sp to end. Do not turn work but cont in sc working 20sc evenly along side of pocket, 27sc across lower edge and 20sc up other side. Fasten off.

Left front border

Using No.G hook, ch7.

1st row Into 3rd ch from hook work 1sc, 1sc into each ch to end. Turn. 6sc.

2nd row Ch1, work 1sc into each sc to end. Turn.

3rd row (buttonhole row) Ch1, 1sc into next sc, ch2, skip 2sc, 1sc into next sc, 1sc into turning ch. Turn.

4th row Ch1, 1sc into next sc, 2sc into ch2 sp, 1sc into next sc, 1sc into turning ch. Turn.

43 *Classic V-neck cardigan*

Sizes

To fit 38[40:42:44]in chest
The figures in brackets [] refer to the 40, 42 and 44in sizes respectively
Length to shoulder, 26in
Sleeve seam, 19in

Gauge

3 grs and 4½ rows to 2in over patt worked on No.G crochet hook

Materials

7[7:8:8] skeins Columbia-Minerva Nantuk Sports Yarn
One No.G crochet hook
Six buttons

Work 10 rows sc.**
Rep from ** to ** 4 times more, then 3rd and 4th rows once more. Cont in sc until border fits up front edge to center back neck ending with a WS row. Fasten off.

Right front border
Work as given for left front border, omitting buttonholes.

Finishing
Press each piece under a damp cloth using a warm iron. Join shoulder and side seams. Join sleeve seams for 19in. Sew rem of sleeves to ch16 edge at beg of armholes. Sew in sleeve caps. Sew ends of left and right front borders tog and placing seam to center back neck, and with top buttonhole approx 1½in below first front dec, sew front borders in place. Sew on pockets. Press seams. Sew on buttons.

44 *Pullover in patterned stitches*

Sizes
To fit 38[40:42]in chest
The figures in brackets [] refer to the 40 and 42in sizes respectively
Length to shoulder, 26in, adjustable
Sleeve seam, 18in, adjustable

Gauge
8 sts and 5 rows to 2in over dc worked on No.F crochet hook

Materials
13[14:15] skeins Spinnerin Wintuk Fingering
One No.E crochet hook
One No.F crochet hook

Back
Using No.E hook, ch83[87:91].
1st row Into 2nd ch from hook work 1sc, 1sc in to each ch to end. Turn. 82[86:90]sc.
2nd row Ch1 to count as first sc, 1sc into each sc to end. Turn.
Rep 2nd row 4 times more. Change to No.F hook. Commence patt.
1st row Ch2 to count as first dc, 1dc into each of next 12[14:16]sc, *1tr into each of next 2sc, 1dc into next sc, skip next 2 sts, work 1dc into each of next 2 sts, then 1dc into each of 2 skipped sts working with yarn and hook around back of 2dc just worked – called C4dcB –, skip next 2 sts, 1dc into each of next 2 sts, then 1dc into each of 2 skipped sts working with yarn and hook across front of 2dc just worked – called C4dcF –, 1dc in next sc, 1tr into each of next 2sc, *, 1dc into each of next 28sc, rep from * to * once more, 1dc into each of next 13[15:17]sc. Turn.
2nd row Ch2 to count as first dc, 1dc into each of next 12[14:16]dc, *(yrh twice, from behind work insert hook into sp before next tr, around front of this tr and back to behind work, yrh and draw up a loop then complete tr in usual way – called trB –,) twice, 1dc into each of next 10dc, (1trB) twice, *, 1dc into each of next 28dc, rep from * to * once more, 1dc into each of next 13[15:17]dc. Turn.
3rd row Ch2 to count as first dc, 1dc into each of next 12[14:16]dc, *(yrh twice, from front of work insert hook into sp before next tr, around back of this tr to front of work, yrh and draw up a loop then complete tr in usual way – called trF –,) twice, 1dc in next dc, C4dcF, C4dcB, 1dc in next dc, (1trF) twice, *, 1dc into each of next 28dc, rep from * to * once more, 1dc into each of next 13[15:17]dc. Turn.
4th row As 2nd.
5th row Ch2 to count as first dc, 1dc into each of next 12[14:16]dc, *(1trF) twice, 1dc in next dc, C4dcB, C4dcF, 1dc in next dc, (1trF) twice, *, 1dc into each of next 28dc, rep from * to * once more, 1dc into each of next 13[15:17] dc. Turn.
Rows 2-5 inclusive form patt. Cont in patt until work measures 16in from beg, or desired length to underarm ending with a WS row.

Shape raglan
1st row Ss over first 2[4:6]dc, 1dc in next dc, 1trF to form raglan edge, patt to last 4[6:8]dc, 1trF to form raglan edge, 1dc in next dc, turn.
2nd row Ch2 to count as first dc, 1trB, work next 2 sts leaving last loop on hook for each st, yrh and draw through all 3 loops on hook – called dec 1 –, patt to last 4 sts, dec 1, 1trB, 1dc in turning ch. Turn.
3rd row Ch2 to count as first dc, 1trF, dec 1, patt to last 4 sts, dec 1, 1trF, 1dc in turning ch. Turn.
Rep 2nd and 3rd rows until 28 sts rem. Fasten off.

Front
Work as given for back until front measures same as back to underarm.

Shape raglan
Work 1st and 2nd rows as given for back.
Shape neck
1st row (RS) Ch2 to count as first dc, 1trF, dec 1, patt 31 sts, dec 1, 1dc in next dc, turn.
2nd row Patt to last 4 sts, dec 1, trB, 1dc in turning ch. Turn.
3rd row Ch2 to count as first dc, 1trF, dec 1, patt to last 3 sts, dec 1, 1dc in turning ch. Turn.
Rep 2nd and 3rd rows until 11 sts rem.
Next row (RS) Ch2 to count as first dc, 1trF, dec 1, patt to last 3 sts, dec 1, 1dc in turning ch. Turn.
Next row Dec 1, patt to last 4 sts, dec 1, 1trB, 1dc in turning ch. Turn.
Rep last 2 rows until one st rem. Fasten off.
With RS of work facing, attach yarn to rem sts.
1st row Ch2 to count as first dc, dec 1, patt to last 4 sts, dec 1, 1trF, 1dc in turning ch. Turn.
2nd row Ch2 to count as first dc, 1trB, dec 1, patt to end. Turn.
Rep 1st and 2nd rows until 11 sts rem.
Next row (RS) Ch2 to count as first dc, dec 1, patt to last 4 sts, dec 1, 1trF, 1dc in turning ch. Turn.
Next row Ch2 to count as first dc, 1trB, dec 1, patt to last 3 sts, dec 1, 1dc in turning ch. Turn.
Rep last 2 rows until one st rem.
Fasten off.

Sleeves
Using No.E hook, ch37[39:41].
Work first 2 rows as given for back. 36[38:40]sc.
Rep 2nd row 9 times more.
Next row (inc row) Ch1 to count as first sc, 1sc in each of next 3[0:1]sc, *2sc in next sc, 1sc in each of next 8[6:4]sc, rep from * 2[4:6] times more, 2sc in next sc, 1sc to each sc to end. Turn. 40[44:48]sc.
Change to No.F hook.
Commence patt.
1st row Ch2 to count as first sc, 1dc in first sc to inc 1, 1dc into each of next 12[14:16]sc, (1tr in next sc) twice, 1dc in next sc, C4dcB, C4dcF, 1dc in next sc, (1tr in next sc) twice, 1dc into each of next 12[14:16]sc, 2dc into turning ch to inc 1. Turn.
2nd row Ch2 to count as first dc, 1dc into each of next 13[15:17]dc, (1trB) twice, 1dc into each of next 10dc, (1trB) twice, 1dc into each of next 14[16:18]dc. Turn.
3rd row Ch2 to count as first dc, 1dc into each of next 13[15:17]dc, (1trF) twice, 1dc in next dc, C4dcF, C4dcB, 1dc in next dc, (1trF) twice, 1dc into each of next 14[16:18]dc. Turn.
4th row Ch2 to count as first dc, 1dc in first dc to inc 1, 1dc into each of next 13[15:17]dc, (1trB) twice, 1dc into each of next 10dc, (1trB) twice, 1dc into each of next

1dc into each of next 13[15:17]dc, 2dc in turning ch to inc 1. Turn.
5th row Ch2 to count as first dc, 1dc into each of next 14[16:18]dc, (1trF) twice, 1dc in next dc, C4dcB, C4dcF, 1dc in next dc, (1trF) twice, 1dc into each of next 15[17:19]dc. Turn.
6th row Ch2 to count as first dc, 1dc into each of next 14[16:18]dc, (1trB) twice, 1dc into each of next 10dc, (1trB) twice, 1dc into each of next 15[17:19]dc. Turn.
Keeping patt panel correct, cont to inc in this manner every 3rd row until there are 24[26:28]dc at each side of center panel. Cont without shaping until sleeve measures 18in from beg, or desired length to underarm, ending with a WS row.

Shape raglan
Work as given for back until 8 sts rem. Fasten off.

Neckband
Join raglan seams, Using No.E hook and with RS of work facing, attach yarn at left back raglan seam.
1st round Work 6sc across top of left sleeve, 48sc down left front, 48sc up right front, 6sc across top of right sleeve and 26sc across back neck. Join with a ss to first sc.
2nd round Work 1sc into each of next 78sc, skip next 3sc, 1sc into each sc to end. Join with a ss to first sc.
3rd round Work 1sc into each of next 51sc, skip 3sc, 1sc into each sc to end. Join with a ss to first sc.
4th round Work 1sc into each of next 76sc, skip 3sc, 1sc into each sc to end. Join with a ss to first sc.
5th round Work 1sc into each of next 49sc, skip 3sc, 1sc into each sc to end. Join with a ss to first sc.
Fasten off.

Finishing
Press under a damp cloth with a warm iron. Join side and sleeve seams. Sew in sleeves.

45 *Wide handsome tie*

Size
4in wide at bottom edge by 55in long, when pressed
Gauge
6 sts and 3 rows to 1in over dc worked on No.D crochet hook
Materials
2 balls Unger English Crepe in main color, A
Small amount of contrasting color, B, for trimming
One No.D crochet hook
Tie
Using No.D hook and A, ch47.

Join with a ss into first ch to form circle.
1st round Ch3 to count as first dc, work 1dc into each of next 21ch, (yrh, insert hook into next ch, yrh and draw through loop, yrh and draw through 2 loops on hook) 3 times, yrh and draw through all 4 loops on hook – called 1gr –, work 1dc into each of next 22ch. Join with a ss to 3rd of first ch3.
2nd round Ch3, work 1dc into each of next 21dc, ch1, skip 1gr, work 1dc into each of next 22dc. Join with a ss to 3rd of first ch3.
3rd round Ch3, work 1dc into same space as ss of previous round, work 1dc into each of next 20dc into next 1dc, ch sp and 1dc work 1gr, work 1dc into each of next 20dc, work 2dc in last dc. Join with a ss to 3rd of first ch3.

Rep 2nd and 3rd rounds 3 times more, then 2nd round once more.

Next round Ch3, work 1dc into each of next 20dc, into next 1dc, sp and 1dc work 1gr, work 1dc into each of next 21dc. Join with a ss to 3rd of first ch3.

Next round Ch3, work 1dc into each of next 20dc, ch1, skip 1gr, work 1dc into each of next 21dc. Join with a ss to 3rd of first ch3.

Rep last 2 rounds 14 times more, noting that there will be 1dc less at either side of center gr on next and every other row. 15 sts.

Next round Ch3, work 1dc into each of next 6dc, 1dc in ch sp, 1dc into each of next 7dc. Join with a ss to 3rd of first ch3.

Cont in rounds of dc on these 15 sts until work measures 53in from beg.

Last round Ch2, work 1sc into each of next 2dc, work 1hdc into each of next 3dc, work 1dc into each of next 3dc, work 1hdc into each of next 3dc, work 1sc into each of last 3dc. Join with a ss to 2nd of first ch2. Fasten off.

Finishing
Press under a damp cloth with a warm iron, keeping join of each round at center back. Cut B into 9 strands of approx 24in long. Tie 9 ends tog. Take 3 ends into each strand and plait tog for approx 15in. Tie 9 ends tog. Trim ends. Thread plait through holes at center front and sew on WS at top and bottom.

46 Tie in random colors

Size
2in wide at bottom edge by 55in long, when pressed

Gauge
4 sts and 2 rows to 1in over dc worked on No.F crochet hook

Materials
1 ball Reynolds Firefly in main color, A
Small amount in solid collar yarn, B
One No.D crochet hook
One No.F crochet hook

Tie
Using No.F hook and A, ch191.

1st row Into 2nd ch from hook work 1hdc, work 1hdc into each of next 48ch, 1sc into each of next 50ch, 1hdc into each of next 10ch, 1dc into each of next 80ch. Turn.

2nd row Ch3, work 1dc into each of next 84 sts, 1hdc into each of next 4 sts, 1sc into each of next 50 sts, 1hdc into each of next 5 sts, 1dc into each st to end. Turn.

3rd row Ch3, work 1dc into each of next 44 sts, 1hdc into each of next 5 sts, 1sc into each of next 50 sts, 1hdc into each of next 5 sts, 1dc into each st to end. Turn.

4th row Ch3, work 1dc into each of next 79 sts, 1hdc into each of next 10 sts, 1sc into each of next 50 sts, 1hdc into each st to end. Break off A. Turn.

Edging
Using No D hook and B, attach yarn with a ss, work 1sc into each st to end working last sc in turning ch, ch3, 1sc in turning ch, *work 1sc in next row end, ch3, 1sc in same row end*, rep from * to * along lower edge, work 1sc into each ch along other side and rep from * to * along other short end. Join with a ss to first sc. Fasten off.

Finishing
Press under a damp cloth with a warm iron. Run in all ends.

47 Slim tubular tie

Size
2¼ in wide at bottom edge by 55in long, when pressed

Gauge
7 sts and 9 rows to 1in over st st worked on No.4 needles

Materials
2 balls Unger English Crepe
One pair No.4 knitting needles
One No.E crochet hook

Tie
Using No.4 needles cast on 24 sts.

1st row *K1, ytf, sl 1 p-wise, ytb, rep from * to end.

This row forms patt and is rep throughout. Cont in patt until work measures 24in from beg.

Shape neckband
Next row K3 tog, *ytf, sl 1 p-wise, ytb, K1, rep from * to last 3 sts, ytf, P3 tog.

Work 7 rows patt without shaping. Rep last 8 rows once more, then first of them again. 12 sts.

Cont without shaping until work measures 40in from beg.

Shape end
Next row Inc in first st, patt to last st, inc in last st.

Next row *Sl 1 p-wise, ytb, K1, ytf, rep from *to end.

Rep last row 6 times more.

Next row Inc in first st, patt to last st, inc in last st. 16 sts.

Cont in patt without shaping until work measures 54in from beg. Weave sts tog.

Edging
Using No.E hook and with RS of work facing, work a row of sc around all edges, working 1sc into every other row end along sides. Fasten off.

Finishing
Press under a damp cloth with a warm iron. Run in all ends.

48 Hexagon motif floor rug

Size
About 52in diameter.

Gauge
One motif measures about 5½in diameter when pressed

Materials
J & P Coats "Knit-Cro-Sheen"
30 balls
One No. G crochet hook
Note. 3 balls are used together throughout

Hexagonal motif
Using No. G hook and 3 strands of cotton ch5. Join with a ss into first ch to form a circle.

1st round Ch2, work 11dc into circle. Join with a ss into 2nd of first ch2.

2nd round Ch2, 1dc into same st inserting hook into back loop only, * 2dc into next dc inserting hook into back of loop only, rep from * 10 times more. Join with a ss into 2nd of first ch2. 24dc.

3rd round Ch4, 1dc into same st, 1dc into each of next 3dc working into both loops of all dc to end of motif, * (1 dc, ch2, 1dc) all into next dc,

1dc into each of next 3dc, rep from * 4 times more. Join with a ss into 2nd of first ch4.

4th round Ch4, 2dc into loop, * 1dc into each of next 5dc, (2dc, ch1, 2dc) all into next loop, rep from * 4 times more, 1dc into each of next 4dc, 2dc into last dc. Join with a ss into 2nd of first ch4.

5th round Ch4, 2dc into loop, * 1dc into each of next 9dc, (2dc, ch1, 2dc) all into next loop, rep from * 4 times more, 1dc into each of next 8dc, 2dc into last dc. Join with a ss into 2nd of first ch4. Break yarn and finish off.

Work 60 motifs more.

Finishing
Press motifs on wrong side, under a damp cloth with a warm iron.
Sew 6 motifs around center motif working on wrong side so that the seams are invisible.
Sew 12 motifs around the outside of the 6 already sewn, then 18 and finally 24 motifs around the outside edge. Re-press seams.

49 Circles and bands floor rug

Size
50in diameter
Gauge
4sc to 1in
Small circle measures 5¼in diameter

Materials
Coats & Clark's O.N.T. "Speed-Cro-Sheen"
41 balls
One No.F crochet hook
Note. Yarn is used double throughout.

Central circle
Using No.F crochet hook and double yarn begin at center, ch5. Join with a ss into first ch to form a circle.

1st round Ch1, 8sc into circle. Join with a ss into first ch.

2nd round Ch1, 1sc into same st, 2sc into each sc to end. Join with a ss into first ch. 18sc.

3rd round Ch1, 2sc into next sc, *1sc into next sc, 2sc into next sc, rep from * to end. Join with a ss into first ch. 27sc.

4th round Ch1, 1sc into next sc, 2sc into next sc, *1sc into each of next 2sc, 2sc into next sc, rep from * to end. Ss into first ch. 36sc.

5th round Ch1, 1sc into each sc to end. Join with a ss into first ch.

6th round Ch1, 1sc into each of next 2sc, 2sc into next sc, *1sc into each of next 3sc, 2sc into next sc, rep from * to end. Join with a ss into first ch.

7th round Ch1, 1sc into each of next 3sc, 2sc into next sc, *1sc into each of next 4sc, 2sc into next sc, rep from * to end. Join with a ss into first sc.

8th round Ch1, 1sc into each of next 4sc, 2sc into next sc, *1sc into each of next 5sc, 2sc into next sc, rep from * to end. Join with a ss into first ch.

9th round Ch1, 1sc into each sc to end. Join with a ss into first ch.

10th round Ch1, 1sc into each of next 5sc, 2sc into next sc, *1sc into each of next 6sc, 2sc into next sc, rep from * to end. Join with a ss into first ch.

Continue working in rounds inc 9 times in each of every 3 rounds, then working 1 round without inc, until work measures 20in across circle. Finish.

Small circles
Work as given for central circle from first to 9th rounds. Work 15 circles. Finish off ends. Join into a circle by sewing a few sts at sides of each circle together. Sew the base of each circle at equal intervals to central circle.

Band
Using No.F crochet hook and double yarn join with a sc to center st at outside edge of any circle, 1sc into each of next 2sc towards left on same circle, ch20, *1sc into 5 center sts at outside edge of next circle, ch20, rep from * until all circles are joined, 1sc into each of

2 sts before joining st at beg of round. Join with a ss into first sc.
Work in rounds as for central circle inc 9 times in each of 3 rounds and 1 round without inc, working more or less increases if necessary to keep mat flat. Work until band measures 4in. Join with a ss at each end of last round. Finish off.
Outer circles
Work as for central circle from first – 10th round. Finish off. Work 25 circles.

Finishing
Finish off all ends.
Sew outer circles together into a circle as for inner circle and sew evenly to outside edge of band. The wrong side of work is used as the right side of the mat.

NO.49 *Assemblage chart for circles and bands rug. The pieces are sewn and crocheted together.*

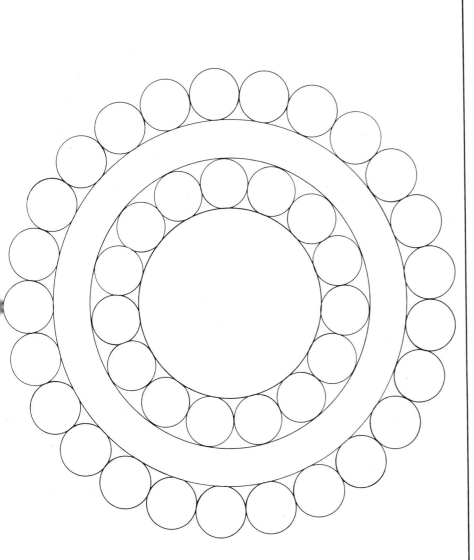

50

Granny squares afghan

Size
About 40in by 60in
Gauge
One motif measures 2in square
Materials
Bernat Sportspun
10 skeins main color, A
2 skeins contrast shade, B, for edging
9 skeins mixed colors for motif centers
One No.D crochet hook
Note. This afghan may be made to any size desired. About 23 motif centers can be edged with 1 ball of main color. If remnants of yarn are used for motif centers hook size must be altered if necessary so that all motifs are exactly the same size.

Square motif
Using No.D crochet hook and first contrast ch4. Join with a ss into first ch to form a circle.
1st round Ch2, 2dc into circle, ch2, * 3dc into circle, ch2, rep from * twice more. Join with a ss into 2nd of first ch2. Break off yarn.
2nd round Attach 2nd contrast with a ss into any ch2 loop, ch2, (1dc, ch2, 2dc) all into same loop, ch2, * into next ch loop work (2dc, ch2, 2dc, ch2), rep from * twice more. Join with a ss to 2nd of first ch2. Break off yarn.
3rd round Attach A with ss to corner ch loop, ch2, into same loop work (2dc, ch2, 3dc), ch1, 3dc into next ch loop, ch1, * into next corner ch loop work (3dc, ch2, 3dc), ch1, 3dc into next ch loop, ch1, rep from * twice more. Join with a ss to 2nd of first ch2. Break off yarn.
Run in ends. Work 600 squares altogether, or number required for size desired.

Finishing
Sew squares together on the wrong side using A. For given size there will be 30 rows each of 20 motifs.

Edging
Using No.D crochet hook and B join with a ss into any square. Work 4 rows sc around complete afghan, working 3sc into each corner st and joining each round to first st of round with a ss.

51

Striped textured pillow

Size
About 24in by 32in
Gauge
13hdc and 8 rows to 4in worked with No.H crochet hook using Bernat Dundee
Materials
Bernat Dundee
6 balls
Bernat Venetian
15 skeins
One No.H crochet hook
One No.J crochet hook
One foam form to fit
Note Venetian is used double throughout.

Front
Using No.H crochet hook and Dundee ch80.
1st row Into back loop of 3rd ch from hook work 1hdc, *1hdc into back loop of next ch, rep from * to end of row. Turn. 79hdc including turning chain.
2nd row Ch2, *1hdc into back loop of next hdc, rep from * to end of row. Turn.
Rep 2nd row 8 times more.
Change to No.J crochet hook and double Venetian.
Next row Ch2, *skip next hdc, 1hdc into both loops of next hdc, rep from * to end. Turn. 40 hdc including turning ch.
Work 2 rows more working 1hdc into each hdc.
Change to No.H crochet hook and Dundee.
Next row Ch2, *2hdc into next hdc, rep from * to end of row. Turn. 79hdc including turning ch.
Work 4 rows more working 1hdc into each st.
Continue in stripe pattern in this way working 3 rows Venetian and 5 rows in Dundee until 5 Venetian stripes have been worked. Finish with 10 rows in Dundee.
Finish off ends.

Back
Work as given for front.

Finishing
With right sides of front and back touching, sew around sides and one end, matching stripes carefully. Turn right side out and insert foam form. Ss remaining opening together.

52

Checkered pillow

Size
About 26in by 26in
Gauge
3hdc and 2 rows to 1in worked with No.H crochet hook using Dundee.
Materials
Bernat Dundee
10 balls
Bernat Venetian
3 skeins
One No.H crochet hook
One No.J crochet hook
One foam form

Front
Using No.H crochet hook and Dundee ch89.
1st row Into 3rd ch from hook work 1hdc, *1hdc into next ch, rep from * to end of row. Turn. 88hdc including turning ch.
2nd row Ch4, skip 1hdc, 1hdc into next hdc, *ch2, skip 1hdc, 1hdc into next hdc, rep from * to end of row. Turn.
3rd - 14th rows Ch2, 1hdc into each of next 15hdc, *ch2, skip 2hdc, 1hdc into each of next 16hdc, rep from * 3 times more.
15th row As 2nd row.
Rep 3rd – 15th rows 3 times more.
Last row As first row. Finish off.

Back
Using No.H crochet hook ch76.
1st row Into 3rd ch from hook work 1hdc, *1hdc into next hdc, rep from * to end of row. Turn.
2nd row Ch2, *1hdc into next hdc, rep from *

to end of row. Turn.
Rep 2nd row until back measures same length as front.
Finish off.
Trim
Edge strips
Using No.J crochet hook and double Venetian ch64.
1st row Into 3rd ch from hook work 1hdc, *1hdc into next ch, rep from * to end of row. Finish off.
Work 3 more strips in same way. Thread through ch loops around the 4 edges.
Center strips
Work as for edge strips beg with ch60. Work 7 strips. Thread through holes to give checkered effect as in illustration.

Finishing
Place front and back together with right sides touching. Sew around 3 sides. Turn right side out and insert foam form. Slip stitch remaining opening.

53

Fringed bedside rug

Size
About 24in by 14in without fringe
Gauge
6dc to 4in
Materials
Unger's Roxanne
4 balls in each of 2 colors, A and B
One No.K crochet hook

Rug
Using No.K crochet hook and 4 strands of A beg at center, ch17.
1st row Into 3rd ch from hook work 1dc, 1dc into each of next ch14, ch2, 1ss into end of ch. Break off A.
2nd round Using 4 strands of B join with a ss between first and 2nd dc, ch3, 1dc between each dc into ch loop at end of first row, 4dc into ch loop, 1dc between each dc along 2nd side and 4dc into other end of first row. Join with a ss into 3rd of first ch3. Break off B.
3rd round Using 4 strands of A join with a ss between first and 2nd dc of 4dc at one end, ch3, 2dc into same place, 1dc between next 2dc, 3dc between 3rd and 4th of 4dc, 1dc between each dc along first side, 3dc between first and 2nd dc of 4dc at other end, 1dc between next 2dc, 3dc between 3rd and 4th of 4dc, 1dc between each dc along other side. Join with a ss into 3rd of 1st ch3. Break off A.
4th round Using 4 strands of B join with a ss between first and 2nd of 3dc group at right hand corner of one end, ch3, 1dc into same sp, 2dc between next 2dc, 1dc between each of next 2dc, 2dc between each of next 2dc, 1dc between each dc along side, 2dc between each of next 2dc, 1dc between each of next 2dc, 2dc between each of next 2dc. Join with a ss into 3rd of first ch3. Break off B.
5th round Using 4 strands of A join with a ss between first 2dc group at one end, ch3, (1dc, ch1, 2dc) all into same sp, work 1dc between each dc along ends and sides working (2dc, ch1, 2dc) between each 2dc in the other 3 corners. Join with a ss into 3rd of first ch3. Break off A.
6th round Using 4 strands of B work as for 5th round. Break off B.

7th round Using 4 strands of A work as for 5th round. Break off A.
8th round Using 4 strands of B work as for 5th round. Break off B.
9th round Using 4 strands of A work 1 round sc working (1sc, ch1, 1sc) into each corner. Join with a ss into first sc. Break off A.
Finish off all ends.

Finishing
Fringe
Cut 11in lengths of A and B. Using 4 strands of B and 2 strands of A draw center of threads through edge of rug and knot. Rep along both ends.

Star spangled rug

Size
Each square measures about 6½in
Complete rug 5 squares by 7 squares
32½in by 45½in
Gauge
About 11sc and 11 rows to 2in
Materials
Columbia-Minerva Featherweight
Knitting Worsted
5 skeins main color, A
2 skeins, contrast, B
One No.D crochet hook

Square
Using No.D crochet hook and A, ch35.
1st row Into 2nd ch from hook work 1sc, *1sc into next ch, rep from * to end of row. Turn.
2nd row Ch1, *1sc into next sc, rep from * to end of row. Turn.
Rep 2nd row twice more.
Continue to work in sc, working 2 color pattern from chart.
Work over thread not in use on every row, carrying it along the entire row. Always join the next color into the last step of the stitch *before* it is required so that it is in position otherwise the design will not have such clear edges.

Finishing
Work 1 row sc using A round each square, working 32sc along sides and 3sc in each corner.
Press all squares on the wrong side under a

damp cloth using a warm iron.
Join squares together by working 1 row sc using A on right side.
When all squares are joined work edging.
Edging
Using No.D crochet hook and A, work around edge. Join with a ss to any st.
1st row Ch2, 1dc into next sc, *ch1, skip 1sc, 1dc into each of next 2sc, rep from * around all edges working (2dc into same sc, ch1) 3 times into 3 corner sc. Join with a ss to 2nd of first ch2.
2nd row Using B, join with a ss into ch loop between dc, ch2, 1sc into same loop, ch1, skip 1dc, *2sc into next loop, ch1, skip 1dc, rep from * around all edges. Break off B.
3rd row Using A join with a ss, ch1, *1sc into next st, rep from * to end of row working 4sc into each ch loop at corners.
Finish off ends.
Press as before.

See next page for chart for star spangled rug.

Round multi-colored floor rug

Size
As required
Materials
Cotton, nylon or suitable material torn into strips about ¾in wide, or rug wool
For fine work – Bernat No.K crochet hook
For coarser work – Bernat No.P crochet hook

Rug
Using suitable hook ch4. Join with a ss into first ch to form a circle.
1st round Work 8sc into circle. Join all rounds with a ss into first sc.
2nd round On this and every round work into back loop of each sc only, * 1sc into next st, 2sc into next st, rep from * to end.
3rd round Work in sc, inc 1sc in every 3rd sc.
4th round Work in sc, inc 1sc in every 4th sc.
5th round Work in sc, inc 1sc in every 5th sc.
Continue in this way until rug is desired size.
It is sometimes necessary to work 1 round without inc in order to keep the rug flat, depending on the width of the material used.

Rings-of-color pillow

Size
About 16in diameter
Gauge
5 rounds to 2in
Materials
Columbia-Minerva Featherweight Knitting Worsted
1 skein dark blue
1 skein brown
1 skein cream
1 skein turquoise
One No.E crochet hook
One 16in foam form
Pillow front
Using No.E crochet hook and blue begin at center, ch4. Join with a ss into first ch to form a circle.
1st round Ch3, work 11 dc into circle. Join with a ss into 3rd of first ch3. 12dc.
2nd round Ch3, 1dc into same st, *2dc into next dc, rep from * to end. Join with a ss into 3rd of first ch3. Break off blue. 24dc.
3rd round Join cream with a ss into last st, ch3, 1dc into same st, 1dc into next dc, *2dc into next dc, 1dc into next dc, rep from * to end. Join with a ss into 3rd of first ch3. Break off cream. 36dc.
4th round Join turquoise with a ss into last st, ch3, 1dc into same st, 1dc into each of next 2dc, *2dc into next dc, 1dc into each of next 2dc, rep from * to end. Join with a ss into 3rd of first ch3. Break off turquoise.
5th round Join brown with a ss into last st, ch3, 1dc into same st, 1dc into each of next 3dc, *2dc into next dc, 1dc into each of next 3dc, rep from * to end. Join with a ss into 3rd of first ch3. Break off brown.
Continue in rounds inc 12 sts on every round so that each round has one more st between each inc and working in stripes of 1 round cream, 1 round brown, 1 round blue, 1 round turquoise, 1 round blue, 1 round cream, 1 round turquoise, 1 round brown, 1 round cream, 1 round brown, 1 round blue, 1 round turquoise, 1 round blue, 1 round cream, 1 round turquoise.

Back
Work as given for front.

Finishing
Finish off all ends. Press both sections on wrong side under a dry cloth with a warm iron.
Sew together around half of edge. Insert foam form and slip stitch remaining edges together.

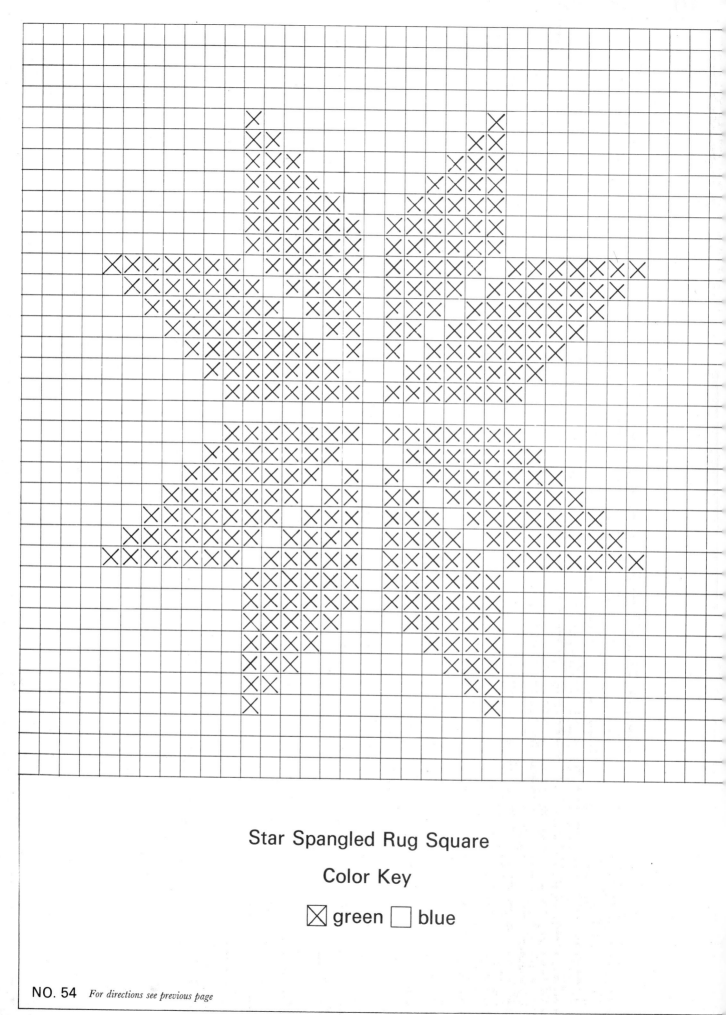

Star Spangled Rug Square

Color Key

⊠ green ☐ blue

with a ss into 2nd of first ch2.

3rd round Ch2, 1dc into next dc, 5dc into next dc, remove hook from last loop and insert it into first of 5dc and into last loop, yrh and draw through both loops forming a bobble – called 1B, 1dc into each of next 2dc, *4dc into next dc, 1dc into each of next 2dc, 1B into next dc, 1dc into each next 2dc, rep from * twice more, 4dc into last st. Join with a ss into 2nd of first ch2.

4th round Ch2, *1B into next dc, 1dc into each of next 2dc, 1B into next dc, 1dc into each of next 2dc, 4dc into next dc, rep from * 3 times more, 1dc into next dc. Join with a ss into 2nd of first ch2.

5th round Ch2, 1dc into each of next 2dc, *1B into next dc, 1dc into each of next 5dc, 4dc into next dc, 1dc into each of next 5dc, rep from * twice more, 1B into next dc, 1dc into each of next 5dc, 4dc into next dc, 1dc into each of next 2dc. Join with a ss into 2nd of first ch2.

6th round Using dark green, ch2, 1dc into each of next 10dc, *4dc into next dc, 1dc into each of next 14dc, rep from * twice more, 4dc into next dc, 1 dc into each of next 3dc. Join with a ss into 2nd of first ch2.

7th round Using turquoise, ch1, 1sc into each of next 12dc, *4sc into next dc, 1sc into each of next 17dc, rep from * twice more, 4sc into next dc, 1sc into each of next 5dc. Join with a ss into first ch.

8th round Using green, ch2, 1dc into next 2dc, 2dc into next dc, 1dc into each of next 10dc, *4dc into next dc, 1dc into each of next 9dc, 2dc, into next dc, 1dc into each of next 10dc, rep from * twice more, 4dc into next dc, 1dc into each of next 6dc. Join with a ss into 2nd of first ch2.

9th round Ch2, (1dc into each of next 2dc, 1B into next dc) 5 times, 1dc into next dc, *4dc into next dc, 1dc into next dc, (1B into next dc, 1dc into each of next 2dc) 8 times, rep from * twice more, 4dc into next dc, 1dc into next dc, (1B into next dc, 1dc into each of next 2dc) twice, working 1B into same st as first ch2. Join with a ss into 2nd of first ch2.

10th round Ch2, 1dc into each of next 18dc, *4dc into next dc, 1dc into each of next 27dc, rep from * twice more, 4dc into next dc, 1dc into each of next 8dc. Join with a ss into 2nd of first ch2

11th round Using turquoise, ch2, 1dc into each of next 20dc, *4dc into next dc, 1dc into each of next 30dc, rep from * twice more, 4dc into next dc, 1dc into each of next 9dc. Join with a ss into 2nd of ch2.

12th round Ch2, 1dc into each of next 22dc, *4dc into next dc, 1dc into each of next 33dc, rep from * twice more, 4dc into next dc, 1dc into each of next 10dc. Join with a ss into 2nd of first ch2.

13th round Ch2, 1dc into each of next 24dc, *4dc into next dc, 1dc into each of next 36dc, rep from * twice more, 4dc into next dc, 1dc into each of next 11dc. Join with a ss into 2nd of first ch2.

14th round Ch2, 1dc into each of next 26dc, *4dc into next dc, 1dc into each of next 39dc, rep from * twice more, 4dc into next dc, 1dc into each of next 12dc.
Join with a ss into 2nd of first ch2.

15th round Using dark green, ch1, 1sc into each of next 28dc, *2sc into next dc, 1sc into each of next 42dc, rep from * twice more, 2sc into next dc, 1sc into each of next 13dc. Join with a ss into first ch.

16th round Using yellow, ch1, 1sc into each of next 29sc, *2sc into next sc, 1sc into each of next 43sc, rep from * twice more, 2sc into next sc, 1sc into each of next 14sc. Join with a ss to first ch.

17th round Using dark green, ch2, 1dc into each of next 29sc, *4dc into next sc, 1dc into each of next 44sc, rep from * twice more, 4dc into next sc, 1dc into each of next 14sc. Join with a ss into 2nd of first ch2.

18th round Ch2, 1dc into each of next 31dc, *4dc into next dc, 1dc into each of next 47dc, rep from * twice more, 4dc into next dc, 1dc into each of next 15dc. Join with a ss into 2nd of first ch2.
Crochet back and forth along each side of square in rows as follows.

1st row Using yellow, join into first st in from right hand corner, 1sc, (insert hook into next st, yrh and draw through loop) twice, yrh and draw loop through all loops to dec 1sc, 1sc into each of next 44dc, dec 1sc as before, 1sc into next dc. Turn.

2nd row Using green, ch2, 1dc into next sc, skip 1dc, 1dc into each of next 44dc, skip 1dc, 1dc into next dc.
Turn.

3rd row Ch2, 1dc into next dc, dec 1dc, *1B into next dc, 1dc into each of next 2dc, rep from * ending 1B into next dc, dec 1dc, 1dc into next dc. Turn.

4th row Ch2, 1dc into next dc, dec 1dc, 1dc into each of next 38dc, dec 1dc, 1dc into next dc. Turn.

5th row Using yellow, ch1, 1sc into next dc, dec 1sc, 1sc into each of next 36dc, dec 1sc, 1sc into next dc.
Turn.

6th row Using dark green, ch2, skip 1sc, 1dc into each of next 36sc, skip 1sc, 1dc into next sc. Turn.

7th row Ch1, 1sc into next dc, dec 1sc, 1sc into each of next 32dc, dec 1sc, 1sc into next dc.
Turn.

8th row Using turquoise, ch2, 1dc into next sc, skip 1sc, 1dc into each of next 32sc, skip 1sc, 1dc into next sc.
Turn.

9th row Ch2, 1dc into next dc, dec 1dc, *1B into next dc, 1dc into each of next 2dc, rep from * ending 1B into next dc, dec 1dc, 1dc into next dc. Turn.

10th row Ch2, 1dc into next dc, dec 1dc, 1dc into each of next 26dc, dec 1dc, 1dc into next dc.
Turn.

11th row Using dark green, ch1, 1sc into next dc, dec 1sc, 1sc into each of next 24dc, dec 1dc, 1sc into next dc.
Turn.

12th row Ch2, 1dc into next sc, dec 1dc, 1dc into each of next 22sc, dec 1dc, 1dc into next sc.
Turn.

13th row Using yellow, ch1, 1sc into next dc, dec 1sc, 1sc into each of next 20dc, dec 1sc, 1sc into next dc.
Turn.

14th row Ch1, 1sc into next sc, dec 1sc, 1sc into each of next 18 sc, dec 1sc, 1sc into next sc. Turn.

15th row Ch1, 1sc into next sc, dec 1sc, 1sc into each of next 16sc, dec 1sc, 1sc into next sc. Turn.

16th row Ch1, 1sc into next sc, dec 1sc, 1sc into each of next 14sc, dec 1sc, 1sc into next sc.
Turn.

17th row Using dark green, ch1, 1sc into next sc, dec 1sc, 1sc into each of next 12sc, dec 1sc.
Continue using dark green working in sc and dec one st at each side on every row until 4 sts rem.

Last row 1sc into first st, dec 1sc, 1sc into last st.
Finish off.
Work other sides in the same manner.

Back
Work as given for front.

Finishing
Press both pieces lightly on wrong side under a damp cloth using a warm iron. Seam around 3 edges. Insert foam form and slip-stitch 4th side together.

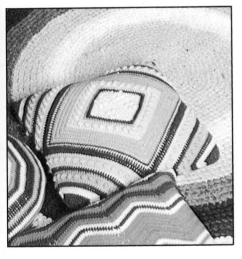

57

Diamond pattern bobble pillow

Size
16in square
Gauge
5dc to 1in
Materials
Unger's Roxanne
1 ball dark green
1 ball yellow
2 balls green
2 balls turquoise
One No.D crochet hook
One 16in square foam form

Front
Using No.D crochet hook and yellow begin at center and ch4. Join with a ss into first ch to form a circle.

1st round Ch2, 11dc into circle. Join with a ss into 2nd of first ch2.

2nd round Ch2, *1dc into each of next 2dc, 4dc into next dc for corner, rep from * twice more, 1dc into each of next 2dc, 3dc into last dc. Join

58

Zigzag patterned pillow

Size
16in square
Gauge
5dc to 1in
Materials
Columbia-Minerva Featherweight
Knitting Worsted
3 skein white
2 skein orange
2 skein pink
2 skein dark red
One No.D crochet hook
One 16in foam form

Pillow

Using No.D crochet hook and red ch91.
1st row Into 3rd ch from hook work 1dc, 1dc into each of next ch8, *3dc into next ch, 1dc into each of next ch9, work (1dc into each of next ch2 leaving last loop of each on hook, yrh and draw through loops) twice, 1dc into each of next ch9, rep from * twice more, 3dc into next ch, 1dc into each of next ch10.
Turn.
2nd row Ch3, skip next dc, 1dc into each of next 9dc, *3dc into next dc, 1dc into each of next 9dc, work next 2dc together twice, 1dc into each of next 9dc, rep from * twice more, 3dc into next dc, 1dc into each of next 9dc, skip 1dc, 1dc into last st.
Turn.
Repeat 2nd row working in stripes thus – *2 rows orange, 2 rows red, 4 rows white, 1 row pink, 1 row white, 4 rows pink, 4 rows orange, 1 row white, 1 row red, 1 row white, 2 rows pink, 2 rows red. Rep from * until work measures 32in.
Finish off.

Finishing

Press if desired under a dry cloth with a warm iron.
Fold work so that ends fit together in center of back.
Sew side seams.
Slip foam form inside pillow and slip-stitch cast-on and bound-off edges together across center back.

59

Small squares afghan

Size
One square measures 4in square
Afghan may be made any size desired
Gauge
5dc to 1in
Materials
Columbia-Minerva Nantuk Sports
Oddments in various colors
One No.E crochet hook

Square

Using No.E crochet hook ch22.
1st row Into 4th ch from hook work 1dc, * 1dc into next ch, rep from * to end. Turn.
2nd row Ch3, * 1dc into next dc picking up back loop only, rep from * to end. Turn.
Rep 2nd row until square measures just about 4in.
Last row Work 1 row sc using contrast color. Finish off.

Finishing

Sew or crochet the squares together alternating the placement of the squares as in illustration.

60

Flowered wall panel

Size
29½in by 19½in
Gauge
Flower center: 3in diameter
Background: 5dc and 5sp to 2in
Materials
Bernat Sportspun
2 skeins red for background, A
1 skein wine, B, 1 skein pink, C
1 skein tangerine, D, 1 skein black, E
1 skein navy blue, F
2 skeins mid blue, G
1 skein white, H

One No.G crochet hook

Large center motif

Using No.G crochet hook and B begin at center, ch4. Join with a ss into first ch to form a circle.
1st round Work 8sc into circle. Do not join.
2nd round Working into back loop of each st only throughout, work 2sc into each of next 8sc. Break off B leaving an end for darning in.
3rd round Using C work 1sc into each sc and 2sc into every 4th sc. 20sc.
4th round Work 1sc into each sc and 2sc into every 5th sc. 24sc. Break off C leaving an end.
5th round Using D work 1sc into each sc and 2sc into every 6th sc. 28sc.
6th round Work 1sc into each sc and 2sc into every 7th sc. 32sc. Finish off. This is center of flower 1.
Work 5 more flower centers in this manner as follows:
One using H, G and F. Center of flower 2.
One using C, B and G. Center of flower 6.
One using E, F and G. Center of flower 4.
One using E, B and D. Center of flower 5.
One using B, D and H. Center of flower 3.

Oval petals

Using No.G crochet hook and B begin at center and ch5.
1st round Into 2nd ch from hook work 1sc, 1sc into each of next ch3, 1sc into end of ch, turn and work 4sc along other side of ch. Break off B leaving an end.
2nd round Using C and working into the back loop only of each st throughout, work 2sc into each sc. 18sc.
3rd and 4th rounds Work 1sc into each sc, inc 1sc at each end of each round. Break off C.
5th round Using D work as for 3rd round. Finish off.
Work 7 more petals using same colors for flower 1.
Work 8 petals using H, G and F for flower 2.
Work 8 petals using B, D and H for flower 3.
Work 8 petals using E for 1 round, H for 2 rounds, F for 1 round and G for 1 round for flower 4. Sew petals round center motifs.

Small circles

Work as for flower center working first – 3rd rounds only and changing color after each round. Work 9 circles using C, B and G, petals of flower 6.
Work 9 circles using E, B and D, petals of flower 5. Sew petals around centers.
Work 7 circles using H, D and E for center and petals of flower 7.
Work 7 circles using B, C and G for center and petals of flower 8.
Work 1 circle of 4 rounds using B for 1 round, H for 2 rounds and B for 1 round for center of flower 9.
Work 7 circles of 3 rounds using H for 2 round, and B for 1 round for petals of flower 9. Sew petals around center.
Work 1 circle of 3 rounds using H for 1 round, B for 1 round and H for 1 round for center of flower 10.
Work 6 circles of 3 rounds using B for 2 rounds, and H for 1 round for petals of flower 10. Sew petals around center.

Separate ovals

Work 2 ovals of 4 rounds using H for 1 round, C for 2 rounds and E for 1 round for leaves 11.
Work 2 ovals of 4 rounds using F for 2 rounds, H for 1 round and G for 1 round for leaves 12.
Work 3 rounds of 4 rounds using C for 2 rounds, B for 1 round and G for 1 round for leaves 13.
Work 2 ovals of 4 rounds using G for 1 round, D for 2 rounds and F for 1 round for leaves 14.

Separate circles
Work 1 circle of 3 rounds using C, G and E for circle 15.
Work 1 circle of 3 rounds using D, H and B for circle 16.
Work 3 circles of 3 rounds using B, D and H for circle 17.

Background
Using No.G crochet hook and A ch92.
1st row Into 4th ch from hook work 1dc, * ch1, skip ch1, 1dc into next ch, rep from * to end. Turn.
2nd row Ch3, 1dc into next dc, * ch1, 1dc into next dc, rep from * to end. Turn.
Rep 2nd row until background measures 27½in. Finish off.

Edging
Using No.G crochet hook and G ch6.
1st row Into 2nd ch from hook work 1sc, 1sc into each of next ch3. Turn.
2nd row Ch1, 1sc into each sc to end. Turn.
Rep 2nd row until edging measures same length as bottom of background.
Work another piece for top in same way.
Work 2 pieces for side edges, length of background plus top and bottom edging.

Finishing
Press all pieces under a damp cloth with a warm iron. Sew edges to background. Sew flowers to background as shown in diagram.

The flower wall panel number key is on the next page

61

Moon and stars tablecloth with tassels

Size
About 40in square
Gauge
One motif measures 5in diameter
Materials
Coats & Clark's O.N.T. "Speed-Cro-Sheen"
17 balls
One No.10 steel crochet hook

Large star
Using No.10 crochet hook begin at center, ch6. Join with a ss into first ch to form a circle.
1st round Ch2, work 14dc into circle. Join with a ss into 2nd of first ch2.
2nd round Ch2, 1dc into same st. * picking up back loop only 2dc into next dc, rep from * to end. Join with a ss into 2nd of first ch2. 30dc.
3rd round As 2nd. 60dc.
4th round * Ch3, skip 1dc, 1sc into next dc, ch3, skip 2dc, 1sc into next dc, rep from * ending with ch3.
Join with a ss into first ch. 24 loops.
5th round 2 ss into first loop, 1sc into center of first loop, ch4, * 1sc into next loop, ch4, rep from * to end.
Join with a ss into first sc.
6th round 2 ss into loop, ch5, * 1sc into next ch loop, ch5, rep from * to end. Join with a ss into first ch.
7th round As 6th round.
8th round As 6th round with ch6 between sc.
9th round As 8th round.
Finish off.
Work 63 more large stars.

Finishing
Join 2 large stars together by joining into any ch loop with a sc, ch3, 1sc into loop on 2nd star, ch3, 1sc into next ch loop on first star, ch3, 1sc into next loop on 2nd star, ch3, 1sc into next ch loop on first star, ch3, 1sc into next ch loop on 2nd star. Break off yarn. ch3 loops from each star have been joined together.
Holding the 2 stars so that the joining is in the center between them, attach the yarn with a ss into the next ch loops above on the right hand side star, ch4, work 2tr into same ch loop, work 3tr into next ch loop above joining on left hand star. Break off yarn and finish off. Work 2 groups of 3tr in each ch loop below central join also.
Join all of the large stars to each other in this way.
In each group of 4 stars joined there will be one ch loop not used between each group of tr.

Small stars
Into each space between 4 large stars work 1 small star.
Begin in center, ch6. Join with a ss into first ch to form a circle.

1st round * Ch6, 1sc between 2 groups of 3tr, ch6, 1sc into small circle, ch6, 1sc into empty ch loop on side of large star, ch6, 1sc into small circle, rep from * 3 times more thus joining small star to 4 large stars around it.
Join with a ss to first ch.
Finish off.
Work small stars in space between all large stars.
Work tassels in center of tr groups around edge of cloth.

62

Patchwork bedspread

Size
About 57in by 90in
Gauge
24dc and 14 rows to 5in square
Materials
Reynolds Danksyarn
10 balls dark red, A
8 balls purple, B
6 balls pink, C
5 balls red, D
5 balls white, E
5 balls lilac, F
No.E crochet hook

Bedspread
The bedspread is made of 5in squares using 6 different designs and sewn together as shown by the chart.
Square with wide stripes (design 1)
Using No.E crochet hook and B ch26.
1st row Into 4th ch from hook work 1dc, * 1dc into next ch, rep from * to end of row. Turn.
2nd row Ch3, 1dc into each dc to end. Turn.
Rep 2nd row throughout working 7 rows B, 4 rows D and 3 rows E.
Finish off.
Work 29 squares more in the same manner.
Square with narrow stripes (design 2)
Work as given for square with wide stripes working 2 rows D, 1 row B, 3 rows C, 2 rows D, 2 rows E, 1 row A, 3 rows F. Work 36 squares altogether.
Square with 4 squares (design 3)
Using No.E crochet hook and C ch12, do NOT break off color, ch14 more using A.
1st row Using A, into 4th ch from hook work 1dc, work 10dc along next ch10, change to C and work 12dc into ch12 made with C. Work until 7 rows have been completed. Work another 7 rows using B in place of C, and F in place of A. Finish off Work 30 squares altogether
Square with 9 small squares (design 4)
Work as for last design beginning with ch8 D, ch8 A, and ch10 C.
1st row Using C, into 4th ch from hook work 1dc, work 1dc into each of next ch6, change to

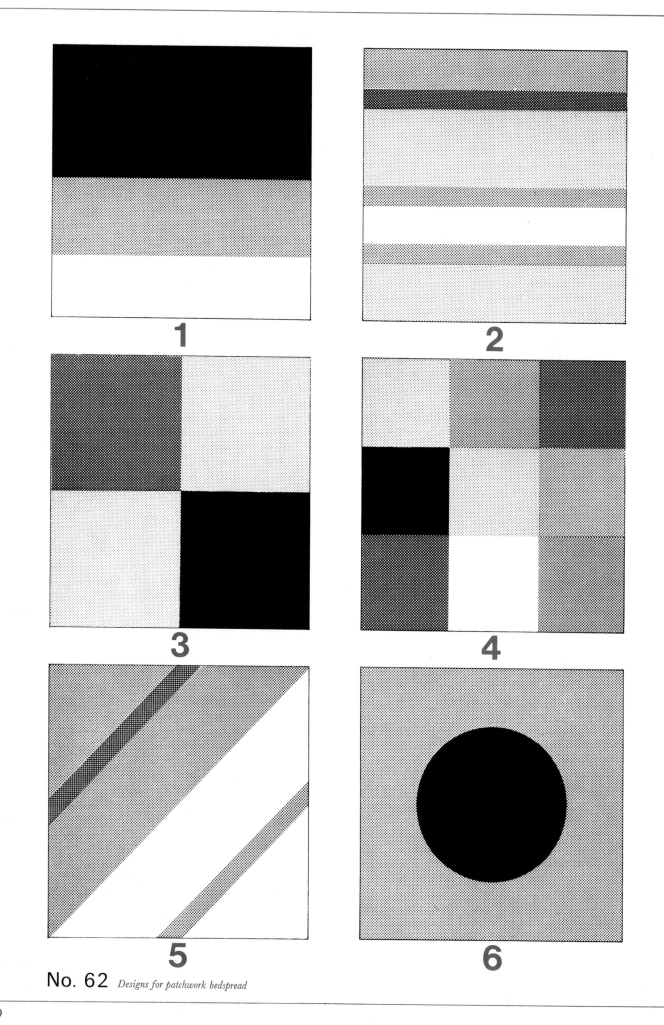

1

2

3

4

5

6

No. 62 *Designs for patchwork bedspread*

and work 1dc into each of next ch8, change
to D and work 1dc into each of next ch8. Turn.
Work 3 rows more using these colors, then
1 row hdc beg with ch2. Change colors to C,
F and B, and work 4 rows dc and 1 row hdc.
Change colors to D, E and A. Work 4 rows
dc and 1 row hdc. Finish off.
Work 36 squares altogether.

Square with diagonal stripes (design 5)
Using No.E crochet hook and D ch3.
1st row Into first of ch3 work 4dc. Turn.
2nd row Ch3, 1dc into first dc, 1dc into each of
next 3dc, 2dc into last dc. Turn.
3rd row Ch3, 1dc into first dc, 1dc into each of
next dc to last dc, 2dc into last dc. Turn.
4th row As 3rd row. 11dc.
5th row Using B, as 3rd row. 13dc.
6th - 11th rows Using D, work as for 3rd row.
25dc.
12th row Using E, ch3, skip 1dc, 1dc into each
of next dc to last 2dc, skip next dc, 1dc into last
dc. Turn. 23dc.
13th and 14th rows As 12th row.
15th row Using A, as 12th row.
16th - 22nd rows Using E as 12th row. 3dc.
Finish off.
Work 30 squares in all.

Square with center circle (design 6)
Using No.E crochet hook and B beg at center,
ch4. Join with a ss into first ch.
1st round Ch2, 11dc into ring, ss to 2nd of ch2
(12 sts).
2nd round Ch2, 1dc into same st, * 2dc into next
dc, rep from * to end. Join with a ss to 2nd of
first ch2. 24dc.
3rd round Ch2, 1dc into same st, * 1dc into
next dc, 2dc into next dc, rep from * to end.
Join with a ss into 2nd of first ch2. 36dc.
4th round Ch2, 1dc into same st, * 1dc into
each of next 2dc, 2dc into next dc, rep from * to
end. 48dc. Break off B. Darn in ends.
5th round Using A join with a ss into last st,
ch1, 1sc into each of next 4dc, * 1dc into next
dc, 3dc into next dc, 1dc into next dc, 1sc into
each of next 9dc, rep from * to end of round
ending last rep with 5sc into last 5 sts. Join
with a ss into first ch.
6th round Ch1, 1sc into each of next 5 sts, *
1dc into next dc, (2dc into next dc) twice, 1dc into
next dc, 1sc into each of next 10 sts, rep from
* to end of round ending last rep with 5sc into
last 5 sts. Join with a ss into first ch.
7th round Ch2, * 1dc into each of next 7 sts,
3dc into next st, 1dc into each of next 15dc, rep
from * to end of round ending last rep with 1dc
into each of last 7 sts. Join with a ss into 2nd
of first ch2.
8th round Ch2, * 1dc into each of next 7 sts,
(2dc into next st) twice, 1dc into each of next
16 sts, rep from * to end of round ending last
rep with 1dc into each of last 8 sts. Join with a
ss into 2nd of first ch2. Finish off.
Work 36 squares in all.

Finishing
Press squares on wrong side under a damp cloth
using a warm iron. Sew squares together as
shown in chart.

Edging
Using No.E crochet hook and A join with a
ss to edge.
1st round Ch3, work 1dc into every st and 2dc
into every row around all sides. Join with a ss
into 3rd of first ch3
Work 3 rounds more all around blanket working
3dc into each corner Finish off

*Opposite : the designs for each of the six squares; next
page, the chart for assembling the squares : you need
30 No.1 squares ; 36 No.2 squares ; 30 No.3 squares ;
36 No.4 squares ; 30 No.5 squares ; and 36 No.6
squares. Six squares make a pillow 10 by 15 inches.*

Round place mats —orange

Size
About 14in diameter
Gauge
8dc to 1in worked with No.B crochet hook
Materials
Coats & Clark's O.N.T. Pearl Cotton
5 balls will make one mat
One No.B crochet hook
Note Every dc is worked into the back loop
only throughout the design.

Mat
Using No.B crochet hook begin at the center,
ch7. Join with a ss into first ch to form
a circle.
1st round Ch3, work 13dc into circle. Join with
a ss into 3rd of first ch3.
2nd round Ch5, * 1dc into next dc picking up
back loop only of each dc, ch2, rep from * 12
times more. Join with a ss into 3rd of first ch5.
14 loops.
3rd round Ch3, 1dc into next ch, ch2, 1dc into
next ch, * 1dc into next dc, 1dc into next ch,
ch2, 1dc into next ch, rep from * 12 times more.
Join with a ss into 3rd of first ch3. 14 loops.
4th round Ch7, * skip ch loop and dc on each
side of loop, 1dc into next dc, ch4, rep from * 12
times more. Join with a ss into 3rd of first ch7.
5th round Ch3, * 1dc into each of first and 2nd
ch of ch loop, ch3, 1dc into each of 3rd and 4th
ch of loop, 1dc into next dc, rep from * 13 times
more skipping 1dc into next dc at end of last
rep. Join with a ss into 3rd of first ch3.
6th round Ch6, 2dc into ch loop, ch3, * 1dc into
3rd of next 5dc, ch3, 2dc into next ch loop, ch3,
rep from * 12 times more. Join with a ss into
3rd of first ch6. 14 groups of 2dc.
7th round 1 ss into each of next ch2 of first
loop, ch7, * 1dc into next ch loop, ch4, rep
from * 26 times more. Join with a ss into 3rd
of first ch3.
8th round 1 ss into each of next ch2 of first ch
loop, ch3, 1dc into next ch, ch4, * 1dc into each
of 2nd and 3rd ch of next ch loop, ch4, rep
from * 26 times more. Join with a ss into 3rd
of first ch3.
9th round Ch3, 1dc into each st to end of
round. Join with a ss into 3rd of first ch3. 168dc

including first ch3.
10th round Ch3, 1dc into each of next 2dc, ch6,
* skip 5dc, 1dc into each of next 3dc, ch6, rep
from * 19 times more. Join with a ss into 3rd
of first ch3. 21 dc groups.
11th round Ch3, 1dc into each of next 2dc, ch4,
skip 4dc, 1dc into each of 5th and 6th ch of ch
loop, * 1dc into each of next 3dc, ch4, skip ch4,
1dc into each of 5th and 6th ch of next ch loop,
rep from * 19 times more. Join with a ss into
3rd of first ch3.
12th round Ch3, 1dc into each of next 2dc, *
ch4, skip 3dc, 1dc into 4th ch of ch4 loop, 1dc
into each of next 5dc, rep from * 19 times more,
ch4, skip 3ch, 1dc into last ch of ch loop, 1dc
into each of next 2dc. Join with a ss into first
ch3.
13th round Ch3, 1dc into each of next 2dc, *
ch4, skip 2ch, 1dc into each of 3rd and 4th ch
of ch loop, 1dc into each of next 6dc, rep from *
19 times more, ch4, skip 2ch, 1dc into each of
3rd and 4th ch of next ch loop, 1dc into each of
next 3dc. Join with a ss into 3rd of first ch3.
14th round Ch3, 1dc into next dc, skip 1dc, *
ch4, skip 2ch, 1dc into each of 3rd and 4th ch
of ch loop, 1dc into each of next 7dc, skip 1dc,
rep from * 19 times more, ch4, skip 2ch, 1dc
into each of 3rd and 4th ch of ch loop, 1dc into
each of next 5dc. Join with a ss into 3rd of
first ch3.
15th round Ch7, skip ch2, 1dc into each of 3rd
and 4th ch of ch loop, * 1dc into each of next
8dc, skip 1dc, ch4, skip ch2, 1dc into each of 3rd
and 4th ch of ch loop, rep from * 19 times
more, 1dc into each of next 7dc. Join with a ss
into 3rd of first ch7.
16th round Ss into 4th ch of first ch loop, ch3,
1dc into each of next 9dc, skip last dc, *ch4,
skip ch3, 1dc into 4th ch of ch loop, 1dc into
each of next 9dc, skip last dc, rep from * 19
times more, ch4. Join with a ss to 3rd of first
ch3.
17th round Ch3, 1dc into each of next 8dc, skip
last dc, *ch4, skip ch2, 1dc into each of 3rd and
4th ch of ch loop, 1dc into each of next 9dc, skip
last dc, rep from * 19 times more, ch4, skip ch2,
1dc into each of 3rd and 4th ch of last loop.
Join with a ss into 3rd of first ch3.
18th round Ch3, 1dc into each of next 7dc, skip
last dc, *ch4, skip ch3, 1dc into 4th ch of ch
loop, 1dc into each of next 10dc, skip last dc, rep
from * 19 times more, ch4, skip ch3, 1dc into
4th ch of last ch loop, 1dc into each of next 2dc.
Join with a ss into 3rd of first ch3.
19th round 1 ss into next st, ch3, 1dc into each
of next 2dc, ch5, skip 4dc, 3dc into next ch loop,
ch5, *skip 4dc, 1dc into each of next 3dc, ch5,
skip 4dc, 3dc into next ch loop, ch5, rep from *
19 times more. Join with a ss into 3rd of first
ch3.
20th round 1 ss into 2nd of 3dc, ch7, 3dc into
ch5 loop, ch3, *1dc into 2nd of 3dc group, ch3,
3dc into next ch5 loop, ch3, rep from * 40 times
more. Join with a ss into 3rd of first ch7.
21st round 1 ss into each of next 4 sts, ch1,
1sc into each of next 2dc, ch7, *skip single dc,
1sc into each of next 3dc of 3dc group, ch7, rep
from * 40 times more.
Join with a ss into first ch.
22nd round 1 ss into center dc, ch7, 3dc into
ch loop, ch3, *1dc into 2nd of 3sc group, ch3,
3dc into next loop, ch3, rep from * 40 times
more. Join with a ss into 3rd of first ch7.
23rd round Ch4, *skip 1st, 1dc into next st,
ch1, rep from * to end of round. Join with a ss
into 3rd of first ch4.
Finish off.

Finishing
Darn in all ends.
Press under a damp cloth on wrong side, using
a warm iron.

Patchwork Bedspread Number Key

6	2	4	6	2	4	6	2	4
3	1	5	3	1	5	3	1	5
2	4	6	2	4	6	2	4	6
1	5	3	1	5	3	1	5	3
4	6	2	4	6	2	4	6	2
5	3	1	5	3	1	5	3	1
6	2	4	6	2	4	6	2	4
3	1	5	3	1	5	3	1	5
2	4	6	2	4	6	2	4	6
1	5	3	1	5	3	1	5	3
4	6	2	4	6	2	4	6	2

6	2	4	6	2	4	6	2	4
3	1	5	3	1	5	3	1	5
2	4	6	2	4	6	2	4	6
1	5	3	1	5	3	1	5	3
5	3	1	5	3	1	5	3	1
6	2	4	6	2	4	6	2	4
3	1	5	3	1	5	3	1	5
2	4	6	2	4	6	2	4	6
1	5	3	1	5	3	1	5	3
4	6	2	4	6	2	4	6	2

Chevron striped blanket

Size
About 36in by 52in

Gauge
5sc and 4 rows to 2in over patt worked on No.K crochet hook using yarn double

Materials
Spinnerin Wintuk Sports
4 skeins main color A, pink
4 skeins first contrast B, beige
2 skeins 2nd contrast C, white
One No.K crochet hook

Blanket
Using No.K crochet hook and 2 strands of A ch111.
1st row Insert hook into 2nd ch from hook, yrh and draw through loop, insert hook into next ch, yrh and draw through loop, yrh and draw through all three loops on hook, 1sc into each of next ch5, 3sc into next ch, * 1sc into each of next ch6, (insert hook, yrh and draw through loop) into each of next ch3, yrh and draw through all 4 loops on hook, 1sc into each of next ch6, 3sc into next ch, rep from * 5 times more, 1sc into each of next ch5, (insert hook, yrh and draw through loop) into each of last ch2, yrh and draw through all 3 loops on hook. Turn.
2nd row Ch1, working into back loop of sc only on every row (insert hook, yrh and draw loop through) into each of next 2sc, yrh and draw through all three loops on hook, 1sc into each of next 5sc, 3sc into next sc, * 1sc into each of next 6sc, (insert hook, yrh and draw through loop) into each of next 3sc, yrh and draw through all 4 loops on hook, 1sc into each of next 6sc, 3sc into next sc, rep from * 5 times more, 1sc into each of next 5sc, (insert hook, yrh and draw through loop) into each of last 2sc. Turn.
Rep 2nd row throughout working in stripe sequence thus: * 6 rows A, 6 rows B, 6 rows C, 6 rows B, rep from * until 78 rows in all have been worked. Finish off.

Finishing
Using A make 52 small pompons and sew 26 evenly spaced to either side of blanket.

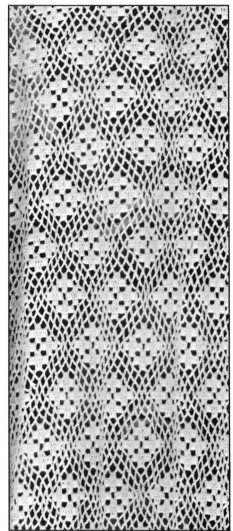

65

Lace curtain

Size
38in by 41in

Gauge
1dc motif and ch2 loops to 4in

Materials
American Thread Puritan Bedspread Cotton, Art. 40
10 balls. One No. C crochet hook

Curtain
Using No.C crochet hook ch218.
1st row * (1sc into next ch, ch7, skip ch3) 5 times, 1sc into next ch, ch3, skip ch2, 1dc into each of next ch3, ch3, skip ch2, rep from * 6 times more, (1sc into next ch, ch7, skip ch3) 5 times, ending with 1sc into last ch Turn.
2nd row Ch10, (1sc into next ch loop, ch7) 4 times, 1sc into next ch loop, ch3, 3dc into next loop, 1dc into each of next 3dc, 3dc into next loop, ch3, rep from * 6 times more, (1sc into next ch loop, ch7) 4 times, 1sc into last loop. Turn.
3rd row Ch10, * (1sc into next loop, ch7) 3 times, 1sc into next loop, ch3, 3dc into next loop, ch3, skip 3dc, 1dc into each of next 3dc, ch3, skip 3dc, 3dc into next loop, ch3, rep from

* 6 times more, (1sc into next loop, ch7) 4 times, 1sc into 4th of 10 turning ch. Turn.
4th row Ch10, 1sc into next loop, ch7, * (1sc into next loop, ch7) twice, 1sc into next loop, (ch3, 3dc into next ch3 loop, 1dc into each of next 3dc, 3dc into next ch3 loop) twice, ch3, rep from * 6 times more, (1sc into next loop, ch7,) 3 times, 1sc into last loop. Turn.
5th row Ch10, * (1sc into next loop, ch7,) 3 times, 1sc into next loop, ch3, skip 3dc, 1dc into each of next 3dc, ch3, 3dc into next loop, ch3, skip 3dc, 1dc into each of next 3dc, ch3, rep from * 6 times more, (1sc into next loop, ch7) 4 times, 1sc into 4th of 10 turning ch. Turn.
6th row As 2nd.
7th row Ch10, (1sc into next loop, ch7) 4 times, * 1sc into next loop, ch5, skip 3dc, 1dc into each of next 3dc, ch5, 1sc into next loop, ch7, 1sc into next loop) 4 times, ch7, rep from * 6 times more, 1sc into last loop. Turn.
8th row Ch10, * 1sc into next loop, ch7, 1sc into next loop, ch5, 1dc into each of center ch3 of next loop, ch5, (1sc into next loop, ch7) 4 times, rep from * 6 times more, 1sc into next loop, ch7, 1sc into next loop, ch5, 1dc into each of center ch3 of next loop, ch5, 1sc into next loop, ch7, 1sc into last loop. Turn.
9th row Ch10, * 1sc into next loop, ch3, 3dc into next loop, 1sc into each of 3dc, 3dc into next loop, ch3, (1sc into next loop, ch7) 4 times, rep from * 6 times more, 1sc into next loop, ch3, 3dc into next loop, 1dc into each of next 3dc, 3dc into next loop, ch3, 1sc into next loop, ch7, 1sc into next loop. Turn.
10th row Ch10, *1sc into next loop, ch3, 3dc into next loop, ch3, skip 3dc, 1dc into each of next 3dc, ch3, skip 3dc, 3dc into next loop, ch3, (1sc into next loop, ch7) 3 times, rep from * 6 times more, 1sc into next loop, ch3, 3dc into next loop, ch3, skip 3dc, 1dc into each of next 3dc, ch3, skip 3dc, 3dc into next loop, ch3, 1sc into last loop. Turn.
11th row Ch3, * (3dc into loop, 1dc into each of next 3dc, 3dc into next loop, ch3) twice, (1sc into next loop, ch7) twice, 1sc into next loop, ch3, rep from * 6 times more, (3dc into loop, 1dc into each of next 3dc, 3dc into loop, ch3) twice, 1sc into last loop. Turn.
12th row Ch10, *1sc into loop, ch3, skip 3dc, 1dc into each of next 3dc, ch3, 3dc into next loop, ch3, skip 3dc, 1dc into each of next 3dc, ch3 (1sc into next loop, ch7) 3 times, rep from * 6 times more, 1sc into next loop, ch3, skip 3dc, 1dc into each of next 3dc, ch3, 3dc into next loop, ch3, skip 3dc, 1dc into each of next 3dc, ch3, 1sc into last loop.
Turn.
13th row As 9th row.
14th row Ch10, 1sc into next loop, ch7, *1sc into next loop, ch5, skip 3dc, 1dc into each of next 3dc, ch5, (1sc into next loop, ch7) 5 times, rep from * 6 times more, 1sc into next loop, ch5, skip 3dc, 1dc into each of next 3dc, ch5, 1sc into next loop, ch7, 1sc into last loop. Turn.
15th row Ch10, *(1sc into next loop, ch7) 4 times, 1sc into next loop, ch5, 3dc into next loop, ch5, rep from * 6 times more, (1sc into next loop, ch7) 5 times, 1sc into last loop.
Turn.
Rep from 2nd row until 9 complete patts have been worked.
Finish off.

Finishing
Finish off ends. Along sides and lower edge work 1 row dc.
2nd row * 1sc into next dc, ch4, 1 ss into first of ch4, to form a picot, 1sc into same st as last sc, rep from * along dc row.
Finish off.
Sew curtain rings as desired to top edge.
Press lightly.

Motif

Using No.D crochet hook begin at center, ch10. Join with a ss into first ch to form a circle.

1st round Ch3, 3dc into circle, *ch3, 4dc into circle, rep from * twice more. Ch3 join with a ss into 3rd of first ch3.

2nd round Ss into 4th dc, ch5, * (1dc, ch4, 1dc) into corner loop, ch2, 1dc into first of next dc group, ch2, skip 2dc, 1dc into next dc, ch2, rep from * twice more, (1dc, ch4, 1dc) into next corner, ch2, 1dc into first dc of next group, ch2. Join with a ss into 3rd of first 3 or ch5 on every round unless otherwise stated.

3rd round Ch5, * 1dc into next dc, (3dc, ch4, 3dc) into corner, (1dc into next dc, ch2) 3 times, rep from * twice more, 1dc into next dc, (3dc, ch4, 3dc) into corner, (1dc into next dc, ch2) twice.

4th round Ch5, * 1dc into each of next 4dc, (ch2, 1dc, ch4, 1dc, ch2) into corner, 1dc into each of next 4dc, (ch2, 1dc into next dc) twice, rep from * twice more, 1dc into each of next 4dc, (ch2, 1dc, ch4, 1dc, ch2) into corner, 1dc into each of next 4dc, ch2, 1dc, ch2.

5th round Ch5, * 4dc, ch2, 1dc into next dc, (3dc, ch4, 3dc) into corner, 1dc into next dc, ch2, 4dc, ch2, (1dc into next dc, ch2) twice, rep from * twice more, 4dc, ch2, 1dc into next dc, (3dc, ch4, 3dc) into corner, 1dc into next dc, ch2, 4dc, ch2, 1dc into next dc, ch2.

6th round Ch5, * 4dc, ch2, 4dc, ch2, 1dc, ch4, 1dc, ch2) into corner, (4dc, ch2) twice, (1dc, ch2) twice, rep from * ending last rep (1dc, ch2) once.

7th round Ch5, * (4dc, ch2) twice, 1dc into next dc, (3dc, ch4, 3dc) into corner, 1dc into next dc, ch2, (4dc, ch2) twice, (1dc, ch2) twice, rep from * ending last rep with (1dc, ch2) once.

8th round Ch5, * (4dc, ch2) 3 times, (1dc, ch4, 1dc) into corner, ch2, (4dc, ch2) 3 times, (1dc, ch2) twice, rep from * ending last rep (1dc, ch2) once.

9th round Ch5, * (4dc, ch2) 3 times, 1dc into next dc, (3dc, ch4, 3dc) into corner, 1dc into next dc, ch2, (4dc, ch2) 3 times, (1dc, ch2) twice, rep from * ending last rep (1dc, ch2) once.

10th round Ch5, * (4dc, ch2) 4 times, (1dc, ch4, 1dc) into corner, ch2, (4dc, ch2) 4 times, (1dc, ch2) twice, rep from * ending last rep (1dc, ch2) once.

11th round Ch5, * (4dc, ch2) 4 times, 1dc into next dc, (3dc, ch4, 3dc) into corner, 1dc into next dc ch2 (4dc, ch2) 4 times, (1dc, ch2) twice, rep from * ending last rep (1dc, ch2) once.

12th round Ch5, * 1dc, ch2, skip 2dc, 1dc, ch2, (4dc, ch2) 4 times, (1dc, ch4, 1dc) into corner, ch2, (4dc, ch2) 4 times, 1dc into dc, ch2, skip 2dc, 1dc, ch2, 1dc into dc, 2dc into next sp, 1dc into dc, ch2, rep from * ending last rep with 2dc into last sp.

13th round Ch3, 2dc into first sp, * (1dc into dc, ch2) twice, (4dc, ch2) 4 times, 1dc into dc, (3dc, ch4, 3dc) into corner, 1dc into dc, (ch2, 4dc) 4 times, (ch2, 1dc into dc) twice, 2dc into sp, 1dc into dc, ch2, 1dc into dc, 2dc into next sp, rep from * ending with ch2 over center dc group.

14th round Ch5, * 1dc into 4th dc, 2dc into sp, 1dc into dc, ch2, 1dc into next dc, ch2, skip 2dc, 1dc, ch2, (4dc, ch2) 4 times, (1dc, ch4, 1dc) into corner, ch2, (4dc, ch2) 4 times, 1dc into dc, ch2, skip 2dc, 1dc, ch2, 1dc into dc, 2dc into sp, (1dc into dc, ch2) 3 times, rep from * ending (1dc, ch2) twice.

15th round Ch5, * 1dc into dc, ch2, skip 2dc, 1dc, 2dc into sp, (1dc into dc, ch2) twice, (4dc, ch2) 4 times, 1dc into dc, (3dc, ch4, 3dc) into corner, 1dc into dc, (ch2, 4dc) 4 times, (ch2, 1dc into dc) twice, 2dc into sp, 1dc into dc, ch2, skip 2dc, 1dc into next dc, 2dc into sp, 1dc into dc, ch2, 1dc into dc, ch2, rep from * ending 2dc into last sp.

16th round Ch3, 2dc into sp, 1dc into dc, ch2, * 1dc into dc, ch2, skip 2dc, 1dc, 2dc into sp, (1dc into next dc, ch2) twice, skip 2dc, 1dc, ch2, (4dc, ch2) 4 times, (1dc, ch4, 1dc) into corner, ch2, (4dc, ch2) 4 times, (1dc into next dc, ch2, skip 2dc, 1dc, ch2, 1dc into dc, 2dc into sp) twice, 1dc into dc, 2dc into sp, 1dc into next dc, ch2, rep from * ending with ch2 over center group.

17th round Ss into 4th dc, ch3, 2dc into sp, 1dc into dc, * ch2, 1dc into dc, ch2, skip 2dc, 1dc, 2dc into sp, (1dc, ch2) twice, (4dc, ch2) 4 times, 1dc into dc, ch2, (1dc, ch4, 1dc) into corner, ch2, 1dc into dc, ch2, (ch2, 4dc) 4 times, (ch2, 1dc into dc, ch2, 1dc into dc, 2dc into sp, 1dc into dc) twice, ch4, 1hdc into sp between dc groups, ch4, skip 3dc, 1dc, 2dc into sp, 1dc into dc, rep from * ending with ch4.

18th round Ss into 4th dc, ch3, 2dc into sp, 1dc into dc, * ch2, 1dc into dc, ch2, skip 2dc, 1dc, 2dc into sp, 1dc into dc, ch2, skip 2dc, 1dc, ch2, (4dc, ch2) 3 times, (1dc, ch2) twice, (1dc, ch4, 1dc) into corner, (ch2, 1dc) twice, (ch2, 4dc) 3 times, ch2, 1dc into dc, (ch2, skip 2dc, 1dc, ch2, 1dc into dc, 2dc into sp, 1dc into dc) twice, ch5, 2hdc into ch4 loop, 2hdc into next ch4 loop, ch5, skip 3dc, 1dc, 2dc into sp, 1dc into next dc, rep from * ending ch5.

19th round Ss into 4th dc, ch3, 2dc into sp, 1dc into dc, * ch2, 1dc into dc, ch2, skip 2dc, 1dc, 2dc into sp, (1dc, ch2) twice, (4dc, ch2) 3 times, (1dc, ch2) 3 times, (1dc, ch4, 1dc) into corner, (ch2, 1dc) 3 times, (ch2, 4dc) 3 times, (ch2, 1dc into dc, ch2, 1dc into dc, 2dc into sp, 1dc into dc) twice, ch6, 2hdc into loop, 3hdc one between each of next 4dc, 2hdc into next loop, ch6, skip 3dc, 1dc, 2dc into sp, 1dc into next dc, rep from * ending ch6.

20th round Ch5, skip 2dc, 1dc, 2dc into sp, 1dc into dc, * ch2, 1dc into dc, ch2, skip 2dc, 1dc, 2dc into sp, (1dc, ch2) twice, skip 2dc, 1dc, ch2, (4dc, ch2) twice, (1dc, ch2) 4 times, (1dc, ch4, 1dc) into corner, (ch2, 1dc into next dc) 4 times, (ch2, 4dc) twice, ch2, 1dc into dc, (ch2, skip 2dc, 1dc, ch2, 1dc into dc, 2dc into sp, 1dc into dc) twice, ch2, skip 2dc, 1dc, 3dc into loop, ch5, skip 2hdc, 4hdc one between each of center 5hdc, ch5, 3dc into end of loop, 1dc into next dc, ch2, skip 2dc, 1dc, 2dc into sp, 1dc into dc, rep from * ending 3dc into last loop.

21st round Ss into 4th of first dc group, ch3, 2dc into sp, 1dc into dc, * ch2, 1dc into dc, ch2, skip 2dc, 1dc, 2dc into sp, (1dc, ch2) twice, (4dc, ch2) twice, (1dc, ch2) 5 times, (1dc, ch4, 1dc) into corner, (ch2, 1dc) 5 times, (ch2, 4dc) twice, (ch2, 1dc) twice, 2dc into next sp, 1dc into dc, ch2, skip 2dc, 1dc, ch2, 1dc into dc, 2dc into sp, 1dc into dc, 2dc into sp, 1dc into dc, 1hdc into next sp, ch4, skip 3dc, 1dc, 3dc into loop, ch4, 1hdc between center hdc, ch4, 3dc into loop, 1dc into next dc, ch4, 1hdc into next sp, ch4, skip 3dc, 1dc, 2dc into next sp, 1dc into next dc, rep from * ending ch4

22nd round Ss into 4th dc, ch3, 2dc into sp, 1dc into dc, * ch2, 1dc into dc, ch2, skip 2dc, 1dc, 2dc into sp, (1dc, ch2) twice, skip 2dc, 1dc, 2dc, 4dc, ch2, (1dc, ch2) 6 times, (1dc, ch4, 1dc) into corner, (ch2, 1dc) 6 times, ch2, 4dc, ch2, 1dc into dc, (ch2, skip 2dc, 1dc, ch2, 1dc into dc, 2dc into sp, 1dc into dc) twice, ch5, 2hdc into loop, 2hdc into next loop, ch5, skip 3dc, 1dc, 3dc into loop, ch2, 3dc into end of next loop, 1dc into dc, ch5, 2hdc into loop, 2hdc into next loop, ch5, skip 3dc, 1dc, 2dc into sp, 1dc into next dc, rep from * ending ch5.

23rd round Ss into 4th dc, ch3, 1dc into dc, 2dc into sp, 1dc into dc * ch2, 1dc into dc, ch2, skip 2dc, 1dc, 2dc into sp, (1dc into dc, ch2) twice, 4dc, ch2, (1dc, ch2) 7 times, (1dc, ch4, 1dc) into corner, (ch2, 1dc) 7 times, ch2, 4dc, (ch2, 1dc into dc, ch2, 1dc into dc, 2dc into sp, 1dc into dc) twice, ch6, 2hdc into loop, 3hdc one between each

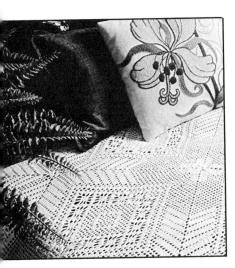

Large
lacy diamonds
bedspread

Size
About 80in by 96in
Motif about 24in square

Gauge
1 block of 4dc plus 1 open work square to 1in

Materials
Coats & Clark's O.N.T. "Speed-Cro-Sheen" 98 balls
One No.D Crochet hook

of 4hdc, 2hdc into next loop, ch6, skip 3dc, 1dc, 2dc into ch2, 1dc into next dc, ch6, 2hdc into loop, 3hdc one between each of center 4hdc, 2hdc into loop, ch6, skip 3dc, 1dc, 2dc into sp, 1dc into dc, rep from * ending ch6.

24th round Ss into 4th dc, ch3, 2dc into sp, (1dc into dc, ch2) twice, * 1dc into dc, 2dc into sp, 1dc into dc, ch2, (1dc into dc, ch2) twice, (1dc, ch4, 1dc) into corner, (ch2, 1dc) 10 times, ch2, 1dc into dc, 2dc into sp, 1dc into dc, ch2, skip 2dc, 1dc, ch2, 1dc into dc, 2dc into sp, 1dc into dc, (ch2, 1dc into dc, 3dc into loop, ch5, 4hdc one between each of center 5hdc, ch5, 3dc into loop, 1dc into next dc) twice, ch2, 1dc into dc, 2dc into sp, (1dc, ch2) twice, rep from * ending ch2.

25th round Ss into 4th dc, ch3, 2dc into sp, 1dc into dc, * (ch2, 1dc) twice, 2dc into sp, 1dc into dc, ch2, (1dc, ch2) 10 times, (1dc, ch4, 1dc) corner, (ch2, 1dc) 11 times, 2dc into sp, 1dc into dc, (ch2, 1dc) twice, 2dc into sp, 1dc into dc, ch5, 1hdc into next sp, ch4, skip 3dc, 1dc, 3dc into loop, ch4, 1hdc into center of hdc, ch4, 3dc into loop, 1dc into dc, ch2, skip 2dc, 1dc, 3dc into loop, ch4, 1hdc into center of hdc, ch4, 3dc into loop, 1dc into dc, ch5, 1hdc into next sp, ch5, skip 3dc, 1dc, 2dc into sp, 1dc into dc, rep from * ending ch4.

26th round Ss into 4th dc, ch3, 2dc into sp, 1dc into dc, * ch2, 1dc into dc, ch2, skip 2dc, 1dc, 2dc into sp, 1dc into dc, ch2, (1dc, ch2) 10 times, (1dc, ch4, 1dc) into corner loop, ch2, (1dc, ch2) 10 times, 1dc into dc, 2dc into sp, 1dc into dc, ch2, 1dc into dc, ch2, 1dc into dc, 2dc into sp, 1dc into dc, ch5, 2hdc into loop, 2hdc into next loop, ch5, skip 3dc, 1dc, 3dc into loop, ch2, 3dc into next loop, 1dc into dc, ch2, (1dc, ch2) 4 times, 1dc into dc, 3dc into loop, ch2, 3dc into next loop, 1dc into dc, ch5, 2hdc into loop, 2hdc into next loop, ch5, skip 3dc, 1dc into dc, 2dc into sp, 1dc into dc, rep from * ending ch5.

27th round Ss into 4th dc, ch3, 2dc into sp, 1dc into dc, * ch2, 1dc into dc, ch2, skip 2dc, 1dc, 2dc into sp, 1dc into dc, ch2, (1dc, ch2) 10 times, (1dc, ch4, 1dc) into corner, (ch2, 1dc) 10 times, ch2, 1dc into dc, 2dc into sp, 1dc into dc, (ch2, 1dc) twice, 2dc into sp, 1dc into dc, ch6, 2hdc into loop, 3hdc one between each of 4hdc, 2hdc into next loop, ch6, skip 3dc, 1dc, 2dc into sp, 1dc into dc, ch2, (1dc, ch2) 6 times, skip 3dc, 1dc, 2dc into sp, 1dc into next dc, ch6, 2hdc into loop, 3hdc one between each of 4hdc, 2hdc into loop, ch6, skip 3dc, 1dc, 2dc into sp, 1dc into dc, rep from * ending ch6.

28th round Ss into 4th dc, ch3, 2dc into sp, 1dc into dc, * (ch2, 1dc) twice, 2dc into sp, 1dc into dc, ch2, (1dc, ch2) 10 times, (1dc, ch4, 1dc) into corner, (ch2, 1dc) 10 times, ch2, 1dc into dc, 2dc into sp, 1dc into dc, (ch2, 1dc) twice, 2dc into sp, 1dc into dc, ch2, skip 2dc, 1dc into loop, ch5, 4hdc one between each of 5hdc, ch5, 3dc into loop, 1dc into dc, ch2, (1dc, ch2) 8 times, skip 2dc, 1dc, 3dc into loop, ch5, 4hdc one between each of 5hdc, ch5, 3dc into loop, 1dc into dc, ch2, skip 2dc, 1dc into next dc, 2dc into sp, 1dc into dc, rep from * ending ch2.

29th round Ss into 4th dc, ch3, 2dc into sp, 1dc into dc, * ch2, 1dc into dc, ch2, skip 2dc, 1dc, 2dc into sp, 1dc into dc, (ch2, 1dc) 10 times, (3dc, ch4, 3dc) into corner, (1dc, ch2) 10 times, 1dc into dc, 2dc into sp, 1dc into dc, (ch2, 1dc) twice, 2dc into sp, 1dc into dc, ch4, 1hdc into next sp, ch4, skip 3dc, 1dc, 3dc into loop, ch4, 1hdc into center of hdc, 3dc into loop, 1dc into dc, ch2, (1dc, ch2) 4 times, 1dc into dc, 2dc into sp, 1dc into dc, ch2, (1dc, ch2) 4 times, skip 2dc, 1dc, 3dc into loop, ch4, 1hdc into center of hdc, ch4, 3dc into loop, 1dc into dc, ch5, 1hdc into next sp, ch4, skip 3dc, 1dc, 3dc into loop, ch4, 1hdc into center of hdc, ch4, 3dc into loop, 1dc into dc, ch5, 1hdc into next sp, ch4, skip 3dc, 1dc, 2dc into sp, 1dc into next dc, rep from * ending ch4.

30th round Ss into 4th dc, ch3, 2dc into sp, 1dc into dc, * ch2, 1dc into dc, ch2, skip 2dc, 1dc, 2dc into sp, 1dc into dc, (ch2, 1dc) 9 times, 1dc into

each of next 3dc, (3dc, ch4, 3dc) into corner, 1dc into each of next 4dc, (ch2, 1dc) 9 times, 2dc into sp, 1dc into dc, ch2, skip 2dc, 1dc, ch2, 1dc into dc, 2dc into sp, 1dc into dc, ch5, 2hdc into loop, 2hdc into next loop, ch5, skip 3dc, 1dc, 3dc into loop, ch2, 3dc into next loop, 1dc into dc, ch2, (1dc, ch2) 4 times, (1dc into dc, 2dc into sp, 1dc into dc) twice, (1dc, ch2) 4 times, skip 2dc, 1dc, 3dc into loop, ch2, 3dc into next loop, 1dc into dc, ch5, 2hdc into loop, 2hdc into next loop, ch5, skip 3dc, 1dc, 2dc into sp, 1dc into dc, rep from * ending ch5.

31st round Ss into 4th dc, ch3, 2dc into sp, 1dc into dc, * ch2, 1dc into dc, ch2, skip 2dc, 1dc, 2dc into sp, 1dc into dc, (ch2, 1dc) 8 times, 1dc into each of next 6dc, (3dc, ch4, 3dc) into corner, 1dc into each of next 7dc, (ch2, 1dc) 8 times, 2dc into sp, 1dc into dc, ch2, skip 2dc, 1dc, ch2, 1dc into dc, 2dc into sp, 1dc into dc, ch6, 2hdc into loop, 3hdc one between each of 4hdc, 2hdc into loop, ch6, skip 3dc, 1dc into dc, 2dc into sp, 1dc into dc, ch2, skip 2dc, 1dc, (ch2, 1dc) 5 times, 2dc into sp, 1dc into dc, (ch2, 1dc) 3 times, 2dc into sp, 1dc into dc, (ch2, 1dc) 5 times, 2dc into sp, 1dc into dc, ch6, 2hdc into loop, 3hdc one between each of next 4hdc, 2hdc into loop, ch6, skip 3dc, 1dc, 2dc into sp, 1dc into dc, rep from * ending ch6.

32nd round Ss into 4th dc, ch3, 2dc into sp, 1dc into dc, * ch2, 1dc into dc, ch2, skip 2dc, 1dc, 2dc into sp, 1dc into dc, (ch2, 1dc) 7 times, 1dc into each of next 9dc, (3dc, ch4, 3dc) into corner, 1dc into each of next 10dc, (ch2, 1dc) 6 times, (ch2, 1dc into dc, 2dc into sp, 1dc into dc, ch2, skip 2dc, 1dc) twice, 3dc into loop, ch5, 4hdc between center 5hdc, ch5, 3dc into loop, 1dc into dc, (ch2, 1dc) 5 times, 2dc into sp, 1dc into dc, (ch2, 1dc) 5 times, 2dc into sp, 1dc into dc, (ch2, 1dc) 5 times, 3dc into loop, ch5, 4hdc between center 5hdc, ch5, 3dc into loop, 1dc into dc, ch2, skip 2dc, 1dc, 2dc into sp, 1dc into dc, rep from * ending ch2.

33rd round Ss into 4th dc, ch3, 2dc into sp, 1dc into dc, * ch2, 1dc into dc, ch2, skip 2dc, 1dc, 2dc into sp, 1dc into dc, (ch2, 1dc) 8 times, 1dc into each of next 6dc, (3dc, ch4, 3dc) into corner, 1dc into each of next 7dc, (ch2, 1dc) 8 times, (2dc into sp, 1dc into dc, ch2, skip 2dc, 1dc, ch2, 1dc into dc) twice, ch2, skip 2dc, 1dc, 3dc into loop, ch4, 1hdc into center of hdc, ch4, 3dc into loop, 1dc into dc, (ch2, 1dc) 5 times, 2dc into sp, 1dc into dc, (ch2, 1dc) 7 times, 2dc into sp, 1dc into dc, (ch2, 1dc) 5 times, 3dc into loop, ch4, 1hdc into center of hdc, ch4, 3dc into loop, 1dc into dc, (ch2, 1dc) 3 times, 2dc into sp, 1dc into dc, rep from * ending ch2. Finish off.
Make 11 more squares in the same manner.

Finishing
Darn in all ends. Pin out squares and press on wrong side under a damp cloth using a warm iron. Sew squares together in 3 strips of 4 squares.

Edging
Using No.D crochet hook ch8.
1st row Into 4th ch from hook work 1dc, 1dc into next ch, ch4, 1dc into each of next ch3. Turn.
2nd row Ch3, 1dc into first dc, ch2, skip 1dc, 1dc, (2dc, ch4, 2dc) into ch4 loop, 1dc into each of next 3dc. Turn.
3rd row Ch4, 1dc into 3rd dc, (2dc, ch4, 2dc) into ch4 loop, 1dc into next dc, ch2, skip 1dc, 1dc, ch2, skip ch2, 1dc into each of next 2dc. Turn.
4th row Ch3, 1dc into next dc, ch2, 1dc into dc, ch2, 1dc into next dc, ch2, skip 1dc, 1dc, (2dc, ch4, 2dc) into loop, skip 2dc, 1dc into last dc, ch2, 1dc into edge ch sp. Turn.
5th row Ch4, 1dc into next dc, (2dc, ch4, 2dc) into loop, 1dc into next dc, ch2, skip 1dc, 1dc, (1dc into next dc, ch2) twice, 1dc into each of last 2dc. Turn.

6th row Ch3, 1dc into next dc, (ch2, 1dc into dc) 4 times, ch2, skip 1dc, 1dc, (2dc, ch4, 2dc) into loop, skip 2dc, 1dc, ch2, 1dc into last sp. Turn.
7th row Ch4, 1dc into next dc, (2dc, ch4, 2dc) into loop, 1dc into next dc, ch2, skip 1dc, 1dc, (1dc, ch2) 4 times, 1dc into each of last 2dc. Turn.
8th row Ch3, 1dc into next dc, (ch2, 1dc) 6 times, ch2, skip 1dc, 1dc, (2dc, ch4, 2dc) into loop, skip 2dc, 1dc, ch2, 1dc into last sp. Turn.
9th row Ch4, 1dc into next dc, (2dc, ch4, 2dc) into loop, 1dc into next dc, ch2, skip 1dc, 1dc, ch2, (1dc, ch2) 6 times, 1dc into each of last 2dc. Turn.
10th row Ch3, 1dc into next dc, (ch2, 1dc) 8 times, ch2, skip 1dc, 1dc, (2dc, ch4, 2dc) into loop, skip 2dc, 1dc, ch2, 1dc into last sp. Turn.
11th row Ch4, 1dc into next dc, (2dc, ch4, 2dc) into loop, 1dc into next dc. Turn.
12th row Ch3, 1dc into first dc, ch2, skip 1dc, 1dc, (2dc, ch4, 2dc) into loop, skip 2dc, 1dc, ch2, 1dc into last sp. Turn.
Rep from 3rd – 12th rows until edge is desired length. Finish off.
Sew on around edge.

Flower petal table runner and mats

Size
Table runner 6in by 27in
Single mat about 7in diameter
Gauge
After 2 rounds circle should measure about 1¾in diameter

Materials
Clark's Big Ball Mercerized Cotton No.30

Table runner 2 balls
Mat 1 ball
One No.B crochet hook
Note. 2 strands of cotton are used together throughout.

Table runner
Using No.B crochet hook and 2 strands of cotton begin at center and ch5. Join with a ss into first ch to form a circle.
1st round Ch7, * 1tr into circle, ch4, rep from * 4 times more. Join with a ss into 3rd of first ch7.
2nd round Ch3, 5tr into first sp, ch8, * 6tr into next sp, ch8, rep from * 4 times more. Join with a ss into 3rd of first ch3.
3rd round Ss into 2nd ch of first ch8 loop, ch3, 9tr into same loop, ch8, * 10tr into next ch8 loop, ch8, rep from * 4 times more. Join with a ss into 3rd of first ch3.
4th round Ch3, 1tr into each of next 9tr, ch4, 1sc into ch8 loop, ch4, * 1tr into each of next 10tr, ch4, 1sc into loop, ch4, rep from * 4 times more. Join with a ss into 3rd of first ch3. Finish off.
Work 2nd motif in same manner, do not break yarn. Join first and 2nd motifs together by working a row of ss along next 10tr working through edges of both motifs at the same time. Finish off. Work another 6 motifs and join to the preceding motif in the same way.
5th round Attach yarn with ss into first tr of group to right above join between first 2 motifs, ch3, 1tr into each of next 9tr, * ch4, 1sc into next ch loop, ch4, 1sc into next loop, ch3, 1sc into first loop across join on next motif, ch4, 1sc into next loop, ch4, 1tr into each of next 10tr, ch4, 1sc into next loop, ch4, 1sc into next loop, ch4, 1tr into each of next 10tr, rep from * to end motif, work around motif to first joining on next side and rep along other side and end of runner until round is completed, ending with a ss into 3rd of first ch3.
6th round Ss into 2nd tr, ch3, 1tr into each of next 3tr leaving last loop of each tr on hook, yrh and draw through loops, (1tr into each of next 4tr leaving last loop of each tr on hook, yrh and draw through all loops – called 1cl –), *(ch5, 1sc into next loop) twice, ch3, 1sc into first loop on next motif, ch5, 1sc into next loop, ch5, (1cl into next 4tr) twice, (ch5, 1sc into next loop) 3 times, ch5, (1cl into next 4tr) twice, rep from * along side work around motif as for sides in loop spaces where there are no joinings. Work along the other side and end to correspond. Join with a ss into 3rd of first ch3.
7th round Ss to center of leaf shape, *1sc in center st of leaf, (ch6, 1sc into next loop) twice, ch3, (1sc into next loop, ch6) twice, 1sc into top of next leaf shape, (ch6, 1sc into next loop) 4 times, ch6, rep from * along side and at end work as for loop sp where there are no joinings, work along other side and end to correspond. Join with a ss into first sc.
8th round Ss to center of first loop, (1sc into loop, ch6) rep into each loop except on sides above joinings, ch3 as before. Join with a ss into first sc.
9th round Into each ch6 loop work (4sc, ch4, 4sc), and into ch3 loops above joinings work 3sc. Join with a ss into first sc. Finish off.

Single mat
Work as given for table runner from first – 4th rounds.
5th round Inserting hook into both loops of previous round, ch3, 1tr into each of next 9tr, (ch4, 1sc into next loop) twice, ch4, *1tr

into each of next 10tr, (ch4, 1sc into next loop) twice, ch4, rep from * 4 times more. Join with a ss into 3rd of first ch3.
6th round Ss into 2nd tr of previous round, ch3, 1tr into each of next 3tr leaving last loop of each tr on hook, yrh and draw through all loops, 1tr into each of next 4tr leaving last loop of each tr on hook, yrh and draw through all loops, (ch5, 1sc into next loop) 3 times, ch5, * (1tr into each of next 4tr leaving last loop of each tr on hook, yrh and draw through all loops) twice, (ch5, 1sc into next loop) 3 times, ch5, rep from * 4 times more. Join with a ss into 3rd of first ch3.
7th round Ss into center of leaf shape, * 1sc into center st, (ch5, 1sc into next loop) 4 times, ch5, rep from * 5 times more. Join with a ss into first sc.
8th round Ss into center of next ch loop, * 1sc into centre of loop, ch6, rep from * to end. Join with a ss into first ss.
9th round As 8th round.
10th round As 9th round working ch7 in place of ch6.
11th round Into each loop work (4sc, ch4, 4sc). Join with a ss into first sc. Finish off.

Finishing
Run in all ends.
Press on wrong side under a damp cloth with a warm iron.

Napkin ring

Size
1½in by 6in before seaming
Gauge
Strip measures about 1½in in width
Materials
Clark's Big Ball Mercerized Cotton No.30
1 ball
One No.10 steel crochet hook

Ring
Using No.10 steel hook ch4.
1st row Into first ch (4th from hook) work 2dc, ch2, 3dc into same ch, ch12, 3dc into 9th of ch12 (3rd ch from hook), ch2, 3dc into same ch. Turn.
2nd row Ch3, 3dc, ch2, 3dc all into first ch2 loop, ch4, 1sc into 4th (center ch of previous row, ch4, 3dc, ch2, 3dc all into next ch2 loop. Turn.
3rd row Ch3, 3dc, ch2, 3dc all into first ch2 loop, ch7, 3dc, ch2, 3dc all into next ch2 loop. Turn.
4th row Ch3, 3dc, ch2, 3dc all into first ch2 loop, ch4, 1sc into 4th of ch7 of previous row, ch4, 3dc, ch2, 3dc all into next ch2 loop. Turn.
Repeat 3rd and 4th rows until strip measures 6in in length.
Finish off.

Finishing
Pin out and press under a damp cloth using a warm iron. Seam ends neatly together to form a circle.

Rajah lampshade

Size
To fit Tiffany lampshade 14in diameter
Materials
Reynolds Danskyarn.
3 balls
One No.H crochet hook

Lampshade
Using No.H crochet hook ch16. Join with a ss into first ch to form a circle.
1st round Work 24sc into circle. Join with a ss into first sc.
2nd round Ch5, * skip 1sc, 1dc into next sc, ch2, rep from * 10 times more. Join with a ss into 3rd of first ch5. 12 spaces.
3rd round Ss into first sp, ch3, (1dc, ch1, 2dc) into first sp, (2dc, ch1, 2dc) into each of next 11 sp. Join with a ss into 3rd of first ch3.
4th round Ss into first ch sp, (ch5, 1dc) into first sp, ch1, * (1dc, ch2, 1dc, ch1) into each of next 11sp. Join with a ss into 3rd of first ch5.
5th round Ss into first sp, (ch3, 2dc, ch1, 3dc) into first sp, (3dc, ch1, 3dc) into each of next 11sp. Join with a ss into 3rd of first ch3.
6th round Ss into first ch1 sp, (ch6, 1dc) into first sp, ch2, (1dc, ch3, 1dc, ch2) into each of next 11sp. Join with a ss into 3rd of first ch6.
7th round Ss into first ch3 sp, (ch3, 2dc, ch2, 3dc) into first sp, (3dc, ch2, 3dc) into each of next 11sp. Join with a ss into 3rd of first ch3.
8th round Ss into ch2 sp, (ch7, 1dc) into first sp, ch3, (1dc, ch4, 1dc, ch3) into each of next 11sp. Join with a ss into 3rd of first ch3.
9th round Ss into first ch4 sp, (ch4, 2tr, ch2, 3tr) into first sp, ch1, (3tr, ch2, 3tr, ch1) into each of next 11sp. Join with a ss into 4th of first ch4.
10th round Ss into first ch2 sp, (ch7, 1dc) into this sp, * ch2, 1dc into ch1 sp, ch2, (1dc, ch4, 1dc) into next sp, rep from * 10 times more, ch2, 1dc into next ch1 sp, ch2. Join with a ss into 3rd of first ch7.
11th round Ss into first ch4 sp, (ch4, 3tr, ch2, 4tr) into first sp, ch1, (4tr, ch2, 4tr, ch1) into each of next 11sp. Join with a ss into 4th of first ch4.
12th round Ss into first ch2 sp, (ch7, 1dc) into this sp, * ch3, 1dc into ch1 sp, ch3, (1dc, ch4, 1dc) into next ch2 sp, rep from *10 times more,

ch3, 1dc into ch1 sp, ch3. Join with a ss into 3rd of first ch7.

13th round Ss into ch4 sp, (ch4, 4tr, ch2, 5tr) into first sp, ch2, (5tr, ch2, 5tr, ch2) into each of next 11 four ch sp. Join with a ss into 4th of first ch4.

Rep 12th and 13th rounds twice more.

18th round Ch9, * 1sc into ch2 sp center of shell group, ch5, 1dc between shell groups, ch5, rep from * 10 times more, 1sc into center of shell group, ch5. Ss into 3dr of first ch9.

19th round Ch3, * 1dc into next st, rep from * to end. Join with a ss into 3rd of first ch3.

20th round * Ch5, skip 2dc, 1sc into next dc, rep from * to end. Join with a ss into 2nd of first ch5.

21st round Ss along ch2, * ch5, skip 5sts, 1sc into next st, rep from * to end. Join with a ss into 2nd of first ch5.

22nd round * Ch2, skip 5sts, 1sc into next st, rep from * to end. Join with a ss into 2nd of first ch2.

23rd round Ch3, * 1dc into next st, rep from * to end. Join with a ss into 3rd of first ch3. Finish off.

Finishing
Place shade over frame and secure at top and lower edge.

Fringe
Cut 8 lengths of yarn 10in long and knot through lower edge between dc. Knot 1 group of threads into every 3rd space.

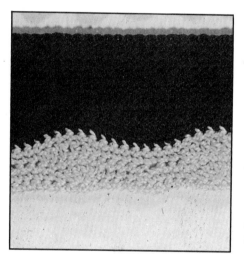

Two color wave braid

Size
3in deep
Materials
Coats & Clark's O.N.T. "Speed-Cro-Sheen"
1 ball brown, A; 1 ball beige, B
One No.E crochet hook

Braid
Using No.E crochet hook and B work a ch 24in long (for extra length work 15sc for every patt).

1st row 1sc into each ch to end. Turn.
2nd row Ch1, 1sc into each of next 9sc, *1dc into next sc, 3dc into next sc, 1dc into next sc 1sc into each of next 10sc. Rep from * to end.

Turn.

3rd row Ch1, 1sc into each of next 3sc, skip 2sc, 1sc into each of next 4sc, * 1sc into each of 5dc, 1sc into each of 4sc, skip 2sc, 1sc into each of 4sc, rep from * to end. Turn.

4th row Ch1, 1sc into each of next 8sc, * 1dc into each of 5sc, 1sc into each of 8sc, rep from * to end. Turn.

5th row Ch1, 1sc into each sc to end. Finish off. Turn.

6th row Attach A and work 1sc into each sc.

7th row Ch3, 1dc into each of 8sc, * 1sc into each of 5dc, 1dc into each of 8sc, rep from * to end. Turn.

8th row 1sc into each st to end. Turn.

9th row 1sc into each sc to end. Turn.

Rep last row until work measures 3in from beg. Finish off.

Finishing
Press lightly on wrong side under a damp cloth with a warm iron.

Knitted edge with cable center braid

Size
4in wide by 25in long
Materials
Coats & Clark's O.N.T. "Speed-Cro-Sheen"
3 balls beige, A
2 balls camel, B
2 balls brown, C
No.3 knitting needles
One cable needle

Cable center
Using No.3 needles and C cast on 12 sts.
1st row K.
2nd row K4, P4, K4.
Rep first and 2nd rows once more.
5th row K4, slip next 2 sts onto cable needle and hold at back, K2, K2 from cable needle. K4.
6th row As 2nd row.
Rep from first to 6th rows until work measures 22in, ending with a 2nd row.
Bind off.

Panel
Using No.3 needles and A, cast on 20 sts.
1st row K.

2nd row K2, P16, K2.
Rep first and 2nd rows until work measures 23in ending with a first row.
Bind off.
Using B and with RS panel facing pick up and K one st in between every row along one edge.
K 4 rows.
Bind off.
Work the other edge in the same manner.
Work the ends in the same manner.

Finishing
Press pieces lightly on wrong side under a damp cloth with a warm iron.
Sew cable strip into center of panel.

Three color braid with fringe

Size
3in wide by 21in long
Materials
Coats & Clarks' O.N.T. "Speed-Cro-Sheen"
1 ball camel, A
1 ball beige, B
1 ball brown, C
No.3 knitting needles
Bernat Aero Jackpin needles ½in
One cable needle

Braid
Using No.3 needles and A cast on 126 sts.
K 2 rows, P 1 row.
4th and 5th rows Using C, K.
6th row Using A, K.
7th row Using A, P.
Rep 6th and 7th rows once.
10th row Using B, K.
11th row Using B, P.
12th row Using B and Jackpins, K.
13th row Using B and No.3 needle, * slip 3 sts onto a cable needle and leave these sts at back of work, K3, K3 from cable needle, rep from * to end.
Rep 10th and 11th rows once.
Rep 6th and 7th rows twice.
20th row Using B, K.
Using A, K 1 row, P 1 row, K 2 rows. Bind off.

Finishing
Press lightly on wrong side under a damp cloth with a warm iron.

Fringe
Using each color cut 8in lengths. Using one strand of each color (3 in all) fold in half and knot through edge to form fringe.

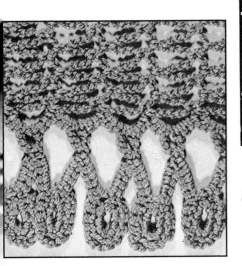

73

Classic pattern braid

Size
About 4½in deep
Materials
Coats & Clark's O.N.T. "Speed-Cro-Sheen"
1 ball
One No.D crochet hook

Braid
Using No.D crochet hook ch14.
1st row Work 1sc into each ch to end. Turn.
2nd row * Ch8, skip 1sc, 1sc into next sc, rep from * to end. Turn. 6 loops.
3rd row Ch6, 1sc into loop, * ch3, 1sc into next loop, rep from * to end. Turn.
4th row * Ch8, 1sc into next loop, rep from * ending with ch8, 1sc into sc. Turn. 6 loops.
Rep 3rd and 4th rows until work measures 24in, or length desired. Finish off.

Side edging
Along sides work 3sc into each ch3 sp.

Lower edging
Working into ch6 sp along lower edge
1st row * 3sc, ch6, 3sc, rep from * into each sp to end. Turn.
2nd row Ss into 2nd sc and ch2, 1sc into sp, * ch10, 1sc into next sp, rep from * to end. Turn.
3rd row * 5sc into loop, ch8, ss into 8th ch from hook, turn, 8sc into loop, 1sc into sc, turn, 1sc into 4sc, ch4, 1sc into 4sc, 5sc into same loop, rep from * to end. Finish off.

Finishing
Press lightly under a damp cloth with a warm iron.

74

Granny squares potholders

Size
About 7¼in by 7¼in
Gauge
One square motif measures about 3¼in by 3¼in
Materials
Reynolds Danksyarn
1 ball main color, A
1 ball each of 2 contrast colors, B and C
No.E crochet hook
This quantity makes 2 potholders

Square motif
Using No.E crochet hook and B begin at center, ch7. Join with a ss into first ch to form a circle.
1st round Ch5, * 1dc into circle, ch2, rep from * 6 times more. Ss into 3rd of first ch5.
2nd round 1 ss over first dc, 1 ss into first ch sp, ch3, 3dc into same ch sp as ss, * ch1, 4dc into next sp, rep from * 6 times more, ch1. Join with a ss into 3rd of first ch3. Break off yarn.
3rd round Attach C with a ss into first ch sp of previous round, ch3, 5dc into same ch sp, 6dc into next ch sp, * 6dc into next ch sp, 6dc into next ch sp, rep from * twice more, ch1. Ss into 3rd of first ch3. Break off yarn.
4th round Attach A with a ss into sp formed by last ch1, ch3, (1dc, ch1, 2dc) all into same sp, * ch2, skip 3dc, 1sc between dc, ch2, skip 3dc, 1sc into ch sp, ch2, skip 3dc, 1sc between dc, ch2, skip 3dc, (2dc, ch1, 2dc) all into next ch sp, rep from * twice more, ch2, skip 3dc, 1sc between dc, ch2, skip 3dc, 1sc into ch sp, ch2, skip 3dc, 1sc between dc, ch2. Join with a ss into 3rd of first ch3.
5th round 1 ss into first dc, 1 ss into ch sp, ch3, (1dc, ch1, 2dc) all into corner sp, * 1dc into sp between next 2dc, (2dc into next ch sp) 4 times, 1dc between next 2dc, (2dc, ch1, 2dc) all into next corner sp, rep from * twice more, 1dc between next 2dc, (2dc into next ch sp) 4 times, 1dc between next 2dc. Join with a ss into 3rd of first ch3. Break off yarn.
Work 1 more square using B as first color.
Work 2 more squares using C in place of B, and B in place of C.
Join 4 squares together on wrong side using A and working 1sc into each sp between dc.

Back
Using No.E crochet hook and A begin at center, ch4. Ss into first ch to form circle.
1st round Ch1, work 7sc into circle. Join with a ss into first ch.
2nd round Ch3, (1dc, ch2, 2dc) into first sc, * 1dc into next sc, (2dc, ch2, 2dc) into next sc, rep from * twice more, 1dc into last sc. Join with a ss into 3rd of first ch3.
3rd round 1 ss into first dc, 1 ss into next ch sp, ch3, (1dc, ch1, 2dc) all into corner sp, * 1dc between each dc to next corner, (2dc, ch2, 2dc) all into next ch sp, rep from * twice more, 1dc between each dc to end of round. Join with a ss into 3rd of first ch3.
Rep 3rd round until back measures same size as front. Finish off.

Edging
1st round Hold back and front together with wrong sides touching and right side of front facing. Join A to any st with a ss, ch1, 1sc into each st through back and front together. Join with a ss into first ch. Break yarn.
2nd round Join in B with a ss to first sc after any corner, (allow 3sc to count as 1 corner), ch2, 1hdc into same sc, skip 1sc, * 1hdc into next sc, skip 1sc, rep from * to next corner, ch7, skip 3 corner sc, sep from * twice more, (2hdc into next sc, skip 1sc) to end of round, ch7. Ss into 2nd of first ch2. Break off B.
3rd round Join in C with a ss between first 2hdc groups, ch2, 1hdc into same sp, *2hdc into each sp to corner, 12sc into corner loop, rep from * 3 times more. Join with a ss into 2nd of first ch2.

Finishing
Darn in all ends. Press under a damp cloth with a warm iron.
Make the second potholder in the same manner using C for the 2nd round of edging and B for the 3rd round.

75

String Bag

Size
16in long, excluding handles
Gauge
7 sts to 2in
Materials
Coats & Clark's O.N.T. "Speed-Cro-Sheen"
3 balls main color, A; 1 ball contrast, B
Coats & Clark's O.N.T. Pearl Cotton
8 balls main color, A; 1 ball contrast, B
One pair No.10 knitting needles
One No.D crochet hook
One Bucilla Flower Loom No.4616
Main part
Using No.10 needles and one strand each of "Speed-Cro-Sheen" and Pearl Cotton A, cast on 104 sts. K 1 row.
1st patt row * K2 tog, y2rn, sl 1, K1, psso, rep

from * to end.
2nd patt row *K1, K the first loop and P the 2nd loop of y2rn, K2, rep from * to end.
3rd patt row K2, * K2 tog, y2rn, sl1, K1, psso, rep from * to last 2 sts, K2.
4th patt row K3, * K the first loop and P the 2nd loop of y2rn, K2, rep from * to last st, K1.
These 4 rows form the patt and are rep throughout. Continue in patt until work measures 20in, ending with a 2nd or 4th patt row. Bind off loosely.

Handles
Using No.D crochet hook and one strand each of "Speed-Cro-Sheen" and Pearl Cotton color B, work in sc along one side edge of main section, working into every other row end, thus drawing up edge.
Next row Ch1, 1sc into first sc, * skip 1sc, 1sc into next sc, rep from * to end.
Next row Ch1, * 1sc into next sc, rep from * to end. Rep last row once more.
Without breaking yarn ch50 for handle, work 1sc into opposite end of row from beg of handle, 2sc down side of border, turn.
Next row 1sc into each of first 3sc, 1sc into each of next ch50, 3sc down side of border, turn. Work 1 row sc into each st. Fasten off.
Work handle at other side edge to correspond.

Finishing
Fold bag with handles together. Seam sides, leaving 5in open at the top. Press lightly.

Flower
Using one strand each of "Speed-Cro-Sheen" and Pearl Cotton color B, work 1 flower on loom (instructions with loom), using center ring only and working around circle 3 times to make a small flower.
Repeat as desired and sew onto bag.

Bordered dishcloth

Size
18in square
Gauge
4 sts to 1in
Materials
Coats & Clark's O.N.T. "Speed-Cro-Sheen", 2 balls main color A
1 ball contrast color, B; No.6 knitting needles

Dishcloth
Using No.6 needles and B double, cast on 66 sts. K 1 row.
2nd row K2, * y2rn, K2 tog, rep from * to end. K 1 row. Break off B. Attach 2 strands of A leaving ends to run in.
1st patt row (RS) *K2 tog, yrn, P2, yon, sl1, K1, psso, rep from * to end.
2nd patt row P2, K2, * P4, K2, rep from * to last 2 sts, P2.
Rep first and 2nd patt rows until work measures 17½in, ending with a 2nd patt row. Break off A and attach B. K 2 rows.
**** Last row** K2, * y2rn, K2 tog, rep from * to end. Bind off loosely knitwise, dropping extra loop of yrn.**
Side borders
Using B double and with RS facing pick up and K 72 sts evenly along side between borders. K 1 row.
Rep from ** to **.
Work other side in the same manner.
Finishing
Run in ends and sew corners together.

77
Lattice squares bedspread

Size
52in by 80in
Gauge
One motif measures 4in square
Materials
Coats & Clark's O.N.T. "Speed-Cro-Sheen"
44 balls
One No.B crochet hook
Note. One ball will make a total of 5 squares.

Lattice square
Using No.B crochet hook
ch23.
1st row Into 8th ch from hook work 1dc, * ch2, skip ch2, 1dc into next ch, rep from * 4 times more.
Turn. (6 spaces).
2nd row Ch5, 1dc into top of next dc, * ch2, 1dc into top of next dc, rep from * 4 times more. Turn.
3rd, 4th, 5th and 6th rows As 2nd row.
7th row Ch1, 2sc into sp, * 2sc into each of next 3 sp, ch10, turn, 1sc between sc immediately above 2nd dc in from left, turn, into ch10 loop work (2sc, ch3) 5 times, 2sc into same loop, 2sc into next sp to left, 6sc into corner, rep from * 3 times more ending 3rd rep with 3sc into corner instead of 6sc. Join with a ss into first ch.
8th row Ch1, * ch8, 1sc into 2nd of ch3 loop around circle, ch10, 1sc into 4th of ch3 loop around circle, ch8, 1sc between 3rd and 4th sc in corner sp, rep from * 3 times. Join with a ss into first ch.
9th round * 8sc into ch8 loop, 10sc into ch10 loop, 8sc into ch8 loop, rep from * 3 times. Join with a ss into first sc.
Finish off.
Make the required number of squares in the same manner.

Finishing
Press each square with wrong side up under a damp cloth using a warm iron.
Be careful that all squares are the same size.
Crochet squares together using sc.

Crash course in crochet

Everything a beginner needs to know and a comprehensive reference for the expert

How to begin.

The materials required are a crochet hook, yarn, a pair of scissors and a large eyed, darning needle.

There are many sizes of hook available ranging from the fine steel hooks for cotton or fine yarns to the larger alloy ones for use with thicker yarns. However, to practise it is perhaps easiest to work with a sports yarn and No.F crochet hook.

Placing yarn on hook.

Crochet works on the principle of one loop being pulled through another and all crochet stitches are simply varying permutations of this.

Start with a slip loop to place the yarn into the hook. Hold the end of the yarn between the thumb and forefinger of the left hand. Using the right hand, form a loop and hold this in position with the left hand, making the long end of the yarn fall behind the loop.

Hold the crochet hook in your right hand with the thumb and forefinger positioned on the flat bar. Insert the hook through the loop and behind the long end, catching it in the curve of the hook. Pull the hook out of the loop, thus bringing the long end through to form another loop. Keep-

ing this loop on the hook, pull the short end downward to tighten the loop around the curve of the hook.

Holding the work.

The hook is held in the right hand in the same way as a pencil, gripping the flat bar between thumb and forefinger and resting the hook against the second finger.

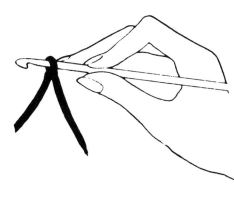

It is with this finger that the hook is controlled and guided through the loops. The left hand holds the work and controls the yarn. Pass the long

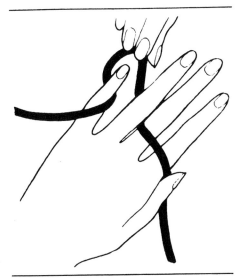

end of the yarn around the little finger, across the palm, through between the second and third fingers. Catch the

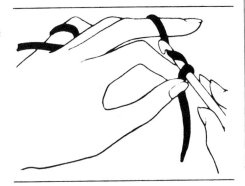

knot of the loop between thumb and forefinger.

Stitches.

Chain. This forms the foundation of crochet work. Pass the hook under

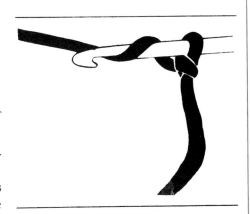

the yarn which lies between the left hand and the hook, catching the yarn in the curve of the hook. This is called "yarn around hook". Draw the yarn through the loop already on the hook. This forms one chain stitch which can be repeated indefinitely.

Crash course in crochet

continued from previous page

To work a practice sampler, chain twenty-two.

Turning chain. Because there are varying depths to crochet stitches and they are worked from the top down, at the beginning of a row the hook has to be taken up to the correct level. This is done with chain which then lie up the side of the next stitch and these are called "turning chain". The number depends on the stitch to follow.

These chain count as the first stitch of the row and the last one is worked into at the end of the next row.
Double crochet. For double crochet 3 turning chain are required.

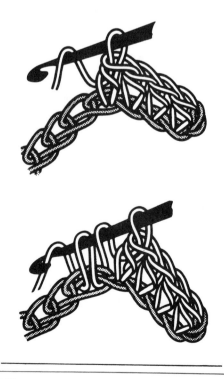

Pass the yarn around the hook and insert hook into fourth chain from the hook, yarn around hook and draw loop through (three loops on hook), yarn around hook and draw through two loops (two loops on hook), yarn around hook and draw through two loops (one loop on hook).

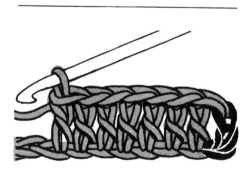

On the sampler, working first double crochet into fourth chain from hook, work one double crochet into each chain. 20 stitches.

Working into spaces.
When following a pattern it is often necessary to work into a space made on the previous row rather than into a stitch.

In such cases the hook is inserted into the actual space and not the chain running over the top of it.

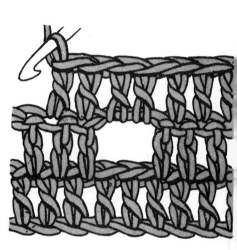

On practice sampler, turn, chain 3 and work one double crochet into each of the next 8 double crochet, chain 2, skip 2 double crochet, work one double crochet into the next double crochet to the end, finishing with one double crochet into the 3rd of 3 turning chain.

Turn, chain 3, work one double crochet into each of the next 8 chain, two double crochet into chain 2 space, one double crochet into each double crochet to end working last double crochet into 3rd of 3 turning chain.

Slip stitch. This stitch is most often used for joining the end of a round to the beginning, attaching or repositioning the yarn without adding to the dimension of the work. It can also be used to give a firm edge and is the flattest stitch of all.

Insert the hook into the next stitch, yarn around hook and draw loop through the stitch and the loop

already on the hook. On the practice sampler, turn and work a row of slip stitches across top of double crochet. Slip stitch requires no turning chain.

Fastening off. Cut the yarn about six inches from the work. Thread the end through the one remaining loop and pull tight. The end can later be run in.

How to work a Granny square.
Although there are several other stitches which will follow, with the information already given here it is possible to work a Granny square. Chain five and join with a slip stitch to form a ring.

1st round. Chain three which will count as the first dc, work 2dc into the ring, *chain 2, work 3 dc into the ring, repeat from * twice more, chain 2, join the three chain.

2nd round. Chain 2, *work 3 dc, chain 2 and another 3 dc all into the next chain 2 space, chain one, repeat from* 3 times more skipping one chain at the end of the last repeat, join with a slip stitch into the first of the first 2 chain.

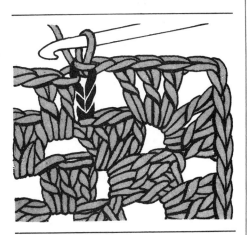

3rd round. Work chain three to count as first dc, into the chain space immediately to the left of the hook work 2 dc, * chain one, work 3 dc, chain 2 and 3 dc into the corner chain 2 space, chain one, work 3 dc into next chain one space, repeat from * twice more, chain one, work 3 dc, chain 2 and 3 dc all into the corner chain 2 space, chain one, join with a slip stitch into the third of three chain.

4th round. Chain 2, * work 3 dc into next chain one space, chain one, work 3 dc, chain 2 and 3 dc all into corner, chain one, work 3 dc into next chain one space, chain one, repeat from * 3 times more skipping the one chain at the end of the last repeat, join with a slip stitch into the first of first chain two.

Crash course in crochet

continued from previous page

Joining the squares.

The squares can be joined either by backstitching together right sides facing or by crocheting. Place two

squares right sides together and work a slip stitch through the double thickness, working into the top of the dc on the last round.

Gauge.

This refers to the number of stitches and rows to the square inch. If the gauge is not correct as given in the directions, the garment will not fit. If by using the number of hook suggested, the gauge does not work out accurately, adjust the size of hook as required.

Abbreviations

alt   — alternative
beg   — beginning
ch   — chain

Stitches.
Single crochet. Two turning chain are required.

Insert the hook into the next stitch to the left of the hook, yarn round to the left of the hook, yarn around loops on hook), yarn around hook and draw through two loops (one loop on hook).

Half double crochet. Two turning chain are required with this stitch.

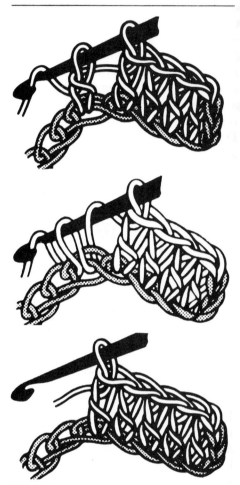

Yarn around hook, insert hook into stitch, yarn around hook into stitch, yarn around hook and draw loop through (three loops on hook), yarn around hook and draw through all three loops (one loop on hook).

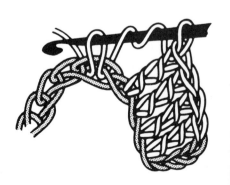

Treble crochet. This stitch requires four turning chain. Pass yarn around hook twice, insert hook into next stitch, yarn around hook and pull through (four loops on hook), yarn around hook and pull through two loops (three loops on hook), yarn around hook and pull through two loops (two loops on hook), yarn around hook and pull through both remaining loops (one loop on hook).

Double treble. Five turning chain are required.

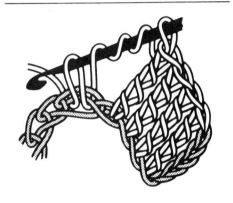

Pass yarn around hook three times, insert hook into next stitch, yarn around hook and draw through (five loops on hook), yarn around hook and draw through first two loops (four loops on hook), yarn around hook and draw through next two loops (three loops on hook), yarn around hook and draw through next two loops (two loops on hook), yarn around hook and draw through remaining two loops (one loop on hook).

Triple treble. This stitch requires six turning chain. Pass the yarn over the hook four times. Insert

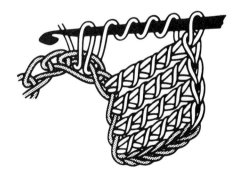

hook into next stitch, pass yarn around hook and draw loop through (six loops on hook), pass yarn around hook and draw through the first two loops (five loops on hook), yarn around hook and draw through next two loops (four loops on hook), yarn around hook and draw through next two loops (three loops on hook), yarn around hook and draw through next two loops (two loops on hook), yarn around hook and draw through remaining two loops (one loop on hook).

Picots.

Picots can be used within a pattern to give an interesting bobble effect. They are also frequently used to give an attractive edging.

The picot is formed by a chain of three, four or five stitches depending on the size of picot desired, and these are formed into a circle by working a single crochet into the first chain.

Clusters.

Sometimes several stitches are worked in a group, usually dc or tr. Work three or more of the stitch, each time leaving the last loop of the stitch on the hook. Finally, pass yarn around hook and draw through all loops on the hook.

Increasing.

It is usual for specific directions for increasing to be included in pattern directions. However as a general rule, two or more stitches can be worked into the same foundation. Sometimes in an open piece of work additional chain stitches are added at the end of a row and used as a foundation chain on the

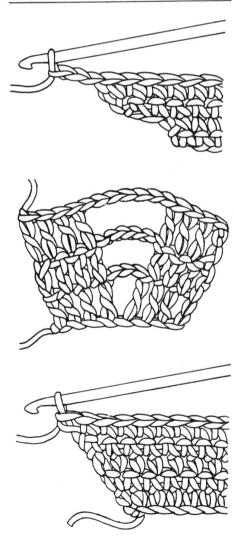

125

Crash course in crochet

continued from previous page

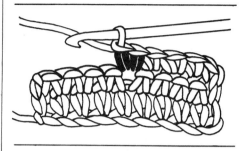

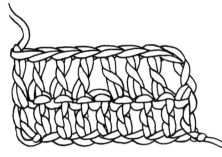

next row. An alternative method is to simply change to a larger hook to give a slightly bigger gauge.

Decreasing.

As with increasing, directions are given specifically with individual patterns. One method is to simply skip a stitch, either at the end of a row or when the resulting space is not too obvious. Sometimes several stitches are worked into one, and to do this the last loop of each stitch is left on the hook in addition to the one already there, and when all the stitches are worked to within the last stage, then the yarn is passed around the hook and pulled through all loops. Occasionally, at the beginning of a row, slip stitch is worked over the top of several stitches and then they are skipped on the next row.

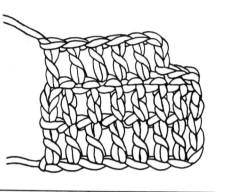

As with increasing, by changing the size of the hook, to alter the gauge, this time to a smaller one, the overall size of the work is altered.

Attaching new yarn.

In crochet it is better not to tie knots to attach new yarn. When there is still about three inches of the first yarn left, lay it across the top of the previous row, lay a similar length of the second yarn with it and work over both ends with the second ball of yarn. If the join comes

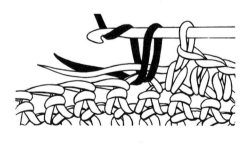

when chain is being worked, lay the new thread alongside the first one, the ends pointing in opposite directions, and work with the double thickness until the first thread runs out.

Blocking.

Most crochet, especially when it is very open in texture, should be blocked. Using a clean, flat surface into which you can stick rustless dressmaking pins, pin the piece out to the correct measurements.

Cover with a damp cloth and leave until the cloth is absolutely dry.

Pieces of crochet can be joined by a crocheted slip stitch as illustrated in the first part of this crochet crash course or by sewing with overcasting stitch for a flat seam, or by using a backstitch seam.

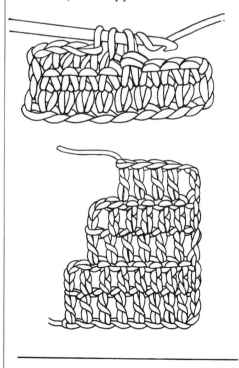

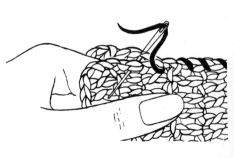

Cotton crochet for such things as edgings or cloths often look better for a light starching. Use a solution of starch—about two teaspoonsful to 2½ cups of hot water. Dab the solution over the article when it is blocked.

Left-handed workers.

When following directions, read left for right and right for left. Wherever there are diagrams, hold them up in front of a mirror and follow the reversed reflection. However, many left-handed people find that they can crochet in exactly the same way as right-handed people, so it is worth trying first.

Abbreviations

sc	—	single crochet
dc	—	double crochet
tr	—	treble crochet
hdc	—	half double crochet
dtr	—	double treble
trtr	—	triple treble

Filet crochet.

In this technique the shapes in the patterning are formed by solid and open squares formed by blocks and spaces. The result is similar to a coarse net. This type of crochet is always worked in straight rows.

The blocks are formed by dc and the spaces by chain, each space divided from the next one by one dc.

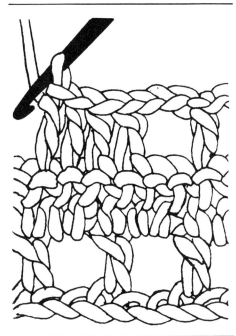

Very often the directions consist only of a chart but whereas in knitting each square would represent one stitch, here it represents a block or space. Each block consists of a given number of dc.

Tunisian crochet.

This form of crochet is a marriage between crochet and knitting. It is worked with a crochet hook which is similar in length to a knitting needle. The basic principle is to work one row forward and then another one back through the center of the first loops. This results in a rich and firm texture which can be varied for different effects. As each loop is drawn through the next stitch it is left on the needle until the end of the row.

1st row. Begin with a length of chain. Insert hook into second chain from hook, yarn over hook and draw loop through, insert hook into each chain in same way.

2nd row. Chain 1, *yarn over hook, draw through two loops on hook, repeat from * to end.

3rd row. Chain 1, *insert hook into vertical loop, yarn over hook and draw yarn through, rep from * to end, insert hook into chain at end of row, draw yarn through. Repeat 2nd and 3rd rows.

Hairpin crochet.

This technique is worked on a tool which looks like a very large hairpin. The knots are formed down the center with loops stretching out on either side to the prongs of the hairpin. The work forms into long strips which can then be joined together and there are many variations of grouping the loops.

Make a slip knot in the yarn and place the loop on the right-hand rod. Draw the loop out so that the knot is exactly central between the bars.

Crash course in crochet

continued from previous page

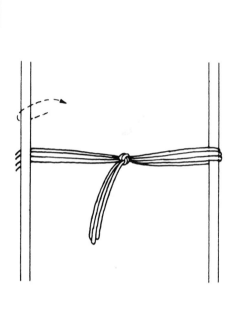

*Insert the crochet hook through loop and draw a single thread through so that there are two loops on the hook, yarn around hook and draw through both loops to complete one single crochet. Keeping loop on hook, pass the hook through to the back of the frame and turn the frame toward you from right to left as before.

Repeat from * turning the frame after each stitch. The frame is always turned the same way.

Hold the yarn behind the left rod with the first finger and thumb of the left hand and turn the frame towards you from right to left until the right-hand rod has reversed to the left side. The yarn will now pass around the other rod and should be held again by the left hand behind the left-hand rod.

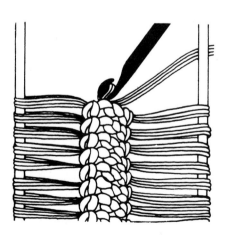